JOSH DOUGLAS

Career Planning For Teens

practical tips for applications,
job and career
from an experienced personnel consultant

Career Planning: Thatconcept

What are we even talking about here?
definition of terms"Career"; oddities of the system; Planning as a mandatory basis for success

"Career" has an elitist touch

It can't cause any damage to initially explain what a "profession" really is. The word reference is definitely less clear in its definitions than one would trust: the quickest walk of the pony, the quick expert vocation, the profession related with headway and the especially effective profession.

The clarifications of pony walkingApart from that, they all share one center for all intents and purpose that separates vocations from the normal: it's either about incredibly quick or potentially especially effective expert headway. This is the assertion: The people who cause a profession to accomplish more than numerous others. This overall definition as of now tends a piece towards elitism. I utilize this emotive word deliberately to flag all along: any individual who needs a vocation ought not fear contact when terms become an integral factor that have essentially pessimistic meanings for specific individuals: top entertainers, especially fruitful, more than others, quicker, better.

Regardless, a profession is something beyond strolling along a foreordained vocation way. How about we settle on this for this book:

A profession is an especially effective vocation that is related with the presumption of steadily expanding material and, generally speaking, likewise staff liabilities. The outside sign is the constant ascent in the order framework.

To say it straight away: Accomplishing something like this despite steady contest from others is difficult - however most certainly conceivable. The situations being referred to are there, they must be filled regardless, and they become empty over and over at various times. You simply must be among the people who are decided to be reassigned.

This isn't quite so troublesome as it initially shows up. What's more, whenever you have gotten to know a few bosses in practice, you will always think: I can do that too. That would be a good start.

The "system" is full of surprises

The professional system discussed here is part of our economic system. The problems begin with the completely different objectives in the two areas. Let's take the company and its employees as an example:

The company, which is commercially oriented in its classic form, has profit maximization as its central goal, which can be supplemented by other goals depending on the specifications of the owner.

The purpose of the company is not to employ as many people as possible and make them happy at the same time. On the other hand, they are indispensable, but also a central cost factor, sometimes to often annoying with their demands and, once you have them, often stand in the way of what you would like to do in the short term: e.g. B. in the event of a sudden drop in sales, the personnel costs can be reduced just as suddenly.

Companies move in markets. By definition, these are hardly predictable, often moody, don't know the concept of justice (are not unjust, just don't know what to do with the word), and are constantly changing. What was a market hit yesterday is no longer bought by anyone today - and anyone who wants to venture onto a very complicated minefield should deal with the stock exchange, which is so important for the economy.

Our professional system is now established as part of these very special structures and somehow always dependent on them. Can it meet the highest standards of logic, absolute clarity, convincing justice or even just comprehensibility? If that's what's added - as given here – that people with different qualifications are everywhere, making decisions, shaping the rules and determining destinies, then you have the answer: it can't.

If someone has the necessary information, knows the respective power constellations as well as the strengths, weaknesses and ambitions of the managers involved, then he sees that things follow their own logic. There but if you are often groping in the dark when it comes to the details mentioned, professional life is always full of surprises.

Only seemingly unorganized, I am listing some "insights", employee sayings and experiences here, which should at least give you an insight into the world of the professional system, which at first seemed a bit "brittle":

- If you have to analyze a difficult constellation, think too(and above all) beyond conventional arguments and solutions. Things are sometimes easier and more difficult at the same time. Example: Which system does this series of numbers follow and what would be the next number after that?

  8 th 3 1 5 9 6 7

  If you've tried the usual mathematical methods and haven't had success, the solution will astonish you: the numbers are arranged quite simply in the alphabet of their spelling, "four" would come next (I read this problem somewhere decades ago and can unfortunately no longer name the creator; but the example shows how easy it is to slip into familiar thought patterns and then

get stuck; in the professionally relevant environment this is a constant threat).
- Not everyone who qualifies rises to the top; not everyone that goes up
comes is qualified – that outlines the opportunities and shows the limits.
- The - imperfect - system is of the existing people forexisting humans and suits them quite well. Above all, a better system would require better people.

- Don't waste your time looking at arranged in-house
Changes the - often small - recognizable advantages against the - often large ones
– Spontaneously visible disadvantagesto weigh. It was mostly important that something was changed. What that is is considered less important. When there are problems, the motto is: "Something has to be done." Many months have passed before you notice what has happened and the time is ripe for a new change.
- All management decisions follow a certaingik, which is often only revealed to those who have been there. The others are then left with comments like: "A big house can offer big things."
Nothing influences the internal processes that are so important for the employeescircumstances of all kinds as much as the thoughts and actions of the company management. But "only" people sit there, ultimately somehow "like you and me". Despite all their professionalism, they have remained what they were before the promotion. Board meetings sometimes run like children's meetings in the sandpit: "If you cut my mold, I'll cut your mold"; also Managing directors are in a bad mood, offended, have toothache or migraines, are

at war with colleagues or the advisory board, fear that their employment contract will be extended, employees simply can't stand them – and have driven entire companies to the wall because they put self-interest above the company's well-being.

- Our quite one-sidedcapital geared towards maximizing sales/incomelistish market economy system works, feeds us all and is currently not threatened by anything even remotely better. But its basic structure is quite simple, and it only partially satisfies the higher demands of people who are looking for ethics and morality, justice, inspiring theoretical approaches, mathematically and logically well-founded processes and mandatory, systematic and convincingly presentable individual measures derived from them. The professional system embedded in it inevitably follows this pattern, and in many areas is also structured rather simply than intellectually extremely demanding. A high level of intelligence, but not necessarily at the highest level, combined with a certain pragmatism, with assertiveness, even with healthy egotism, are almost ideal conditions for those interested in a career. Managers have to decide. Decisions of the type mentioned here are responsibilities to one of a few elective strategies in the event that not a single one of them has the main contentions for itself. As per my definition, the capacity to pursue choices likewise requires "a remainder of idiocy", since the conclusions that are expected consistently are frequently "as a matter of fact" untrustworthy given the data circumstance tended to.

-

- • Particularly unyielding critics who have seen a ton - and who generally havesurvived - remark on choices made by the highest level that remain totally limitless to them in an especially "purposeful" way. With the goal that discoursed of this sort then, at that point, create between associates: "Have you perused what they have now requested once more? That tosses the cycle back for us by aspects!" Then the other individual says quietly: "So what?"
- • In the wake of perusing this section specifically, you ought to in no way, shape or form be stopped,
- however, say: "All things considered, in the event that that is the situation, I can do it as well."

1.1.1 planning must be

The period available for a career between entry into the workforce and retirement is around forty years. In the beginning it's about becoming something, towards the end it's about securing or defending what has been achieved against loss.

During these decades, your personality will change, including your desires and ideas. B. Subject to influences from – perhaps different – partners. At the same time, your professionally relevant environment is changing quickly and permanently. Companies that seemed rock solid when you started are dying, new technologies bring new jobs and careers, and others disappear. Political and social conditions are changing and have different effects. To put it simply: on the day you retire, almost nothing will be the same as it was when you took your final exams.

The whole thing is an ongoing process with an almost infinite number of influencing factors. It is impossible to do justice to this without careful planning that is constantly updated. Of course, you can also simply jump into the professional environment, remain passive and wait and see what comes of it. It's even possible that there will occasionally be a presentable success, albeit rather accidentally. But who wants to waste the one chance they have in life and risk everything on this uncertain card?

The opportunities in professional life are like a widely ramified oneestuary. If you drift, you'll quickly end up in a dead side arm or a bone-crushing waterfall. Only careful planning, observing the rules anchored in the system and taking into account one's own resources, makes success at least likely. Don't forget: Your resources are not unlimited (the system has plenty of wickedness like this in store for you, I'll just get you used to it).

1.2   The indispensable prerequisites for asuccessful planning
1.2.1   The "cake batter principle": threeComponents determine the result

Let's assume that a cake batter consists mainly of flour, eggs and butter. The mixing ratio allows a larger bandwidth, but each component must be involved with a minimum proportion. If the end result is 1kg of dough, you can achieve the goal with different sized component weights, but substituting one "brick" for one or two others ultimately has limitations; Flour, for example, is absolutely essential, nor does it replace an excess of eggs.

That's how it is withthe three essential prerequisites for a career:

- the wanting
- the ability
- knowledge of the rules ofprocess.

All three components are required, the partial replacement of one by another is possible to a certain extent, but here, too, none must go back to zero. In concrete terms: Extremely strong will can definitely cover up weaknesses in ability, intensive will and ability together can fill some gaps in
compensate for the rule application, but they are all needed.

It is not possible to say where the ideal constellation lies, as the requirements in practice vary depending on the company, industry and economic situation. And it is always people with their highly individual standards who decide what is required and what leads to success. There is no absolute scale for this that applies always and everywhere

1.2.2 At the beginningstands the will

I present this aspectconsciously all the way ahead, even ahead of an obvious requirement such as ability: Hardly anything works without your determination, at least nothing that should be successful through systematic planning.

First of all, this secure knowledge is helpful: It is amazing what a person can achieve if he tackles and pursues a project like his career "with every fiber of his heart" and with consistent determination, not getting discouraged by – unavoidable – setbacks and is always willing to pay the required price.

A contribution like this one can perhaps encourage you to be a little more resolute in pursuing your career goals, but I cannot initiate this desire in you. You either have it or you don't, no one can force oneself to do it in the long run, neither seminars nor books can help.

Let's just assume that without a career drive, people wouldn't read a book like this. As a reader, you have basically fulfilled this first requirement.

The will that we are addressing here is fundamentally indispensable, but it does not have to reach the point of fanaticism in the sense of our project and outshines or covers all other human characteristics, abilities and impulses. A healthy mediocrity is enough for a "medium career", what should go well beyond that needs an equally clear plus in wanting.

To cite a borderline example: A CEO certainly needs a very pronounced desire for a career, one could also write will for power.

If he's not the most sophisticated ruler, that's

fine, he doesn't live according to rules at the culmination, he rather makes them. Be that as it may, he can't manage without it possibly: we've seen a couple of vocations of this sort reach a revolting conclusion recently. Frequently the reason is the "sovereign negligence" of a couple of essential standards that generally exist, even at the extremely top.

The overall guideline is: This eagerness, which shows itself in the dynamic quest for a vocation, shouldyou don't likecarry a light before you, however you shouldn't conceal it tensely by the same token. Most importantly, the climate that is significant for the acknowledgment of such a venture (managers) ought to definitely realize that you have desire and are keen on additional advancement. As "respectable" as it might appear to stay humble behind the scenes and hold back to be inquired: in an open society, the people who don't effectively deal with the fulfillment of their objectives are not entirely obvious.

What's more: Assuming you carry the will with you, terms like
- Perfomance,
- Aspiration,
- Victory,
- World class,

incessant delay of private concernsprofessional

1.2.3   It is not possible without skill

I deliberately worded this headline in a somewhat provocative way. The unbiased observer in particular may see this prerequisite for a career as the central aspect of all. But it is not that easy.
Two questions need to be clarified:

- What do you have to be able to do and
- what role do training, learning processes, accumulated experience play?
-
- And it has to be taken into account that almost every working person likes and often says that he has (had) bosses who were completely free of any ability to convincingly fill the position(s) held in the context of their respective career. does it exist Unfortunately, in principle yes - but you must not rely on the fact that you will succeed. Rather, let's analyze the requirements:
- As we defined above, a career is ultimately the continuous ascent in the hierarchy associated with the assumption of increasing material and personnel responsibility. If you want to be able to do that, you have to be willing to take on responsibility, you have to motivate, direct, control other people and lead them to high performance, you have to assert yourself in front of them. He must have a feeling for power, want to make a difference, be able to make decisions that are often quick and by no means always secure.
- That sounds very challengingIn principle, it is, after all – as evidenced by their pay – the executives are a kind of elite in the company.
- But don't worry, because:

- The jobs in the management careers will be filled in any case, in everyonevintage again. It's not about whether there are enough candidates among every 100 employees or among the students: they will be found. It's all about whether you ultimately belong or not. Self-critical questioning of one's own abilities, strengths and weaknesses is permitted and even advisable. However, this is not an ideal playground for people with pronounced self-doubt or inferiority complexes. But that's the same for athletes who only compete in the club championship.

- Before you are allowed to "build a career" you must be in standard functions for yearsRelang first of all "simply work in execution". You do that – a basic requirement – excellently. In doing so, you will acquire security in your professional field, your personality will mature – and you will gain a wide range of career-related experience. Whereby it is less about you than about others: Colleagues want to be promoted, but cannot make it; You see newcomers in positions of advancement, experience their victories and defeats; You watch your bosses lead and – above all – you are led. After five years you know almost everything about the subject. At least that's what you think - and that's what matters most.

  In case that's still not enough for you: you'll find out that tooYour bosses, ultimately only equipped with this imperfect tool, were one day thrown in at the deep end - and they are the proof that very successful careers can be designed on this basis. My urgent recommendation: Use this still quite "carefree" pre-career phase to observe and plan right away what you want to do differently or what you want to do differently. want to do better.

- "To whom God gives an office, he also gives understanding" - like many of our old onesProverbs also has a very high hit rate. It is said that whoever does something often also acquires a respectable degree of skill. That alone doesn't make you an expert, but many people who were considered completely untalented do at least do a tolerable job "in office".
- Shaping a successful career – that is ultimately onecombination of talent as
  Basis and experience through practice, many years of doing.
- And as the last consolation in this series: The standard requirements for careerthose interested are aligned with the average skills of well-educated young people. If you only let established "experts" into a career, 80% of the corresponding positions would remain vacant.
- And the above question about training and learning processes?
- The cautious answer: Such help can only do harm if you feel competent afterwards, which you are not at first. But for the inexperienced newcomer they give guidelines, especially for set pieces.
- My experience shows that pronounced talent – which is, however, quite rare – is an almost unbeatable basis for a career; Recognizable talent plus training results in an ideal development. A lack of talent plus a lot of training plus a lot of experience enables the candidate to get by in every day life. Untalented people cannot be helped at all: not through books, not through training, and experience doesn't help them any further. But so much lack of talent is also rare.

- There is another very helpful point of reference when it comes to "ability": I keep emphasizing that a career goes a little to considerably beyond what may be considered a "lower average". "More than many others" is the motto (which every athlete easily strives for without apologies). Anyone who undoubtedly has the necessary skills will notice this in good time or will receive clues before entering the professional world. School and university bring you together again and again in different situations with people of the same age and with the same education and additionally challenge you in daily contact with "superior" teachers, professors and the like.

Anyone who has always been just a "gray mouse" for these many years, has never stuck his head "out of the crowd" in any way, just always went along without ever attracting attention, did not manage a project, organized no celebrations, was not a member of any worked, has never taken responsibility, has never been an informal representative in any conversation, he will in general have a more terrible hand.

To put it another way: In the event that you are as yet adequately youthful, take your risk and reach out, for example B. in youth associations, college divisions or socially. At that age, the relating activities actually have an instructive and preparing impact, not precisely making ability, however reassuring what has been covered.

Or more all there is the acknowledgment that any individual who tries to a profession should show trying and that he/she should not hold on until his/her ability is affirmed for certain. It resembles the following:

"Don't be apprehensive," said the chicken to the worm - and ate it.

Likewise the "vocation potential test"which we have been effectively presenting for a really long time (further streamlined in this book than Section 3) can give significant data.

In the event that you now from thetext length of this section, it was a statement of the emotional significance of this perspective, then that sounds wrong. I simply needed to address any worries you could have that your own ability probably won't be sufficient. Basically: With the people who at last made it, it was frequently not substantially more unmistakable toward the start, some of the time even "the inverse" applies. Also, as you most likely are aware: individuals develop with their errands.

•

1.2.4   Golf follows rules. career too

Let's take road traffic as an additional example: everything you are allowed to do andeven more of what you are not allowed to do is regulated. Violations are punished, from a small amount in euros to being banned from driving. It's similar in sports, in football e.g. B. Half the nation is a rules expert.

Material existence depends on professional life, and a large part of individual satisfaction depends on the fulfillment of essential career dreams. Job and career now also follow rules. What should actually be self-evident surprises many people with this simple statement. If you now ask: "What are these rules? Do you know the details? Are you interested in this?", one often gets nothing more than a shrug of the shoulders. I don't know why that is, but I've set out to do something about it.

First an example: Let's assume that one day you would like to be the top manager of an automobile company. For whatever reason, you start your career in a smaller engineering office specializing in plant construction. There you will solve highly complex, "exciting" tasks. But you will hardly be able to achieve your dream goal - the rules do not allow it.

Or you lose the "red thread" of your career, strive for promotion too early or too late, pursue a goal that doesn't suit your path, change employers too often or too seldom, have bad or no references at all, show in the job interview a "wrong attitude" to career issues, constantly looking for jobs that don't fit your character.

Or on the other hand you need to be an overseeing chief, yet are caught in a vocation that finishes as a "impasse" a couple of levels down. These would all be infringement of the principles, to which the expert framework responds with shifting levels of seriousness.

The organizations apply individual principles, contingent upon the economy, for instance: in the event that there is a deficiency of laborers, and candidates are in this way correspondingly uncommon, the candidates let rule infringement go, which they would somehow rebuff with disdain (a prompt dismissal).

It just so happens, it isn't without reason that I discuss the "rules of the game" in this specific situation. Since I really exhort treating proficient life exceptionally in a serious way, yet additionally seeing it as a major (for example Imposing business model) game and keeping the player as distant from the endlessly processes as could be expected.

End: Regardless, you should know the main principles. As a suggestion: JOSH DOUGLAS, rules of the game for work and profession, fourth release, Springer-Verlag. Everything spins around this subject there. Obviously, I will likewise consider the main principles in this book.

1.2.5   In individual cases of considerable influence: Luck, coincidence & Co.

Even winners admit it, losers with failed plans even mostly see the main reason for the weak results of their career efforts in incalculable additional influencing factors. That's not entirely wrong, but it falls short when you examine these aspects.

People who have had successful careers almost always admit that they were lucky in key situations. If someone wants to be promoted internally, then they need a "here and now" open position in the right category, among other positive factors. And if you apply externally, you have to meet the "right" company from a long-term perspective and find the "right" direct boss there. Happiness? Coincidence? Nobody will be able to definitively clarify this.

I owe my first big promotion in a group to the fact that in a situation within the department that was characterized by general signs of dissolution, my superior now also took over the house left. He left a gap, I was there, there were no alternatives available internally – I was far too young, but I was accepted. I left two companies in good time and voluntarily, which soon fell apart and which have long since ceased to exist. Happiness? luck of the fit? "It could have gone wrong in each case," doubters still say to me today. Not a conspicuously early promotion, shaken by two company failures – that could have happened to me, too. If I were sitting here today, would I be writing this book? Who wants to answer that...

I'm inclined to the following theory in this difficult field: the single case doesn't prove anything, but a number of incidents make up a picture - and you can and should draw conclusions from this. If, as a freelancer in a free country, you decide three times in a row to join a company that subsequently goes bankrupt, leaving you unemployed, then you should realize that you lack the ability to find the right employers. seek. You should seek expert advice the fourth time if you have to make a decision again.

And if you fail several times in the German owner-managed private company, then you must change the type of company (e.g. choose the American subsidiary) and vice versa.

Mistakes are allowed, but you should recognize them from the result patterns - and draw conclusions from them. Many of us succeed in some difficult projects with above-average frequency, while others tend not to do so repeatedly.

Another aspect: We are a successful company. What is needed is success, not a good excuse for failure. Just as one should not belittle one's own successes unduly by referring to "luck" or "coincidence", so one should be careful not to use "bad luck" as a reason for failures: if you have had bad luck several times in a row and corresponding ones had to accept defeats – who then still entrusts you with the responsibility for projects or values that you needed a lucky hand to lead?

The English language knows the "loser" as a designation for a "loser as a guy". Whatever he may have done, it was wrong, the result stands for it.

Working life lasts about 40 years. During this time,

numerous situations of all conceivable kinds will come your way. In the evaluation of the results of your actions, you will recognize a pattern at the latest at the end. And then, at the latest, the statistical basis is large enough to draw conclusions about characteristics and abilities, and the justifications "luck", "coincidence" and "bad luck" lose their power of persuasion.

And when all is not convincing, Shakespeare remains: "There are more things in heaven and earth than your philosophies dream, Horatio" (Hamlet to his friend).

What should be said in this chapter: A career cannot be made with performance alone – and individual defeats are not always due to mistakes on your part. This aspect is "systemic".

1.3   The planning begins
1.3.1   The goal is the central base

Planning a career between the end of your studies (the additional inclusion of the focus of your main studies is recommended) and retirement includes working out a path, a route between the beginning and the end. Everything happens on this path, all intermediate stations are along it, it is the focus of your daily thoughts and actions.

But the way is only the way, it is a means to an end, not an end in itself. The motto "The path is the goal" that comes from another culture does not fit our topic and has no place here.

Career planning is like planning a mountain. It's about ultimately arriving at a certain point. The path taken to this end is also of interest, but ultimately secondary. In the mountains, aligning yourself primarily with beautiful or interesting paths and shrugging your shoulders
"To see where this leads us" is also possible, but it's more of a walk in the mountains than a climb.

Paths, whether in the mountains or in the career field, can be right or wrong, beneficial or misleading. Imagine a local in the mountains meeting an exhausted climber who asks in a dying voice, "Am I on the right path?" The other will inevitably have to ask, "Yes, where are you going? "

That is the core question par excellence, especially in the career area. Only with the answer to this do suitable paths begin to emerge.

That's why you need a career goal right from the

start, which you can then focus your efforts on. Basically, the more precisely the goal is formulated, the better and the easier it is to plan the way there.
Ideally, the target is fixed after:

- Field of activity (example: development/construction),
- Hierarchy level (example: department manager),
- Industry (example:Mechanical engineering),
- Company type (example: international group).

Don't worry, I'm talking about the ideal case here and of course I know that these ideals are only achieved relatively rarely. But you have to know the ideal in order to be able to see your own deficits and, if necessary, develop strategies to eliminate them. But what you also have to remember is that in this ideal example, which is so clear, at least the goal-oriented way to get there is almost "automatic".

We will discuss more examples, first I wanted to clarify the principle.

Now the question arises: How do you even come close to defining such a precise goal? You need information:

a. about himself
What should actually be quite easy, because you should be quite close and know each other quite well, is often quite difficult in practice. Because you need
- a fairly open presentation of your strengths and weaknesses (the yardstick is the many others in your respective environment who are of the same age and are challenged in a similar way);
- a realistic analysis of what you want in life in general and in your professional life in particular (do you really want to be at the head of a group or does not the head of the accounting department meet your requirements much better?);
- at least a preliminary certainty that you are willing to pay the price that the fulfillment of demanding goals inevitably demands (possibly prioritizing professional over private/family concerns; willingness to relocate); provisionally because this aspect is particularly subject

to development in the course of your personal development;

b. about the environment of possible targets
In order to be able to seriously aspire to "board member" or "middle manager" at all, you need to have a basic understanding of what each is, what characterizes these goals, or how they differ.
This also applies to what is typical of a group or private medium-sized companies and also to the special features of certain sectors.
You get this information

– active through early research on the Internet, in literature, in the business section of daily newspapers;
passively by attentively recording and collecting such details as reported by family members and acquaintances; if you take the last three years of school and your entire degree as a basis for this You eight to ten years in which you hear a lot, you have torecord, register and evaluate it only willingly;
– the "silver bullet" are internships during your studies; You get to know different types of companies from your own experience, see e.g. B. the work in controlling or in production, which makes your later choice much easier.

Whatever the case, you need a goal in order to be able to plan your career path sensibly. We shall see in the next chapter that here, too, nothing is eaten as hot as it was cooked - alongside the ideal, as always, there is a practice.

—

1.3.2   Goal Setting: Tips and Tricks

The premise of the arranging system is entirely straightforward: the more definitively the objective is characterized, the simpler it is to decide the way. However, exactly this accuracy is deficient. Mostly due to failure, somewhat as a result of dread of such sweeping choices, yet in addition part of the way due to basic obliviousness about the potential outcomes, possibilities and dangers of a vocation, the exact putting forth of objectives prior to beginning a profession isn't made. What's more, there likely could be the standard late designers, whose craving for headway possibly stirs when they have been able to know proficient life and its extraordinary highlights better. For this multitude of deviations from the ideal, there are arrangements that have their singular qualities - however over all they represent the way that "everything isn't finished" right away,

a.   Stop midway:
The accompanying generally applies: keep the objective you set to yourself, you are the main individual who knows it, regardless of whether your vocation is creating as expected.
If, "as an insurance", you base your way anticipating an

objective that is fairly high for your prerequisites, then you stay allowed to choose one day, pretty much distant from the objective, basically to quit taking a stab at additional expert headway and for you as well as yours current circumstance, that is precisely exact thing you would have needed all along.Example: You are planning – very demanding – "top technical management in a medium-sized company" and off you go. Along the way, you eventually become "Head of Department in Technical Management," declare yourself happy with that, and stop further promotion efforts. In the course of your Due to constant personal development, your expectations of personal success may have changed, you may feel that you are overwhelmed if you continue your career, or you are simply no longer willing to pay the "price" that is constantly being demanded.

Then simply stop where you are now - and nobody will notice that you have fallen significantly short of original goals.

Of course, you could have included this "head of department in technical management" as a goal in the planning. But: At that time you were perhaps unsure how far your ambition would reach one day. And perhaps over the years you have constantly had doubts as to whether you shouldn't have chosen a more challenging goal. But as it was, you were in a much better position compared to the variant of planning carefully at first and having to increase the goal again and again.

The question remains as to where the difference lies between the department head that arose from later self-restraint or the one that should have represented the end of the career path from the start.

There is a difference! Let's assume you had the from the start

"Head of department in technical management" was my goal. One day you would then have received the offer to switch to technical purchasing and, after a certain period of time, to become the successor to the head of department. That would have fitted in well with your plan. But: This head of department in technical purchasing might one day become the head of overall purchasing, but never the technical head or technical managing director ("top technical management"). With the latter goal in mind, you should never have accepted this department head offer.

Therefore, the motto "plan for high goals as a precaution and, if necessary, be satisfied with significantly less" can definitely be a solution if you are still unsure at the time of planning and you are not yet able to correctly assess your abilities.

Conclusion: Choosing a high goal gives you the chance to achieve "a lot" over a long period of time. And you can always stop "in the middle". However, it reduces your chances of responding to a wide range of offers that you come across "on the side of the road". To be on the safe side, the offers must always match the most demanding career goal.

A chosen low goal makes it more difficult to achieve "more" afterwards, but makes it easier to fulfill the - modest - original plan. Defining a variant is also a question of type.

a. "Put the horse before the horse":

Here you do not plan the goal and then take the appropriate path, here you look back at the path you have already taken - mostly without a goal.

ten way. Then find a goal that could fit that path so clearly that an outsider would not realize that there was no systematic planning behind it.

This variantis "very welcome". In addition to the advantage that it is still better than having no concept at all before retirement, there are disadvantages compared to "planning from the beginning":

– Only destinations that fit the rather randomly created path are eligible. Which in turn means that very many conceivable goals simply fail completely.

Example: If, after two years of professional experience in software development andfive other people in internal logistics suddenly dream of the head of development and construction or the technical director, it remains an – unfulfillable – dream.

– The method finds its limits where previously there was a rather confused career path without a clear red thread. Of course, you can still plan ambitiously even then - but it is extremely doubtful whether you will find (employer) partners who will enable you to realize it. But e.g. For example, stumbling into the function of an assistant controller after graduation without a concept, doing it successfully for three years, finding joy in it and now building on that to plan your career up to commercial manager, that is definitely possible. Only in the aspects of company type and size are you already somewhat pre-determined (after ten years there it would hardly be possible to correct this).

b. Appearing without a specific goal, but with high standards, is sometimes also possible:

The combination of great ambition, high willingness to perform and high standards without a defined goal has worked. Such a person does not plan for many years, he always looks for his chances, is open to unconventional possibilities, in an emergency he resolutely takes action where he would not have wasted a look a while ago. He doesn't yet know the position he wants to have one day, but he knows it should be "up".

The problem arises from the description of this procedure: You can't plan something like this - and it can also go horribly wrong. If someone fails, the professional observer (e.g. a job applicant) just shrugs and murmurs that that was to be expected. In retrospect, the result is only classified as a "chaotic career". Especially in the industrial environment, which is the focus of this book, this variant is considered extremely daring. After all, industrial companies are also used to new products, new manufacturing processes and production plants as well as the development of new markets must be carefully and systematically planned. It goes much better with this if the relevant managers proceed in a similarly planned manner on their own behalf.

1.3.3   100% goal attainment remains a beautiful dream

Cautious preparation of a vocation is one side, it is the other to execute the idea.

The issues start with the time period between the beginning of a profession and retirement. Just the last option is really the finish of our arranging project. Albeit the stage that comes into question for effectively molding a lifelong finishes today "around 50", the fifteen to twenty years after that likewise require consideration: It is vital to get what has been accomplished - what you can do at this age lost, you scarcely get it back available.

So did the planningto cover the forty years between the finish of the course and arriving at the outright age limit. Anybody with even a little valuable encounter will promptly acknowledge the impediment: Even in principle, this can't work. The "foes" of long haul arranging are the progressions in practically all boundaries that initially assumed a part in the arranging program - from the organizer's own character to the conditions in the expert climate to the mechanical and social structure conditions.

The arrangement is: Vocation arranging is definitely not an oddball cycle with an exceptionally short idea stage and an incredibly lengthy execution stage. Then again, a consistent cycle should be continually checked and refreshed. Practically speaking, "ceaselessly" signifies about like clockwork, to some degree preferably.

All that inside the past arranging must be scrutinized: from one's own will to the conceivable outcomes of realization with the current employer or on the labor market. A constant with increasing importance for the entire planning process is the previous professional path. Career goals can be redefined, but should always be chosen in such a way that they fit as closely as possible with the previous professional path. Therefore, updating is to be seen more as a process with careful changes than one with constant 90° or even 180° changes in direction.

As a consolation: Hardly anyone finally achieves the goal formulated forty years ago and in doing so follows exactly the path envisaged at the time. But hardly anyone is still the same person when they reach their destination, even when looking at themselves at the start of the "working life rally". Somewhere between melancholy and a smile, the person who has finally reached the goal looks at the ideas he had "back then". But, a separate chapter is dedicated to the warning further ahead, without planning it is much more chaotic. And the chances of success are significantly lower.

Somewhat daring, but formulated quite permissible: Long-term career planningat the beginning of one's career, including constant review and updating, should serve less to achieve that one goal set "in the distant past". On the other hand, it is intended to ensure that, for forty years, we always move within the framework of a carefully planned process and do not stumble around disoriented in the "mined terrain". You realize early enough that this is a dangerous environment.

1.3.4   The Timelineas a benchmark and control instrument

If you present your thoughts about your career to someone, they will first and foremost notice WHAT you are planning or what you are doing there. want to be. The WHEN is just as important and crucial for success.

It starts with the fact that time is limited and cannot be increased: a wasted or lost year is simply "gone" - like the drain from an account that is no longer funded. Income, for example, is subject to completely different rules: If I have earned (too) little in the first ten years of work, this can be compensated for by a very high income in later years. This is not possible if you lose time: A single year that took longer than usual to get your high school diploma or degree is in the "papers" for life – and quickly adds up to other possible abnormalities. This is why the timeline is so important when shaping a career. The corresponding standards are tough: it's easy to be "too young" and very quickly it can mean "too late, the train has left". And not four different employers in the CV are the problem, they will be with the addition "in three years". Whoever says "career" says "performance". The latter is physical/technical work per unit of time. Performance cannot be defined at all without taking time into account. You can definitely equate the WHAT in career planning with the term "work". "I've been promoted to Team Leader" is similar to "I got 500kg of rocks from A to B". Nice that it was achieved, but You can definitely equate the WHAT in career planning with the term

"work". "I've been promoted to Team Leader" is similar to "I got 500kg of rocks from A to B". Nice that it was achieved, but You can definitely equate the WHAT in career planning with the term "work". "I've been promoted to Team Leader" is similar to "I got 500kg of rocks from A to B". Nice that it was achieved, but
any really useful statement is not both.
Only if the conveyedadds "3 years after I started my career" becomes a definable (here positive) achievement. As with the stone Transporter when he adds "in 10 minutes". And the admiration turns into bored yawning, when it says "at 49 years of age" and in the other case
"within severaldays".

The applicable "rules of the game" are also often related to time. The sum of all aspects results in the following recommendations as "rules of thumb":

- The career starter may not be considered by external applicantscatcher after two yearsTerm of service already change employers, the professionally experienced employee should be able to show about five years per employer in the curriculum vitae.
- Very(!) clearly aboveTen years of service per employer shouldwould at least lead to the consideration of whether a change might not be appropriate simply so that one day one does not have to leave and then be regarded as hopelessly inflexible after eighteen years of service; Factual (changing areas of responsibility) and hierarchical (promotions) changes during this time shift this "limit" upwards.
- The first real promotion is possible and therefore plannable after about fiveyears of service; at the age of

45 you should (with a little tolerance upwards) "sit" again in the position from which you can retire "if necessary".

- A promotion every five years until you reach your career goal is a goodThe third point of reference, this frequency is sufficient for the path from clerk to managing director/board member.
- If there has been no promotion in the CV for about ten years,
the "career train" slowly leaves the station without you.

This is accompanied by some additional insights/recommendations:

- What wants to become a checkmark (which means: a career is only
requires a playground for late developers).
- Even with limited goals, it is advisable toand stop climbing once you've achieved what you've planned - and not wait until you're 45 and then suddenly want to become a group leader.
- By the time you're about 35, "ladder" should be on your business card.
- Should an emergency occur at an advanced age and a new oneIf a position has to be found externally, the following applies: A higher rank is easier to market than a lower rank (while managing directors can still find a new job at the age of 52 to 55, clerks sometimes encounter concerns at the age of 45 purely for reasons of age (which no longer often -
may be mentioned, but which of course continue to exist in the mind of the decision-maker).

And at the end of this chapter one more restriction: the publication of – e.g. Experience has shown that those who seek advice welcome rules and recommendations that are partly unwritten but still exist and are seen as a helpful basis for planning. However, I always have a "stomach ache" and am afraid that someone will cling too tightly to a number and see a catastrophe if a size is slightly exceeded. Therefore a restriction to the statements in this chapter:

- All figures are inevitably only general average valuesdepending on the economic situation, industry, type of company and responsible decision-maker: So if it says "five years" somewhere, then six is just as safe as about four, but two or twelve years are then fundamentally associated with problems calculate. However, anyone who finds the specified dimensions in their CV is on the safe side.

1.3.5 Generalists, common threads and which employerwhom "impressed"

In addition to a path leading up in the hierarchy, the classic ascent also largely follows a technical "red thread". It is advisable to follow this system in your own planning; the career that is gradually developing is sought after on the labor market at all times because it is in great demand and is therefore easy to "sell". This common thread is primarily formed by an area of activity that remains the same or is logically based on the previous area of activity in the individual professional stations. A second component of this type, which is not quite as dominant in its effect, is the combination of industry and company type. Positive example:

1. career station: industrial engineer in the machining series production of mechanical engineering, medium-sized company with approx. 2,000 employees;
2. professional position: team leader production in the metal-cutting series production of mechanical engineering, medium-sized company with approx. 1,000 to 3,000 employees (like No. 1 identical);

3. Professional station: Head of production for machining in series production in mechanical engineering, medium-sized company with approx. 1,000 to 3,000 employees (preferably identical with No. 1 and/or 2);

4. professional position: overall production manager of a company with series production in mechanical engineering, approx. 800 subordinate employees in the departments of cutting production, welding, painting, assembly, maintenance in a medium-sized company with approx. 1,000 to 3,000 employees (probably no longer with No. 1 and 2, but maybe still identical to No. 3). You would now be in your early 40s and may have achieved your goal.

Negative example: You dream of generalists.This is someone who can do "everything".
– which is difficult enough, but in any case at the expense of qualifications in a specific field of activity. For some reason, the thought of being a generalist (or wanting to become better) is magically drawn to some people. Those who tend to sift through existing descriptions of positions (in job advertisements). When will a "generalist" ever be sought there?
Two statementsmoreover:

a. There is no such thing as a generalist career path, and hardly any special career path with the express aim of being a generalist.

b. There are generalist positions in top management such as chairman of the board, sole managing director, head of division or similar. However, these positions are usually reached via one of the classic career paths with a common thread. Our overall production manager from just now could also become a plant manager and thus also be responsible for purchasing and the commercial departments, then he could take over another plant with additional responsibility for sales, so he would be responsible for profit + loss - and would be generalist. This part of the career is more difficult to plan because one step no longer leads logically to the next.

A somewhat special element is the company size (which I used in the positive example aboveleft identical). The following applies here:The following applies to external applications (you must reckon with the need for this):
The recipient of the application sees the origin of the applicant from a company of the next higher level particularly positively, this employer "impresses" him. He accepts a current employer of his own size, but he is very critical of coming from a much smaller company. Derived from this, a special long-term career has proven to be almost classic: Start in a 100,000-employee company as Clerk, after five years changeas a team/group or project leader in a company with 10,000 to 20,000 employees, after a further seven years as a department head in a company with 3,000 employees, after a further five years as a division manager in a company with 800 employees. Finally, at the age of about 47, as managing director in a house with maybe 300 "people".

The reverse is not possible: the simultaneous leap up in company size and in the hierarchy ("double leap") only succeeds in exceptional cases.

1.3.6 The implementation of the planning in day-to-day operations

As is almost always the case, the implementation process, which lasted several decades, is the larger problem, which is much more difficult to assess and is influenced by far more different parameters. But the following still applies: Without sensible planning, the extremely complex professional practice can no longer be mastered in such a way that a halfway satisfactory career, which also corresponds to one's own intentions, results afterwards.

While planning is the sole responsibility of the career aspirant, implementation is always in the interests of the respective employer. It is important to move in this very difficult area in such a way that one primarily serves the interests of the much stronger employer and at the same time has one's own interests in mind according to appropriate planning.

Here I list the most important basics, empirical values and recommendations that, in my experience, play a role:

1. Your carefully prepared career planning is of no interest to the employer you are looking for or have found. He is not – not even remotely – a committed partner in fulfilling your concept, but he needs you primarily to fulfill a task he has, to fill an existing and currently vacant position with him. You have to qualify for that, that's what you get paid for. He doesn't want to have anything to do with your long-term plans, he thinks

concrete goals for twenty years later are ridiculous, you would lose your qualifications if you did. You're not even striving for your next career goal for five years – you're starting now to do precisely this new job well and with commitment.

When people ask about your future plans, you tend to be low-key when it comes to talks about standard positions. When applying for junior jobs (trainee, succession), you also first concentrate on the upcoming tasks ahead, but: you definitely have the right level of ambition, want to prove yourself first, gain qualifications, but later (once you have performed well) take on more responsibility. The following always applies: An employer fears nothing more than a young "ambitious man" who "only has his career on his mind" and asks about the next promotion once a week.

2. In today's fast-paced world with its z. T. extremely short change intervals, even the most benevolent employer can no longer be taken for granted as a long-term partner for your career planning. If it turns out, it's good, if not, you have to take action and change if necessary. Attention: Even large and very well-known corporations no longer plan for more than two years when it comes to personnel issues and thus also in terms of the specific development of their employees.

3. The employer is basically not interested in your promotion - certainly not because you "deserve it". You can only "earn" your salary.
An employee is promoted if

a. he has done his previous job excellently as an indispensable prerequisite. The assessment is primarily the responsibility of the supervisor, who has a subjective opinion, but always considers it to be objective.

b. a personal one within the organizational structures of the employer

"Hole" has arisen, for which a "plug" is now being sought. You could offer yourself for this. The employer is interested in the fact that something is happening with his "hole". He tends not to be interested in whether this also coincides with the interests or even the plans of the "tamping". That's his problem.

You ponder the acknowledgment of your profession arranging, the business has his work force association as a top priority. You likewise watch out for it, since it is essential to you, however your drawn out objectives are unique. That might be fine for some time, however most likely not so much for twenty or forty years. Assuming the conceivable vocation way with the business veers off altogether from your profession arranging, either change this preparation or search for another business.

4.   As a safeguard, a representative trying to advancement should as of now work, show up and think (perhaps at the same time look: facial hair/clothing, and so on) in their past position like an individual from the level to which they need to be advanced. He delivers, still at the old compensation, semi fundamental work, through which he qualifies. This is designated "putting resources into your own vocation".

5.   The first advancement to an administrative position is generally the most troublesome. The well established past business is an especially intriguing, yet not by any means the only possible accomplice. You should can to some extent generally plan your arrangements there. In the event that that doesn't work in this House, you need to act.

6.	The execution of your profession planningit expects that you give it a specific need over different issues, for example B. certainly additionally towards the interests of your manager. In the event that you have worked there effectively for the suggested five, perhaps seven or eight years, on the off chance that you are as yet going for the gold one further advancement however it is unimaginable there, then, at that point, you have the "ethical support" to look remotely a superior opportunity to attempt. With a time of administration here, your past business won't be excessively disheartened when you leave.

To put it very clearly: A healthy selfishness is part of a successful strategy in our economic system – your employer acts in the same way towards the partners in his markets.

Career Planning: ThePractice

2.1   About the history of the practice part

Since 1984, VDI nachrichten, the "leading opinion-forming weekly newspaper for engineers and technical management" with over 300,000 readers, has published the "Career Advice" series in every issue. Readers ask questions, JOSH DOUGLAS answers. The topics cover the entire spectrum of "Application, Profession, Career", so far 2,700 questions and answers have appeared there.

Original submissions and replies are printed in the following chapters, e.g. T. slightly revised for this purpose and arranged thematically. The senders remain anonymous in the series, but are known to the publisher and to me.

All questions are authentic, they each reflect excerpts from real working life. When making my selection, when it was printed in the VDI nachrichten and now again for this book, I made sure that the focus was and is on questions that are relevant in practice and by no means completely exotic. These problems affect people who are in the working world and want to achieve something in the long term or maybe "just" want to secure their livelihood in the short term (which is also part of successfully shaping a career).

In the almost thirty years that this series has been running, there have been numerous confirming indications, including from readers who are not engineers and in some cases even come from professional environments that are completely outside of the industry that is always the focus of our attention. These are merchants, lawyers, doctors, teachers in the public sector, etc. They keep saying: That's exactly how it is with us.

My actual target group "academics in industry" shows different reactions when they follow my posts over a longer period of time: clear skepticism to rejection as a student, cautious reluctance in the first years of work, approval to enthusiasm from about ten "service years": "exactly the same" be it in the companies or "actually much worse".

If this is the case, I noted early on, then students experience and know far too little about professional practice "out there", for example. Or also: The typical university teaches hardly anything about later professional life that goes beyond purely technical matters. That's why so many mistakes are made, especially in the first years of work or even when starting out.

And if you come across occasional entertaining effects while reading the individual cases, then they are there on purpose. Keeping a series alive and in the interest of readers over this extremely long period of time takes more than dry imparting of knowledge and constant repetition of cautionary advice.

But since the skepticism of inexperienced first-time readers of my answers sometimes reaches a considerable dimension, I assure you again as a precautionary measure: All my statements, even if they have sometimes been consciously written "with a light pen", are on point completely serious and never meant as a gloss. And this is also a precaution: I didn't do our professional system, I found it that way. Neither individual newspaper articles nor books would have the power to change it emphatically.

2.2 Attunement to the following specific questions

The following cases have been selected twice: First, from the constantly incoming questions on the "Career Advice" series, those suitable for publication and public answering were filtered out. A further selection was made from this for this book.

Despite, or perhaps because of, the double selection, you might be surprised when reading these practical examples: While the first, purely conceptual part of this book calls for systematic, long-term planning geared towards a goal, this is mainly about individual sub-programs. problems and often about difficulties that played no role at all in the beginning of the book. To "compensate" for this, one rarely recognizes a well thought-out planning approach in the concrete descriptions.
These notes on this:

1. 1. The shippers who express their opinion here didn't have the foggiest idea about the initial segment of this book. They typically began their individual expert vocations sooner or later with next to no all-encompassing idea. Assuming there was profession aspiration, they frequently "moved" from one situation to another.
2. 2. The previews that should be visible in the singular inquiries will likewise give you fascinating and, I trust, educational bits of knowledge into training.
3. 3. No matter how cautiously you plan, you can experience issues of the sort depicted by the

submitters whenever en route beginning to end. With my responses I attempt to give potential arrangements. The inquiries and answers imprinted on the accompanying pages showed up in the years 2011 to 2013 in the "Profession Counsel" part of the VDI news. Moreover, under "Notes from training" I once in a while gave answers that rung a bell, regardless of whether there were no specific questions.

2.3 asking andAnswers to the career and related areas from the series "Career Advice" from VDI nachrichten
2.3.1 The career entry

Ideally, this is the first step on the way to the previously carefully defined goal. In practice, however, the typical young academic sees this start as a separate, isolated problem that must be solved somehow. You'll see what comes after that at some point.

2.3.1.1 wanted paradise

Ask

In a few months I will complete my doctorate, after that I
I would like to start a job in industry, preferably in a larger company.

I. Of course I want a great employer
– with viable structures,
– where good work and success are synonymous,
– where employees are treated fairly,
– where teamwork is not just a term that is often mentioned, but actually practiced and
– in which the decisions of the superiors up to the company management are comprehensible.

How do I find a company that meets these requirements as well or as closely as possible? Can you rely on awards for the best employer in Germany?

II. What should I specifically ask about in a job interview without coming across as arrogant?
Can I ask to see the later section once?
I shouldrefuse if my future superior does not take part in the interview?
What kind of salary demand... (that's enough; H. Mell)?

Answer

Two souls live, alas, in your breast (freely based on Goethe, Faust).

There is part I of your question: Intellectually well thought out, correctly formulated and about as practical as little Fritzchen imagining paradise. To relieve you, let me say (CV is available), you are a straight-A candidate (inter alia intermediate diploma 1.1). Something like this happens there. This can get worse later (seriously).

With the malice imposed on me for educational reasons, I point out two facts that are somehow related:

a. You write in your résumé that, according to some statistics, your pre-diploma grade was the only one of this quality.

b. II have been answering questions of this kind here and in public events for more than 25 years. "How do I find paradise?" is extremely rare, just like your intermediate diploma. In general and sincerely, I only mean well, my advice for your later professional life: Always be better and smarter than others - but when you appear, look, general and special professional behavior, when answering questions, orientate yourself on what what the average does. Deviations from this only in homeopathic doses, at least until you are firmly "in" the system.

Well, I said all that to you because you can stand it and didn't ask out of stupidity (although I sometimes believe that cleverness at a certain level runs the risk of being classified as stupid again by those around you - like both would be located on one circle). Now calmly to the point. First to I:

Forget that – both in terms of your ideas and wishes and especially with regard to the possibilities of finding out all this in the interview. Your requirements are unrealistic – something you have to forgive as a career starter – you are naïve when it comes to finding statements about them, the system is not built that way.

But I can reassure you: All large companies - and one of them you want - are broadly similar to each other. It couldn't be any other way: They produce comparable products, work in the same markets, have the same or even the same shareholders, use this one labor market when hiring employees – from the porter to the head of the supervisory board – and provide theirs beginners from the same universities and send their employees to largely comparable seminars. And to a limited extent, they even exchange these employees with each other through dismissals, applications and new hires.

Now my statement, which may not be scientifically based, but is supported by my life experience: If all of this is the case, then the internal conditions of such companies must inevitably be very, very similar, it is inconceivable otherwise ("anyone who knows one, knows all").

Incidentally, it is different with small private companies: there the individual personality of the owner radiates down to the last small detail in the company.

Coming back to your larger companies: random special circumstances in one place (person of your boss or the informal leader of the team of colleagues) mean bigger differences for your journey there than anything you could find out in advance (a bit naively thinking). , if you actually pursued your list of questions. Don't ask these kinds of questions, you'd just come out as a particularly complete beginner. I laughed at first when I read that too. There are no answers.

Part II is from you z. T. less well thought out and sometimes formulated with the wrong terms, but is much more realistic in substance.

Targeted questions in the job interview: as a beginner, above all about the upcoming task, what the boss expects of the new employee, the structure of the department/number and qualifications of colleagues. The rest is easy to find. Attention: For the boss, who is not allowed to admit that, you as a beginner are about as important as another student in the first semester is for the dean at the university.

A look at the future department: Be sure to ask for it politely(!) – you should have seen the future work environment.

If the future boss is not present: Don't sign a contract if you haven't met him, he is more important to you than the rest of the company.

When it comes to salaries, you should know that all large companies have fixed standards by which they pay beginners. You can accept them or leave them as they are - that's all. Actually, a beginner doesn't "earn" anything in the first six months, you only invest in him in order to have an "industrial usable" employee after about one to two years. Start somewhere, do amazing things, become indispensable to your boss, work your way up the career ladder and the higher salary will come "automatically". Senior executives complaining about underpayment are ra

2.3.1.2   contribution to the energy transition

Ask

The energy transition is a topic that is much discussed, especially politically. my goal
and wish is to make an active contribution to the success of the energy transition after graduation.

One constantly reads (e.g. in comments from politicians or experts) and hears (e.g. in discussion rounds on the topic) that this is precisely where junior staff are needed who have a broad education to understand all the different aspects of the own energy transition. In addition, more and more courses are emerging, especially in the field of renewable energies, which do not train classic process engineers or electrical engineers. So there really does seem to be a need for these "jack of all trades".

I'm studying electrical engineering at a TU, am currently writing my master's thesis on the development of lithium-ion batteries and have completed several internships at a power company and a wind turbine manufacturer. When choosing my elective lectures, it was important to me to also acquire theoretical knowledge about energy from other engineering disciplines (mechanical engineering, chemical engineering).

When I was researching job postings that I was interested in, I got the impression that in the end, traditional electrical or mechanical engineers are always wanted in business. By this I mean not only the required field of study, but also refer to the activities described during the recruitment process.

2.3 Questions and answers about careers and related ones…33

So where are the well-trained young professionals looking for – in development, in sales, in project management? Or in the end even in science or politics?

Answer

Read very briefly, your complaint sounds convincing, your argument even seems logical. But: Only someone who doesn't know the practice thinks and writes like this - because it's different, very different in fact. As a student, you get a "discount" for misinterpretations of this kind, but not later. However, since you are about to start your career, you should know more about the conditions "out there".

You have apparently read a book entitled "How I can accommodate as many impractical, even dangerously false statements and arguments as possible in a few lines". In order of presentation, I'll try to put things right:

1. The second sentence of your submission is the "root of all evil", specifically: the cause of all problems that you have already encountered or will encounter.

   You see, the basis of your plan looks like this: you want to be an employee somewhere. The official (actual!) definition for this is: a dependent employee. The key word is "dependent". Your existence depends on finding someone who will hire you, pay you - and keep you as long as possible. You can be fired; You have to fight for other re-employment or for a promotion, often you even have to do so in order to keep your job. You have no "right to work", if you have one, you are bound by instructions. And you are at the mercy of the big and small decisions of the employer: If he wants to close your business unit or sell the whole company to a financial investor, then he closes or sells. And all your planning can be obsolete.

Nevertheless, professional life can be fulfilling, a pleasure, and a pleasure to complete – many people succeed. But your options are overwhelmed, in addition to all the problems mentioned – and there can be many and they can become extremely oppressive – through your work as a Employee of a commercial enterprise wanting to actively advance a (poorly planned) political and social project of enormous proportions.

The companies that will employ you and whose job advertisements you will read have the overriding goal of achieving the highest possible return on their owners' capital in a variety of ways. If the energy transition serves this purpose, then it will be taken along, people will jump on the bandwagon. But energy transition as a corporate goal? If a company said it, I didn't believe it.

The wind turbine manufacturerdoesn't want an energy turnaround, nor does he want as many wind turbines as possible to be set up by his industry - he doesn't benefit from that. He wants a chance to sell as many of his branded assets as possible. If that works as part of an energy transition, it's good, if it's part of a different program, it would be good too. That's how it works, I'm just stating it here - and the principle feeds us all.

But you also understand that you are overtaxing the

system. No employee in the industry can expect to advance politically desired programs in this context "on the side" (because his number one goal must be something else).

In concrete terms: You will work in a commercially oriented company. You can choose. It builds either wind turbines, photovoltaic systems or biogas power plants. You can specialize in this; However, the "energy transition" is a political issue, that is a completely different dimension.

2. In the first and third sentences of your submission, you refer to politicians, perhaps also to media representatives ("discussion groups"). Let's call them together "Group A". But you need a job with a "Group B" business enterprise. Both groups are not necessarily interlinked and are not subordinate to each other, and they often hardly speak to each other. You've accepted a promise of a certain kind of job from group A (which their representatives will always deny), now go to group B and claim the promise. That's naive. At best, you could refer to concrete statements from representatives of the companies that are now supposed to hire someone. Or you apply for a job in the Federal Environment Ministry, for example.

3. This topic keeps coming up here at intervals: "I consciously pursue a broad-based training, then I am also preferably looking for a generalistically oriented position and the subsequent corresponding career path." This is almost always followed by disappointment. Oh, there is nothing, absolutely nothing, that speaks against a broad education with knowledge of this and that. But there are two

limitations to keep in mind:

4. "Broad" alone doesn't count for much. First of all, depth, i.e. special knowledge, has to be found in an area. Additional breadth on this basis is valuable and will definitely help those affected at some point. However, "I see myself as a generalist" is a statement made by young professionals that is feared by applicants.

5. With rather minor and accidental exceptions,there is no career path for generalists in commercial enterprises, i.e. from "junior generalist" to "senior generalist" to "Top managers in generalist management".
However, there are jobs with a clearly generalist orientation. This includes the sole managing director of a small GmbH as well as the CEO of a large corporation. But the way there normally leads through a career with increasing responsibility in a special field (e.g. development, sales, production, project planning, etc.) of an industry. Anyone who wants to become a technical manager, for example, does not start out as a "Managing Director Candidate III. class" and then slowly advances through the II. class. Instead, he starts out as a development engineer specializing in a product or technology. And then he becomes a group and department manager for development, later a development and construction manager, at some point gets the planning/AV, then the production of a plant, plant planning and maintenance, becomes technical manager there and later possibly technical managing director. Then he is a technical generalist. And then, if necessary, gets the management of a subsidiary, which also includes the responsibility for sales and commercial matters. And then he is finally a generalist.

This career description is just an example, but not unrealistic.

6. Now a word about the degree programs that you take as an indication of the justification of your expectations: Normally, universities introduce new degree programs after approval by the Ministry of Education. The economy then hires their graduates – or not. If you're lucky, there was intensive talks between the two parties beforehand. But it is certain that the company you later apply to has never been asked. And certainly no one ever asked the development manager responsible for hiring, I assure you. And then you come and marvel at his disinterest.

I had a conversation with two college professors. They told me:

"If we want to set up a new field of study, the ministry only asks whether we can get enough students to enroll there. However, we are not asked whether the companies 'out there' are like that people who are trained like that." I have no reason to doubt it.

Well, we're a free country. You decide what you want to train in, and you also bear the risk. In a market economy, the fact that an offer exists is no proof that this product or service makes sense or is needed. So be careful with the plan to want to become a "jack of all trades".

2.3.1.3   Group, promotion, consulting?

Ask

I'm going to complete my certification as a modern specialist with a

I got an excellent grade and have in this manner likewise got a large number of offers, including direct section into a gathering, modern advancements and the board consultancy. You could thusly portray my concern as a "extravagance issue", however a choice actually must be made.

In a gathering (like a top games vehicle maker) there are obviously an extensive variety of improvement open doors, however the singular scope of errands is exceptionally restricted toward the start. I'm likewise put off by extensive inside determination (evaluation) processes for the board positions with the comparing rivalry. Be that as it may, it is most likely best to "move away" from an organization on the off chance that you are disappointed.

Notwithstanding the title, the main expert experience that you gain represents a modern doctorate (offer from the top gathering XY AG is accessible). In any case, the doctoral agreement is obviously restricted and the possibilities being taken on would be 50:50, best case scenario. How simple is it really to find a comparatively compensated line of work at different organizations a short time later? Or on the other hand do you experience more significant compensation requests for graduates without a Dr. furthermore, a place that is generally not straightforwardly custom fitted to the subject of the doctorate, rapidly to reservations?

At asmall innovation the board consultancy, I would have the valuable chance to deal with a wide range of ventures in a brief time frame. Be that as it may, could you at any point then change to industry without losing your compensation? All things considered, you have insight, yet just with evolving projects, so you can't "ever figure things out".

In light of your experience, could you at any point give an appraisal of what the later advancement prospects could be for the separate other options or which choice is the right one for whom?

I am grateful for this submission, as I can use it to demonstrate the typical characteristics of a certain group of applicants, here the one-candidate.

Your preparation of the factual information, the presentation of the advantages and disadvantages is almost perfect. This underscores the statement "A-candidates almost never fail in practice because of technical problems". They can even be entrusted with non-specialist tasks without any problems - they dig through to the heart of the matter there, grasp quickly, analyze accurately and almost always produce a presentable result.

This is underlined here bythe exemplary solved – fictitious – task:

"Put together what options such a candidate has and where the advantages and disadvantages of the individual variants lie."

This roughly corresponds to the tasks set during the course (exams, study and diploma thesis). Anyone who manages to do so in a demonstrable way gets their A (I'm concerned with the principle, not with comparing this submission with a scientific elaboration).

Then comes the next step, the decision. she putsAccording to JOSH DOUGLAS, there is more or less a great deal of stupidity left in the decision maker - very clever people would never make a decision at all. Because a decision is not just a commitment to one of several alternative courses of action for which particularly weighty arguments speak. Any fool or computer could do that. No, a decision is due when

Answer

there are almost as many arguments for and against an alternative or for or against several of them.

Then people suddenly ask: the courage, something actuallydoing irresponsible things because they have to be done; the willingness to listen to one's own gut feeling without being able to provide justifications for it; the desire to consciously do unconventional things; the playful effect of also taking risks that

are "actually unreasonable"; the inclusion of rules from practice, where things are just the way they are - and the consideration of the typical behavior of people affected here, who often act completely beyond rationality and logic.

All of this is, to put it mildly, less the strength of straight-A candidates who always want to do everything "right". What was enough in school and university. In the "afterlife" not only is that no longer enough, but these simple categories "right" or "wrong" no longer exist. For this there are the new requirement categories "strategically well thought out", "tactically clever",

"Clever/refined", "cheeky", "risk-taking", "to the weaknesses of fellow human beings

aiming", "having success" or "happily operating". Maybe even truenor "man matures through his defeats".

Now let's move on to the options you correctly presented:

1. Entry into the group:

Anyone who starts at XY AG is initially employed at XY AG. That alone is something - you collect "credit points" for your future professional life. Five years later, should it become necessary, the name of this employer opens many doors out there. There are numerous internal opportunities for advancement, so there are hardly any excuses for not being promoted in the long term.

The "individual range of tasks"? Who cares? In the beginning they do not shape the corporate policy anyway, nor the new series that is to follow the 911 (as an example). Everything goes a bit leisurely, a bit according to official channels, and nobody ever retires from their entry-level position. You first learn "how things work here", is a small light in big projects, has the marshal's baton in your knapsack – and is at XY AG: goosebumps run down the backs of your fellow students when they hear that. And the father-in-law is already thinking about how to tell the story at the regulars' table.

What are you going to do in that corporation? What does a Pope do – must beone, that's what it's all about (if necessary, an archbishop will do it too).

Attention: The chairmanship of the board of directors is basically open to everyone. But the holder of this position does not have the best super exam of all academic employees, has not always solved the most scientifically demanding tasks and is not necessarily the "best do-gooder" imaginable. The same applies to the levels below him, graduated accordingly. Oh, and one more thing: If you were to ask the respective CEO, "a) how important was the entry-level task in professional practice for attaining the current position and b) didn't you also find the lengthy internal selection processes for management positions with the corresponding competition bothering you? ' then you have the rare chance to see such a man laugh. Winners fear nothing, neither temporarily boring work,

I know that my reasoning makes possible replies like:

"I don't even want to be CEO. Head of development department would be enough for me." That wouldn't be relevant, if I may say so. If you want to work in certain structures, you have to accept the principle according to which they work ("You should recognize them by their extremes"). As a rule, the top manager was also once a department head.

And don't be afraid of the selection methods for future leaders. There are always such "methods", whether it is the assessment by a single boss or the objectified judgment within a systematized selection. Everywhere something can only be achieved "who meets our requirements" - sometimes it's this, sometimes it's that. Just trust that the "methods" actually favor people who fit the bill. Promotion is based on entitlement, never on the basis of considerations of fairness. And: Starting a career here is hardly ever a one-size-fits-all "incorrect".

2. Industrial promotion:

Take a look at the job advertisements and see how many industrial engineers with a doctorate are wanted (almost none). So you would have to do it just because it makes you feel better (that can be an argument). If there really is only a small chance of being taken over later in that company, you should be with the people taken over, otherwise you will easily have the image of "weighed and found wanting". You have to have a very good "excuse" why you weren't taken on in order to be of unlimited interest to other employers.

Attention, you develop a kind of fixation on the salary question, this pops upup again later.

After completing your doctorate, you would be an engineer with a doctorate in external eyes, which is traditionally rated somewhat higher by applicants than someone without a doctorate. It is an open question whether the time spent doing your doctorate would also be recognized as full professional experience. This would then be offset by the fact that the renowned group would not take it over, which would reduce its attractiveness.

And the engineer, who earned his doctorate at the university institute, did something there during his years there and gained experience. These are already "priced into" in the typical entry-level salary for beginners with a doctorate. The purpose of an industrial promotion is primarily the promotion, just as a front door is more a door than a house.

If you are so fixated on money, you should – especially as an industrial engineer – prefer to join the group according to 1. Then you will have several years "more correct" by the time the "industrial doctor" is about to complete his doctorate and is worried about being taken on. , unassailable professional practice that is definitely "easily sellable" internally or externally.

By the way, it's better to say "Doctorate" than "title". Also, "I wanted to earn this degree" sounds more distinguished than "I really wanted this title."

3. Advice:
This is where money comes up again, especially when you are just starting your career, other aspects should play a role first. You earn later: managing directors rarely complain.

Working in a consultancy, as long as it does not exceed

two to three years, is often considered a kind of external trainee program. You see a lot and learn accordingly, no question.

In addition to professional qualifications, demeanor, the ability to "sell yourself" and presentation skills are also required. It is often a very strenuous job, if only because of the high (up to 100%) travel and overnight stay rate and a lot of "overtime". It pays well, otherwise many people wouldn't do it. This portion of a "difficulty allowance" actually disappears when you later switch to "stationary" industry; it cannot always be saved.

Many successful, talented consultants then manage to jump into great industry positions, while others do not (model examples are not always representative, don't let yourself be fooled).

Anyone who stays with us for a long time or always needs acquisition potential, ie sales skills (he is then responsible for order procurement, while lower-ranking managers or newcomers take on the implementation of consulting projects). Many well-known major consultancies are tough as nails: If you don't get promoted internally every few years, you have to leave. Then he wasn't good enough.

So, dear sender, now you decide – also based on gut feeling. You'll never know if it was right. You can see what has become of you in twenty years. But you don't see what would have become of you if you had taken an alternative path. The path of former fellow students or later colleagues also proves nothing - these are other personalities who, e.g. T. achieve completely different results with the same opportunities. After all, personality is a decisive factor in career success later on, and the value of the very good exam decreases.

On which "symptoms" do you read chances down?

Referring to an earlier question where you write that in your experience-
If a special talent for languages correlates negatively with managerial qualities, I would like to ask you for further "observations from practice".

I know that I am asking a lot of you when I ask you to print in this newspaper (and therefore possibly the anger of readers who feel addressed at to drag). On the other hand, if I may say so, in an earlier case you "leaned out so far" that you might want to dare to do it again?

I ask this question so that students like me can assess whether their talents, strengths and weaknesses can already serve as an indication of future success in professional life. This is based on the assumption that your employer gives you the opportunity to actually use any managerial skills you may have.

In your experience, are morally "good" people better leaders than those who have less "noble" character traits? That probably sounds naïve to you, because "warriors" can and are good bosses. However, the question then arises as to whether this isn't a dying species on management floors: I think I'm observing a change in the selection of personnel (particularly of junior managers, e.g. trainees). The aim today is to recruit employees who are team players and sociable, ie morally "better" people than, for example, egocentric cholerics.

Answer

Oh man! They produce opposites that are not, lead to evaluation categories
ries that don't fit the topic here for us and in all innocence ask questions that e.g. T. there is no answer at all and where you could fill a whole book with the reason why it doesn't work that way.

And yet you also deserve recognition. Because you at least deal with such topics; while others stumble through their jobs throughout their lives and make mistakes that they don't even recognize as such afterwards. So, first of all, congratulations.

I just have to cover a few aspects side by side, hoping that a) I can make do with the limited space and b) I'll end up with some semi-useful insights:
It is impossible to predict a single person's future career success. It's too complex an area for that, the influencing factors are too numerous, this one person changes too quickly or is too subject to external criteria, luck, coincidence, opportunity, choice of partner (!) etc. play too large a role Role. It is at best possible with a reasonably homogenous group with distinct characteristics and abilities to predict that a larger percentage of their members will probably "end up" one way or the other.

1. Extreme professional situations often bring particular strengths to light or particular weaknesses that would never have come to the surface if the people concerned had only ever faced average challenges. For some, the particular strain was nothing but a curse, as it broke them, while others saw it as a blessing, as it was

precisely at this point that he was able to distinguish himself.

2. As banal as it sounds: Many young people do not know what they are really capable of (where their true talents lie), what is ultimately good for them and/or develop a fatal passion to pursue exactly those goals that they will not achieve and for disregarding brilliant skills with which they might excel.

It helps if you develop a watchful eye for others as a student. They are the benchmark: I'm fast when I can run faster than most of them. And I'm very fast if I beat the other fastest in their classes. This applies accordingly to all other properties and abilities.

And then I can train weaknesses in a targeted manner, but I always have to reckon with opponents who already have their strengths there without being trained. If they only practice specifically in this area, I'm doomed to lose. It is therefore even more important to develop strengths than to train against weaknesses.

You also learn in unloved subjects for class tests, Abitur exams, exams and exams. But you don't become a mathematician if you only have enough skills for a 2.6 in the corresponding advanced course subject.

It is also not enough to enjoy doing something to make a career out of it. You also have to be good at it.

Again, the comforting message: Everyonecan do anything, he just has to find out and want to take the resulting consequences. Many lack this will alone, they prefer to wait for one
"divine inspiration".

Conclusion: Ideally, "I can do that" and "I would like to do that" meet at one point. It can't hurt, absolutely not, if you also let a third line steer towards this intersection, namely "In this area I have informed myself carefully about the job market and I also see opportunities for me there".

In this country, the degree offered in a specialty does not mean that there will be someone who will be able to graduate from that discipline Direction needs and adjusts. That only sounds banal to experienced readers, many students and their parents actually don't know it!

3. I can't claim to have scientifically proven knowledge here, but I can pass on some insights that came to me in an extremely experience-intensive professional life. Of course, they do not apply in every individual case, but they do provide clues for your own orientation or they are at least warnings of a potential hazard:

– A very pronounced aptitude for foreign languages (not just English, but three or four languages spoken fluently and the fifth acquired while on vacation) seems to go hand in hand with management skills that are below average (was already a topic here, but should be included in such a list).

– The Abitur grade gives a good prognosis basis for the exam grade during studies: Abi = Uni (±½ grade), FH degree usually one grade better than Abi (and would have been university). If you want to break these connections, you have to work a lot more than at school. And hardly anyone really does that.

– In practice, top-level candidates (study exams) hardly ever fail due to technical problems, they can also cope with tasks that they are not trained to handle. However, they often have difficulties with the "system" after the first five to ten years of practice. The (industrial) system geared towards average people often cannot meet their high demands, to say the least.

- A candidates "sell nothing" - their sales talent is often weaker. On the other hand, poor exam grades can(!) stand for above-average sales talent – exam grades are only of minor importance in sales.
- "What wants to become a checkmark soon bends": above-average talent, e.g. B. also for leadership, is very often seen at school and during studies, e.g. B. also in the hobby/leisure area, in non-university engagement. Anyone who goes through school and university as a "gray mouse", never sticks his head out of the crowd, never takes on a special office, never stands out for his outstanding performance, is unlikely to suddenly wake up at 35 and qualify as a manager for the head of a unit .
- A notorious "career killer"is "difficulties with authority figures". What later escalates with the boss often shows up in the parental home (e.g. father), at school and university, in the armed forces, during internships.

4.

For times and processes/incidents before the end of the exam, the young person gets a certain amount when assessing his or her career

"Discount". world travel (oppositebut according to a well-established opinion you don't die if you have to grow up without backpacking through Australia), change of studies, "strange" part-time jobs etc. are examples of this. Prerequisite: These things remain "in context" and they are offset by impressive achievements in relevant subjects.

- "Recognize yourself – and know your target environment": If you are still studying, read ten to fifty job offers in the target environment that you would like to work in later. Let's assume you want to work in development, then collect ads from the field of development engineers. Not primarily those for job starters, but for experienced employees. And then analyze a) the outlined field of activity and b) the required personal qualities and skills mentioned in the advertisement. And then you ask yourself: "Do I want this, can I do this, am I this?"

The relatively large number of these advertisementsyou need because ads z. Texts are often thoughtlessly, routinely and uninterestedly written - a single copy could give you the completely wrong impression, the crowd makes up for that.

- It's amazing what a person can achieve when they really want something and work hard, hard, and tirelessly to get it. This also includes not giving up after setbacks, getting up again after defeats – putting other things on the back burner and subordinating them to the main goal. This ability should also have been demonstrated before the end of the course.
- I also recommend our "Career Potential Test" (Chapter 3 in this book). He at least provides clues for your potential - and through his questions alone allows conclusions to be drawn about what is important.
- Now to your other questions:
- Are Morally "Good" People Better Leaders?
- No, you can answer that quite clearly. I don't want to expand the topic endlessly, but I do want to point out that one point in your formulation that you probably didn't see as critical at all is the question: what is a
- "better" leader? Who should it be better for? The system

knows only one answer: A good leader is someone who their boss thinks is a good one. And he doesn't ask for the "better person", he wants results.

Then "warrior" is not the opposite of "better manager" and also not too "morally good". The warhorse can be good-natured, kind, understanding and successful, but also malicious, dangerous and a Failure. A warhorse sees a problem and goes at it with drawn sword (with everything he has), hit it. Without an elaborate strategy, without a grand political concept. There are situations in which this is successful, in others it is wrong. There's nothing more to this trait, it's not generally bad.

People have been looking for employees who are "able to work in a team" for a long time, but this has nothing to do with "morally better". There are or even were gangster structures (pirates, e.g.) that require the ability to work in a team. This only means that you are able to work towards a self-imposed or predetermined goal together with other people, in close coordination and mutual cooperation (see also the Neanderthals hunting mammoths).

Although this quality is almost indispensable today, typical examples of teams are project groups with a heterogeneous composition. Things have to be seen in a differentiated way: the employees should be able to work in a team, i.e. they should be able to fit into and subordinate themselves to working groups. All well and good - but I've never seen a team get promoted to department head. For that goal, it is a) to fit harmoniously into the team and at the same time

b) profile yourself in a way that you stand out in a higher place as someone who has the makings of leadership. By the way, that's entirely possible.

Your egocentric is actually an opposite type to the team player. But if you take a look at who is at the head of large organizations and thus wields power (which they must also enjoy), then you will not come across brutal egocentrics everywhere, but you will come across more often than "morally better people".

Cholerics, on the other hand, are - isolated from everything else - just easily excitable and short-tempered. Not all the time, but when they are or become irritated. In extreme cases, this could even affect saints. Who can indeed be angry. Maybe even suddenly. According to the definition, the negative characteristics of the choleric are limited to this alone. He can also be a tax evader or fare dodger – like many well-balanced people.

Conclusion: The connections are complex, people (change) change, demands vary. In extreme cases it is even possible that we have an academic fail "down" in the hierarchy, who might have had what it takes to become a good manager.

2.3.1.4 Who works less, could achieve more?

Ask

As a mechanical engineer (Master) during an internship, I have
ness in consulting and am enthusiastic about the tasks and challenges.

The fact that beginners in particular naturally spend 60-70 hours theWork week, but does not fit my life model. I don't want to be single and burned out in five years.

For me, the attraction of working in consulting lies neither in the salary nor in the prestige, but solely in the activity itself. I'm willing to put in a maximum of effort and time in hot project phases, but this shouldn't be the norm and should be rewarded by subsequent recovery phases. Countless projects do not have to be running in parallel in order to achieve a maximum of bonuses. The focus should be on concentrating on one or two projects in a strong team instead of handling huge projects single-handedly for reasons of prestige.

It is also known that balanced employees (keyword work-life balance) perform better over a longer period of time. Couldn't you achieve better results for everyone involved in this way?

Hence my question: Is consulting also possible as a 40-hour week and if so: How? Where?

Answer

Asterix knew that the better the army, the worse the food (which made him
newly minted legionnaire after the first food receptionto say, "I didn't know the Roman army was that good"; I quoted that from memory).

And it seems to be appropriate today: The more important the management consultancy, the smaller the proportion of free time that is left to the younger consultants in particular. There are certainly one or two exceptions, but what you report there seems to be almost standard in many cases. It's not just about the weekly working hours in and of themselves – the projects that you have to be present at are also scattered all over Germany or even Europe.

That's how it is. Partly because of tradition and self-image, partly because of the image, partly because more hours at x euros result in more fees than fewer hours. If you want my advice, just take note of this industry's status, take it as fact, you as a beginner are not going to change that. Other circumstances in life are associated with similar constraints: you will not be able to drive a high-performance premium class car without having to bear high costs, you cannot become Federal Chancellor without having to reside in Berlin and you cannot at the same time with an average salary achieve high consumer spending and high savings rates.

There is no point opting out of a "package offer"picking any raisins but not wanting the rest. The vernacular calls this "wash my fur, but don't get me wet". For the time being, the following applies: Your ideas do not fit into this profession.

Of course you can always think about whether you shouldn't ... and how it would be possible ... But as long as you alone think like that, it's no use. Only when the zeitgeist is on your side, when suddenly there are no more elite graduates who want to enter there under the conditions that are usual today, will the situation change.

My consolation for you: It doesn't have to be your destiny to be single in five years. Not only because management consultants have already found long-term partners – but also because in many cases two to three years of consulting are enough in the career. This replaces a trainee program for many newcomers, after which they switch to "stationary" companies. Then they are not "unaffordably expensive" or flexible enough in this area either.

If that appeals to you as a solution, plan two years there and make your dream come true. But: During the application process, do not say that you are planning to leave the company after two years, nor say anything about 40-hour weeks and the importance of orderly free time. You have to accept (and love) your prospective employer for who they are - or you'll go elsewhere.

And remember this principle: If you want to change the rules of tennis, you should first become German champion (or something like that), then you should win Wimbledon and maybe something else like that. Then, but only then, maybe at least someone will listen to you. Beginners, however, may be welcomed with open arms, but never seriously if they want to change the system before anything else.

I can then use this opportunity to say what I think of terms such as "work-life balance":

I am particularly disturbed by the contrast that is constructed by the concept of the balance between work and life. For me and many others, some of whom have helped this country move forward, my "work" is an important, indispensable part of my "life". And if you search, you will surely find a part of our respective way of living in our way of working.

I see professional work and private life as an interlocking unit. If the mixing ratio doesn't meet my own individual requirements, I'm either doing something fundamentally wrong or I have the wrong job or the wrong standards.

PS: And since that fits the topic so well, I'll present a tried and tested piece of wisdom once again: You can hardly ever really change the conditions that prevail in your professional environment. But your demands, the fulfillment of which depends on your satisfaction, you can formulate them differently without any problems. If you, dear sender, decide either to enjoy the splendor of a management consultancy or to aspire to a 40 hour/week job, you have a chance to achieve your goal of "satisfaction" for a limited time. You just mustn't combine wishes in such a way that they become (almost) unfulfillable.

Because you see the danger of being single in five years, allow me to point out that you must also accept potential partners in their entirety. There, too, it doesn't help to consider why Karl can't look like Klaus and doesn't help around the house like Jürgen.

2.3.1.5 Work-Life-B., 100k €/year, management etc

Ask

After a long orientation phase (I'm in my early 30s), I have my
Degree in mechanical engineering from one of the three best-known universities with above-average results.

After a well-executed application process, I have two basic options:

1. Entry into an emergingState of the art technical consulting firm in the emerging market of technical consulting;
2. The classic engineering job at a world-renowned medium-sized company or a large corporation.
In any case, I would like to keep the option open to do an internationally accredited MBA in five to eight years and to switch to management. To explain my situation in more detail, I have created three PowerPoint slides (see attachment).
a. Which of the two career options is better suited for a management career, are the differences significant?
b. The work-life balance sacrifice that I have to make in technical consulting should result in a salary that is twice as high in ten years after the MBA (compared to a classic engineering career without an MBA) of more than €100k per year reflect, is this goal realistic?
2.3   Questions and answers about careers and related ones...49
c. Which salary targets or job positions should one set for the next ten years for the three career perspectives? (You can set yourself salary targets, but not job positions for various reasons. Correct would be: Which

targets for salary or position development should ....";
3. H.Mell).

In question a there are still two career options, in c there are already three career prospects. Also think of the poor other readers who somehow want to follow us. Let's agree on two different possibilities (consulting or "stationary" company), of which the second in turn breaks down into two sub-areas (medium-sized company or group). Then we've done that.

Then I would like to separate the MBA there. First of all, you cannot do a "part-time MBA". Because the MBA is not extra-occupational, the acquisition alone can be. But that's just a small thing. More important is:

The personality makes the career. The professional qualificationit doesn't do it alone, it's just a self-evident prerequisite (and even that only in normal cases, it also works without it, as practice shows).

The MBA alone does nothing. We have thousands of CEOs or directors across the country who don't have an MBA or equivalent qualification. And there are definitely also MBA graduates with a rather modest career. Just as, by the way, there are also college graduates with straight-A exams and a rather modest career (this is a warning). Their "longer orientation phase" certainly gives cause for concern. These concerns may be lost today given the current shortage of engineers that is repeatedly rumored – but they could resurface the next time there is a change of employer in the next crisis. Especially if something should "happens" in your career in the next few years (which I would always count on).

The MBA can never do any harm, but it is neither an

indispensable prerequisite nor a guarantee for a career and/or a high income. It will help you to do your current job better, but it is not an event in the sense of "it's going to be better from now on".

It's a pity that we can't show at least the most beautiful of your slides. It's about the visual representation of your two major variants, about salary expectations in ten years, about "salary per workload in hours" etc.

That's all very nice – but "life" doesn't work that way, it's not at all calculable in such detail. Bosses who support them are fired and they don't like their successors, companies go bankrupt,

of whom one would never have thought, there young hope bearers connect with life partners who introduce them to a completely new world and force a complete change of consciousness. Or your employer misses out on a technical development and, at the worst possible moment, forces you to enter the labor market. Or you win the lottery or become seriously ill. None of this fits with PowerPoint charts saying what you intend to earn a) with and b) without an MBA in ten years.

In addition, there is a flaw in your concept: you plan routes and"squander products"positive vocation improvements like compensations and week after week working hours. The framework works in an unexpected way: you plan objectives, the method for arriving is only a way, a necessary evil, that's it. In the entrepreneur framework, needing to procure "huge amount of cash" (or even the aggregate y in x years) is permitted, however not fitting for individuals with "better than expected college degrees". For instance, on the off chance that you are overflowing with fearlessness, you plan to one day become the specialized head of a bigger medium-sized organization. He then, at that point, procures 120,000 to perhaps 180,000 EUR - on the way there you arrive at such aggregates as a little something extra. At the point when you have gotten this far in your preparation, you totally need to manage the principles of the "game".

- What's more, the most significant of them for this situation are work before reaching the goalin the same size, better still in somethinglarger companies in the sector you are concerned with (objective) and, if in doubt, also select the type of company that corresponds to the objective (although you still have the opportunity to make corrections at the beginning); avoid significantly smaller employers than the target company;

- don't change employers more often than about every five years and thinkIf you have been significantly more than ten years per employer, look for at least one change;

- embark on a career path that consistently leads to the targetposition fits (in the exampleTechnical manager: development engineer yes, technical buyer rather no);

- get that promotion every five years or so, get started so not much later;

- do not lose the technical and hierarchical "red thread" of yourgradually developing career; You must always be attractive to the labor market (by its laws!);

inform yourself in detail every three to six months about advertisedbest positions in your profession; You then see what is in demand and have it Chance to steer your development in such a way that you remain desirable in the market; you could take this opportunity to see how many advertisements for your target position require a

specific additional qualification (MBA);
- revise your goal planning and the resulting path planningincertain distances; You and your desires change, the environment changes, technological development does away with old jobs and entire industries and replaces them with new ones;

on your way you almost constantly need bosses to look after you for a good Retain employees who promote you and give you good references.

And then – this isn't in the rules, but comes from the life experience of many successful people – you not only have to want your goal with passion, you also have to walk the path that is dependent on this goal "with a hot heart" every day . After all, big goals can only be achieved by those who show above-average commitment, are always committed, bring ideas and "do" above-average good work (according to the standards of the bosses) with particular reliability.

And your core question(Career at "stationary" industrial companyor during counseling), you solve them less with the mind, i.e. in the head, but more with the feeling, i.e. in the stomach. None of the variants is better or worse than the respective alternative, but different. There is almost always one direction that suits your personality better.

Let me pick out two aspects from your lists and diagrams:

They list under "per consulting career" among other things:"Unlimited job/salary prospects". Yes, there are industry directors who were previously consultants. But there are also many – good – consultants who don't make the subsequent leap into another career or don't make it as desired. And there are certainly consultants who have made the leap, but then failed miserably in the unfamiliar, different world. So much for the "unlimited job prospects". And neither the junior consultant nor the development engineer can become more than CEO.

Now to the opportunities in terms of salary: That's right, the consultant usually earns a lot with above-average commitment. But let's take the three classic stages of development in the profession. "Consultant" (with sub-levels from junior to senior and project manager), "manager", "partner". The consultant advises, works out technical solutions for existing orders, which he skillfully and convincingly presents to the customer. But the manager does, but certainly the partner (the one with unlimited salary prospects)

hardly advises anymore, he has "people" for that. His job is acquiring new orders, making and using contacts with the aim of concluding consulting contracts. He is responsible for a few teams of employees that he has to keep busy - with orders so that consulting hours can be billed (which is just as important here as it is for the car manufacturer with cars sold).

Various consultants also sat in my consultation and complained: In the beginning it was all fascinating. But after a short time (one to three years), everything repeats itself: join a new company, analyze the situation, work out solutions in the interests of the client management (it will also become routine!), present yourself and the solutions impressively, deliver a report - and out. You never see anything develop, you can't follow the path of the people affected, you can't analyze the value of your own ideas over the long term.

It's not necessarily the case everywhere, and not everyone feels that way either - but if you see it that way, you've probably chosen the wrong career path!

Or let's take one of your arguments "in favor of a classic industrial career". You write e.g. E.g. (seen first, instinctively as the most important argument): "regulated working hours, approx. 40 hours per week".

You can't say that in general. Almost anything is possible, from the operations manager, who drives into the company every Saturday and keeps a watchful eye on ongoing production, to the young beginner, who is expected to work one to three hours of overtime every day and, in the case of dramatic projects, much more. The formula "consultants work overtime, those interested in a career in the classic industrial sector don't" is not tenable.

In general, the following applies to every type of career: You see and want the job and its positive further development and ultimately shrug your shoulders and accept all the stresses that are attached to it. Or can you imagine, for example, a candidate for Chancellor who, shortly before taking the oath of office, asks: "How many hours per week am I expected to work there?"

And before I forget: In the case of particularly demanding positions and sparkling career ambitions, it is better not to ask questions about overtime or remaining time for the family in the interview. From the employer's point of view, it would rather show that people are thinking in the wrong direction.

:Which top group is better to start with?

Ask

I   am a student of mechanical engineering at a technical college and have completed my bachelor's degree with a specialization in production technology (among the 25% of the best in the year).

During this time, I was an intern at car manufacturer A AG for five months (with subsequent inclusion in the talent development pool) and wrote my bachelor's thesis externally at B AG for five months (grade 1.3 and a job reference with grade 1). I really enjoyed the respective areas of activity in both companies and I could well imagine working there later. I am currently studying the consecutive master's degree in my subject at this technical university and am aiming to graduate in about a year and then start my career.

I've set myself the career goal of becoming head of production at a company in the industry to which A and B belong. However, I think it is rather unrealistic that this target company will be an OEM. I'll stick to your promotion formula: Every five years (if necessary) switch to a smaller company and hold a higher position there.

This means that I aim for production manager of a medium-sized company as a realistically achievable goal.

I am aware that one should not limit one's career goals to individual companies, but should consider an entire industry. Nevertheless, I assume that because of my previous performance, entry offers from the two companies A and B mentioned above are not unrealistic.

Perhaps my specific question can therefore also be formulated as a general question about the appropriate company size.

How are the two companies mentioned above to be evaluated when starting a career? Is the different company size a criterion? In my opinion, the larger company offers many more opportunities for internal changes and advancement. With the smaller ones, I see greater competition for jobs and therefore a greater reputation if you manage to get started. Could the even larger parent company play a positive role (opportunities) for the smaller company?

Answer

First of all, we have to do a little preparatory work so that we can devote ourselves to the core question of your submission all the more easily:

1. To you: You have a bachelor's degreefrom 2.4. That can just about be seen; if you have elitist intentions, it's almost a bit thin. Especially if you had a grade of 1.6 in your Abitur. You get a "discount" when you look at your advanced courses in history and English – on the other hand: Why did you choose them at all? As a future qualified engineer and head of production?
Let's agree on the following: Make sure that your master's degree gets closer to the standard that you set yourself with your Abitur. It's never too early to start with top results.
2. Regarding your goal: Most larger companies (from 1,000 employees upwards) are corporations, legal forms are the AG and the GmbH. These companies each

have a "governing body" that manages the company. This is called the board of directors of the AG and management of the GmbH. As a rule of thumb, the vast majority of the very large corporations are AGs; the smaller the companies, the more often they are GmbHs. We can neglect the difference here. For our concerns, the following applies: A board member and a managing director are absolutely equal in terms of the result of their career development, only laypeople often see "more" in the board of directors than in the GF. With your "career goal executive board" you reduce your target company list to AGs, for which there is no reason. It would be better to say "board member or managing director".

Then you write "Head of Production", then reduce that down "Production manager of a medium-sized company". Again, this doesn't add up:

Large corporations – see above – usually have the legal form of an AG, which means they have a board of directors. And they often afford their own board member for production. As I have just explained, medium-sized companies usually do not have a board of directors. But he usually doesn't have something else, namely a pure production man in the organ. So there is hardly a production manager there. Either a "technical manager" covers development, design, production, maintenance and other technical or technology-related fields, or there is just one single manager for everything (including commercial matters and sales), who you then have to do alone -GF calls. This in turn depends on the size of the company – without being subject to a fixed formula.

So, realistically, your goal could be:
- Head of Production (of a major corporation/OEM) or
- Technical director (of a medium-sized company, in which case you would have to have qualified for the additional management of development and design in the course of your career) or

Production manager (of a medium-sized company in a second management level position, usually reporting to a managing director, responsible for all production matters of the company) or– Production manager (of an organizationally defined sub-area, e.g. a division, a plant or a subsidiary of a large company or group of companies).

The differences in the order of z. B. between the first and the last target position are significant!

Of course there are special and exceptional cases in each group mentioned, there are very small AGs as well as corporations in the legal form of a foundation, etc. Why am I going into this in such detail? Because engineers in particular often show a frightening lack of knowledge when it comes to these questions. And because this is dangerous: you only have to answer the question about your long-term goals during an interview in a GmbH: "CEO". Then say something like: "In any case, I want to manage a bigger shop than this one – and of course I won't stay here anyway. But you can, and I'm generous, teach me something and pay me good money."

Aren't you allowed to want to become a board member just because you're in a GmbH? But of course - not wanting or even thinking is forbidden, only when talking does one distinguish between clever, tactically skilful action and the opposite.

In your submission you are working with the real names of corporations, which I am anonymizing here as a question of guideline. Additionally to your greatest advantage. For different perusers: An and B are really top tends to in German industry, which many specialists view as the fantasy managers second to none (particularly for however long they are not previously working there; later you understand that there excessively just overflowed with water). Consider this: In this nation, there's practically nothing better with regards to picture, name allure and brilliance. We should investigate what you've gotten from these houses up until this point:

- From a cross evaluation in 5 levels for understudies. The master checks the more vulnerable, more typical qualities out. You have three of them (strong, the capacity to structure and the capacity to execute) and there is just a single positive, very extraordinary outrageous worth, specifically in relational abilities. The extra verbal evaluation in this record is excellent. This looks very great generally.

- A simply verbal record from B about the time you were composing your single man proposal there. It's awesome with practically no capabilities, adulating you "on all fronts".

Presently for the accomplishment of the objective: On the off chance that you furtively dream - I suspect so - of a creation chief at An or B, you should in this sub-enter the company category and are not allowed to leave it "downwards". This also applies to a possible "alternative target" at the 2nd management level in a company of this type. If none of the companies or anyone else in this category hires you, that's probably the end of your dreams about "Production Director Group" – but not the end of life.

In principle, you can only achieve the alternative goal of "production manager for medium-sized companies" if you plan to change employers. Reason: Companies of this type are too small to give you the security of being able to move up to the next hierarchical level at the right time.

These changes are possible:

— via the gradual path from the entry-level group into companies of ever smaller size (e.g. suppliers) at ever higher hierarchical levels, until you arrive at one of the possible target positions at the last "change in size" or

— about starting after graduation at a medium-sized company of the target type; whenever things don't go according to plan internally, you move up the hierarchy to another (similar) company of the target type until you finally get where you want to be. You don't need companies A and B for that.

The former variant is somewhat easier, but requires fitting in and successful probation in companies of very different sizes, which is not for everyone.

Never aim for a specific target position in a very specific company, as you rightly mentioned. This is not achievable! Neither "Production Director at BMW" nor "Production Manager at Müller & Sohn" are realistically formulated goals for a career starter. And you have to want a lot in order to achieve just a little bit of it. Planning of this kind has to be constantly checked, rethought and adapted to changing framework conditions – which also include your personality development. After all, few retire in the position they dreamed of when they were 26. In between lies what we call "life".

As for the last paragraph of your submission, that's enough, just forget that part of the question. You run the risk of going into so much detail with the analysis that you no longer see the big picture.

The best thing to do is to check at the appropriate time (about six months before your conceivable starting date according to your master's degree) whether both companies actually want you and can hire you. Maybe ste-
we then in the next crisis, whereupon both declare that they now have a hiring freeze.

If both companies would take you, decide "according to gut feeling", that's all you can do. The informal spokesman for the team of colleagues you get when you start at A, or the third manager you will have at B, or the sudden death of a boss that triggers an unplanned round of promotions at A can have a decisive impact on your career , but cannot be planned. Or that "partner for life" that you met in A-town and then later ruined (and who you would never have met in B-town) becomes the decisive criterion.

2.3.2   The first steps are done

With increasing practice, new problems arise and complex questions arise.

2.3.2.1   Get out what's inside!

Ask

I am Dipl.-Ing. (FH) with an additional master's degree (both very good),
te 30, working in a group. At first I worked "outside" in the organization as a project engineer and then moved to the head office a few years ago. As the name suggests, my department has important company-wide planning functions and it started out very promising with interesting tasks.

In the meantime, these have mainly become administrative functions. It's all about the processing of information for various committees and the board of directors, and hardly any impulses are given. Crucial activities take place in the various plants and subsidiaries anyway. It is becoming increasingly difficult for me not to slip into purely administrative activities. However, an advantage is a large network that I was able to build up and also the fact that the workload is not too great, which leaves room for a fulfilling private life.

In the course of a project, I was offered the project management for the development of a new product area at another location. Technically, that would be new territory for me. But our top management wants to see the project through. Since I was instrumental in pushing this topic from headquarters, I should also carry out the implementation. The acceptance of the project ranges from clear approval to the various areas of that work to outright rejection. Basically, a new, small operating unit has to be set up.

The discussion has now reached a new dimension as the topic has become part of a larger transformation concept. So something has to be done now. My boss here at the head office suggested that I be transferred to that location in order to push the concept forward. So far I've had a very decent relationship with him, so I see his pressure on me as basically positive.

a. How do you rate a move to the other location? Generally with regard to my professional perspective in relation to a project that I now have to push forward through active design?

b. My boss will no longer accept a "no" from me, since he has now confirmed my work as a project manager in various management committees. How do you see a possible no from me with regard to my further development in this company? Can there still be a reason that I could "survive"? Or is the risk of being "politically burned" too high?

c. A great career is actually no longer my goal, since my private life has also become important to me. How can my professional life look like, since the slog will probably consist of accepting assignments in new locations such as China or Russia? Should I try to implement this project and then aim for a return to headquarters, or should I keep striving after all?

Answer

You cannot and must not go on like this, under no circumstances! I will here
swing the really big club: Article 14 of the Basic Law states: "Ownership obliges." As always, my argument is not to be seen as a legal one. But: In our central body of law, it is said that the individual person also has an obligation from what he has.

And you have: your youth, a good 30 years of work ahead of you – and skills (both degrees very good). And now I'll tell you something in all serenity: you will use this potential and make something out of it. In your interest and in that of the general public, who let you attend schools and complete studies. Since hardly anyone wants to hear the story with the general public, we focus on your interests:

a. This is the proven basic rule for professional life: Get out what you are made of!

Attention: Wicked people like me go e.g. For example, in the case of application analyses, it is assumed that you have done this as a matter of course. In other words, what was achieved was what was in it. That was all. Don't ever come to us with hidden talents that you just didn't use and don't use sayings like: "If I had wanted to, this and that would have been possible for me at any time." Nobody believes that.

Imagine a man with the ability to move a vehicle around a race track faster than anyone else. If, instead of becoming multiple Formula 1 World Champion, he had retired as the go-kart champion of his hometown, one would have had to say "what a pity". Or not?

So: Stop with the nonsense of your current job and do something with your talents.

And for those who like it a little more educated: The Greek fable writer Aesop is said to be in

6th century BC (later translated into Latin like this): "Hic Rhodus, hic salta!" Behind this is the story of a boastful sportsman who kept saying that he had jumped very far on Rhodes, for which there was probably no proof. He was then told: "Here is Rhodes, jump here!" So much for "if I only wanted to...".

b. In modern company management, employees in a department like yours have no future. At some point there will be a restructuring that will make such rather superfluous staff members fall victim. Or like this: A company management cannot be so blind as not to notice how inefficient work is being done in their immediate vicinity that young (potential) top performers have excessive "freedom for a full private life".

c. I don't begrudge you your "quiet job". But not doing anything constructive as a candidate for a good thirty years, it can't be. You can't stand it either. One strives to have created something within the scope of one's possibilities, to have made something of oneself and to have achieved success.

Do you want your tombstone to read: "He used his talents successfully" or is it enough "He lived, took a wife and died"? (The latter after Gellert, an Enlightenment poet.)

Now I've tickled your ambition enough. Please give me credit for saying all of this quite unselfishly, I don't gain anything if you actually pull yourself together to strive for a new professional environment.

So that you can see how a series author slowly warms up when he is touched by the topic, I will share with you a very special thought that I had in the meantime. At some point, another argument occurred to me: if the great seafaring If explorer Columbus had decided to restrict himself to a career as a bargee, the Americans might still not have been discovered and none of them would have been discovered at all and the Indians would continue to walk across the prairies, but didn't call themselves that I prefer not to use it.) Regarding the offered project management:

1. You should not and cannot stay in your current job. Your boss has made it clear that your "no" would expose him and he will never forgive you for that. So you have to get away from where you are today.

2. I see the project as an opportunity for you. It won't be easy, but you could show what you've got. As a project manager, you are faced with a highly technical challenge, ideal for straight-A graduates. Career would come later.

3. No, you shouldn't "try" to do the project, you should con-consistently lead to success. Of course it's a risk, but obstacles are there to be overcome. Anyone who talks about possible defeats has already lost.

4. They were about to establish themselves as a sort of "professional retiree" at work, with a nice private life and all. Now comes the professional challenge appropriate to your status and age. This is good for your development, also on a personal level. Somehow the change of location is "in front of your head". They don't

name the new seat, but it doesn't seem to be as bad as China or Russia. Such relocations are now part of a positive corporate career. The alternative is a medium-sized company with only one location.

5. What does your statement mean that a career is "actually no longer" your goal? It used to be different and now you are retiring? Mid-30s? And for that, two degrees and two very good degrees? One wants to shake you.

The normal next step after the successful completion of the project could be taking on a line management position in the newly(

6. established project area.

As a warning: Stab is great, Stab is fun. But being an executive on the staff without promotion to retirement is highly dangerous. The head of a staff has made his career there, but is for his employees this is more of a temporary assignment in a kind of "continuous flow heater" until the jump into the line is successful. Of course, this is only an average view. But the job market doesn't like staff with twenty years of experience there. And this market is your "life insurance".

7. Do your project nowsuccessfully done. You have to see what really comes next. If you are given no other chance as a "reward" than to set up a new product line somewhere as a project manager, you will have to leave the group. This is normal today.

2.3.2.2   Wash my fur, but...

Ask

I am an engineer in my early forties and have been employed in sales for ten years (second engineering job of my career). Everything is actually idyllic: a young family with a child has started, a loan-financed apartment has been bought just outside the city, and there is a regular and satisfactory income. I can be at home every evening, which is also very important to me, knowing and accepting that my locality restricts me in the job market.

However, as far as my career is concerned, I feel that I have reached a zenith. After some successes achieved in the company, a certain uniformity, almost "boredom" has set in for about three years and I notice that without an internal or external job change (however, currently no attractive offers) I can neither get new, more interesting tasks nor a change of attitude will be experienced. I also notice that in the long run I will be unhappy without a challenging career change. I am too ambitious and at least ten years too young for a career on the phasing out track.

Because of the risks that would be associated with exchanging the comfortable "idyll" for a new job with a probationary period, I decided on a compromise solution and postponed the job change project until my mid-forties, when the daughter is out of the woods and the loan has largely been paid off - provided, of course, that a really attractive opportunity does not unexpectedly arise beforehand.

Until this change, I would also like to try to get the

best out of the situation and continue my education as universally as possible (e.g. foreign languages, business administration).

What are the risks of my decision to stay put for the time being, and am I perhaps ill-advised to act now, regardless of the risks? If I were in my mid-40s and well over ten years old maybe too old for a change at today's employer or as

classified as "sluggish"? Which part-time additional qualifications would be recommended?

Answer

It's really fun, yoursto read the letter carefully and to follow this ups and downs in your representations and plans. Sometimes you seem to be quite sure, sometimes you question everything.

Let's try to bring some system into this picture of conflicting feelings. First of all and as a side note: I think your formulation "I feel like I've reached a zenith" is unfortunate. In the figurative usage (actually this is the apex of heaven) one is "in" the zenith (in the only one, not "on" and not at one) or one has passed the zenith of life. But of course that doesn't solve the problem.

It's a bit of a shame that you don't reveal more about yourself. B. a designation/paraphrase of today's position; now everything is possible between sales engineer in the field and Head of Sales Germany. It would also have been nice to see what has changed with your first change. Now I have to work with assumptions, and I assume: today a sales engineer in the field in a non-managerial position. I also have to speculate about the goals you would like to have achieved (except "more interesting tasks" and "salary changes"). On this basis, the following comments:

1. You are a man walking towards his mid-life crisis, the – with individual fluctuations – is to be set at around "45". It expresses itself, among other things, in the fact that one asks oneself "questions of meaning", such as this: "Was that about all? I had such great plans when I was young, I wanted to achieve so much - and now I'm stuck somewhere, I'm slowly approaching 50, and then (almost) everything will be over professionally." Such feelings and questions are normal in the sense of usual – most of the others struggle with it too. You have to get through it somehow, there is no patent solution.

2. At some point I realized that in this free market system there (must) be a halfway balanced relationship between opportunity and risk. If you see a great opportunity and have not yet discovered an adequate risk - then you have not searched thoroughly enough. Wanting a chance but not wanting to take any risks is not an option – the system doesn't play along.

   The vernacular calls the attempt to want opportunities without having to take risks: Wash my fur, but don't get me wet. What is not possible will become clear as soon as possible.

   You are stuck in a special constellation of private and professional life. Now you want to change something. But please no probationary risk, no inconveniences for the daughter and no problems when negotiating with the bank about the real estate loan. Wash me... but we already had that.

3. Man stands on two legs. He stands and walks most safely when both legs are cared for equally and are healthy. If he came up with the idea of only taking care

of his left leg, massaging it, training it systematically, fitting him with the best shoes, that would certainly have optimization effects there - but only for this one organ. The second leg would remain undeveloped, and the overall human standing or walking performance would leave a lot to be desired.

The people we take care of here stand and walk on their"legs", which are called "private life" and "profession". Severely neglecting one in favor of the other takes revenge. Today your "left leg" is in top condition, and you have atrophy (or something like that) in your right leg.

4. An important statement at the end of the first printed paragraph of your submission is incorrect: "... knowing and accepting that my locality restricts me in the job market" - not at all! They are only knowing but not accepting (otherwise the whole case would not exist).

5. Your "solution" to postpone measures to improve the professional situation for several years is not a solution! Once you have gotten this far with your thoughts and critical considerations, then this problem will never let you go. Your frustration at work will increase rather than decrease – and in the end your family will no longer benefit from the apartment in a beautiful location and a dissatisfied husband and father who is always at home in the evenings.

6. Continuing education is always good, but it won't solve your problem. After all, there is no guarantee that you will get "the" dream position on this basis in a few years. Then, if a new crisis hits, you may find your whole plan in ruins.

The basic rule is: Once you have recognized and defined

a problem, then immediately start working on the solution. And you have recognized that you will be permanently dissatisfied with your job – if nothing changes. So change something. Now look externally a "better" job, however you define it. If you continue like this, you will waste valuable years of your life – and maybe in four or five years you will be so "broken" that you will no longer be convincing as an applicant for a promotion position.

PS: Your daughter is happy when her dad is happy - if necessary even in another city.

7.

2.3.2.3   Career without personal responsibility?

Ask

The problems of a questioner from your series gave me food for thought. Could you perhaps give some advice to engineers who do not want to take on personnel responsibilities in the course of their "career", but want to become technical experts in their field?

I'm still at the very beginning of my career and don't want to take on any personnel responsibility, not now and not later either. Nevertheless, I would like to still have a certain value on the job market when I am 50.

Answer

What you're about to do isn't that easy. I want to try important as-
to list:

1. The question of whether the term "career" is still justified at all is still relatively harmless. Actually, you put one under it
   "Career with increasing responsibility for things and personnel" You took this into account by putting the term in quotation marks in your letter and then not. Before we get bogged down in a discussion of terms: if you're talking about "career" or "career," then there's no problem.
2. Your "not now and not later" bothers me a bit:
   If you're just starting out in your career, "not now" is hardly original – you wouldn't have been given a managerial position anyway. I would be careful with "not later (also)". With increasing experience and

increasing age, your personality, your attitude towards things, your standards and your demands change. The vernacular says "One should never say never" or "The appetite often comes with eating". And even "Whom God gives an office, he also gives understanding".

Many employees retire from positions they never dreamed of after graduating.

You don't have to rush for leadership right away, but just wait and see how things develop.

3. "Personnel responsibility" is a term whose definition is extremely broad. Nice, there is the development manager of a large company with 300 subordinate engineers, whom he has to lead in a deeply diversified organization ("may" says the right applicant). But there is also the team/group leader, to whom three employees are assigned in his function: He is a senior engineer, one of the members of his group is a young technician, one is an office worker with non-technical training and the third is a technical draftsman in half-day position. And he is only technically superior to them. He works decisively on the problems himself, gives his employees professional guidelines and instructions, and they support him. With disciplinary matters such as hiring, dismissal, As a rule, he has nothing to do with salary increases, etc., that is done by the superior department head. It's not so demanding in terms of "leadership" that a strict rejection could be justified. And: It's not that terribly "different" from the function of the project/sub-project manager that can be seen everywhere today.

4. With the exception of a few very large companies (not all of them!), we don't have any systematic approach to

personnel management. Frequently, the best clerk is simply promoted to one of the lower management levels. There he is considered to serve the company even better there - so he is expected to happily accept such an appointment on behalf of the employer.

You, dear sender, want to be a good clerk. If your superior now offers you a promotion position because he wants to plug a personnel "hole" and thinks you are suitable, then it is not so easy to refuse this boss' request.

Of course, as a precautionary measure, you could always announce: "I don't want any management tasks." Which means something like: "If the company needs me and thinks I'm suitable, I'll refuse." But that's not entirely unproblematic either.

5. So not wanting to is a bit strange in the long run. Not being able to, that's okay. But then the others (the bosses, for example) usually notice that and you don't get any corresponding offers at all. Instead of "I don't want to", "I don't trust myself to do this" is ultimately the more convincing and easily accepted argument.

At the beginning of your career, refusing promotion or deliberately not doing so is relatively unproblematic. But if you are 46, have 20 years of intensive professional practice and you have been given the third In your early thirties" as a group leader who tells you in detail what is "the thing" professionally, it can look different, don't underestimate it.

6. Professional experience is required, without a doubt. But how much of it? After fiveyears of experience in the profession, the gain curve falls; whether you then do the same job for 12 or 18 years is no longer an advantage.

With 18 years of practice, however, you are older, (supposedly) less flexible, (supposedly) less open to new things - and (definitely) more expensive!

Pay attention to job advertisements: the highest number that is usually required for years of professional experience in the executing field is five, rarely ten. Of course, it doesn't say "uninteresting from the age of twelve" anywhere

– but then you often take the younger development engineer with around five years of experience. Also because it is cheaper and presumably easier to manage and has the potential for further development that may be in the interests of the company.

7. Take a look back at #4. This results in the remark that is often heard (not always, but quite often): "Clerical clerk for 17 years. All right. But if he had been very good, someone would certainly have promoted him." A prejudice, no question, but a massive one.

8.

9. Some (large) companies have their own "professional career". principleAt the same time: Tasks more like a clerk, but with increasing experience and competence earn like a group or department manager. That's great, it solves the problem mentioned here for the employees there - and leads to almost unsolvable difficulties if you want or have to change one day (you do it to prevent wanting to). Switching to the majority of companies without a specialist career is almost impossible.

10. So far it has been: Be careful with hasty decisions. If you still want it: Make an effort to stick to a common theme (activity, industry, type of company), show flexibility, take on new tasks every few years (also in other

departments, also in other companies) . Particularly critical: 22 years of work in the same company, the same department in the same job. Nobody likes to "buy" that later on.

11.

2.3.2.4   Should I lead or should I not?

In one of your articles you advise that the decision on whether you want to pursue a career with personnel responsibility should only be made after you have gained some professional experience.

That's what I (w, doctorate) had planned to do as well two years ago when I was just starting my career. However, it is now the case that I am on the "fast track" in terms of career, so to speak, without having made the right decision so far.

At my (large) employer, I very quickly took over the technical coordination of my specialist area for a project. That was a very strenuous time for me, but we brought the project to a successful conclusion. I soon became the deputy leader of our group. My supervisor encourages me to be included in the management trainee pool, which is a virtually indispensable stepping stone to further advancement.

I also received feedback from the next higher manager that I was seen as a future manager.

In my opinion, what speaks in favor of a management career? I can't imagine being a clerk on a topic for the rest of my professional life. A management career is the "natural" way to get new, demanding tasks in the company. The management job is also associated with a higher reputation and salary.

In addition, I will probably have problems with allowing myself to be led by superiors and project managers in the long run, who (in my opinion) sometimes provide suboptimal framework conditions. The thought "I could do better" would probably be difficult to suppress in the long run And what speaks against it? I think leadership requires a commitment that I don't know if I want to do full-time for the next few years as I plan to have children soon. How long I will take a break, whether and when I want to work full-time afterwards, I don't want to have to decide on these questions just yet. I would like to at least keep open the possibility of working part-time as long as I have young children.

At least in the coming years, starting a family is more important to me than a career. But in the longer term I "only" see the path of classic advancement for me. I now see several alternatives:

a. I am aiming to be included in the junior management pool. According to internal practice, I still have about five years until I have assumed a "higher position".
If I decide against management, I can concentrate on my specialist career. And unlike part-time executives, my company has multiple examples of part-time subject matter experts. There are also examples of employees who switched from a specialist to a management career after a few years.

b. I allow myself to be put in the management trainee pool and look for a suitable position in management from the start. If the need arises, I'll aim for a part-time position. My company officially says that it would like to devote more attention to the topic of "part-time manager" in the future. But being one of the first guinea pigs is probably not advisable.

c. I'm moving internally to another area, preferably one

with less direct customer contact. I suspect that a job there can be better combined with a break (pregnancy, maternity leave, parental leave). With such a change, I would have postponed the question of promotion for the time being, since as a new employee I would not immediately be seen as a candidate for promotion again.

d. I'll stay in my current group and tell my boss that I don't want to pursue a career for the time being. He would certainly understand that on a personal level, but I fear that such a statement has stuck with me longer than I would like.

I am very curious about your assessment.

Answer

My advice, which you quoted, not to commit yourself unnecessarily early in your professional life, is primarily aimed at those who have doubts or young people who initially react negatively to the "imposition" of one day being asked to take on managerial tasks.

I "comfort" these people by pointing out that in the first three to maybe five years of work the topic is not even an issue – after all, nobody promotes it anyway. In doing so, I believe that you should first get to know the professional system in practice before you refuse to go the actually quite natural path of gradual advancement. Maybe I'm also betting that the inexperienced beginner should have gotten angry about his first three "stupid bosses" before he squanders his chance to become a "stupid boss" himself.

This advice is less aimed at those young professionals who know from the start that they want to move up. They can and should work consistently towards their goal. For them, the impatient wait for their first promotion ("much too long") comes naturally.

That's how it is (as I keep emphasizing). The only restriction is that you have to want to lead and give the manager responsible for making the appointment the impression that you can do it (you have the potential for it). I have a lot of sympathy for people who freely state that they can not that one. You shouldn't force anyone to do it, especially if they say they're unsuitable.

I have more problems with people who argue offensively that they simply don't want to, but they can. It always reminds me of the athlete who claims that he could become state champion if he wanted to, but he just doesn't want to.

I'm not saying that I could definitely write better and write books with a "Harry Potter edition", but I wouldn't feel like it.

I've always been an advocate of the principle that you should get everything you can out of yourself. The wickedness lies in reverse (It only contains what was taken out. That was all).

The "I could do better" thing is well thought out - and certainly one of the central sources of motivation for striving for advancement. You could sum it up with the slogan "Either I am led or I lead".
Unfortunately, let's just put it that way, the thought is a bit incomplete.

To start with me: Your considerations here were almost entirely correct. I then managed my small company, in which I was an employee and minority shareholder for many years, as boss. And I'm telling you, it's a fascinating climb! Nobody - apart from the not always easy customers - criticizes my work, expresses any kind of displeasure, I implement every technical idea and I decide for myself which company car I drive.

But, and this is the bitter pill for you, you never get that far in a group. You can become a group leader - the department heads above you who specify "sub-optimal framework conditions" remain. You can become a division director, then the executive board is authorized to issue directives to you, including the risk of acting in a suboptimal manner in your eyes. I assure you, the world is full of divisional directors who blush just to say "CEO".

Yes, and you can become CEO and have a supervisory

board, for whose assessment "suboptimal" is still heavily embellished in your eyes.

I don't want to discourage you from climbing, I just want to prevent you from delusional. Should someone give up a career because of this? But no: As a department head, you are subject to the same management principles as a clerk, but even managing a department to a limited extent is more fun than if you are only 100% managed and not able to show yourself how good you are in this " art" is. And
Besides, as a (future) manager you have your instinct for power and you can't help it.

Your thoughts on family planning are understandable, you share them with many other young women. I'll go into your options later.

Let's arrange your planning variants according to the clarity with which I can give an answer:

To d: I would never do that! Anyone who says A must also say B (at some point). And you're not pregnant yet. You also have to reckon with the possibility that nothing will come of it, otherwise "everything" would be ruined. In addition, you only get your boss to look unobtrusively at your stomach every day. Regarding c: That is far too complicated for me and is based on the principle "from behind through the chest into the eye". All good plans are simple ("We'll go in, we'll smash everything, and we'll get out," Asterix), but your plan is an extremely multifaceted strategy just to avoid promotion.
With a little bit of bad luck it still works...

I prefer a combinationfrom a + b. Take the opportunity to join the junior pool, show that you are interested in a career within reason (ambitious, but not unconditionally fanatical) - and don't talk about pregnancy and part-time work.

Aim for your two – inevitably on separate planning pathsTop goals "Family" and "Career". In both cases, you can only control the implementation to a limited extent. And if starting a family is number one on your priority list, then do it accordingly.

But: If you want to lead (later), then don't turn down any opportunities that arise in this regard. If you become pregnant before then, then first realize your main goal "Family" and make as much as possible out of No. 2 (career).

However, keep in mind that you have several unknowns in your calculation. A mathematically unambiguous solution to the problem is therefore not possible. These unknowns are:

- do you ever get pregnant and when?
- what development has your career made at this point in time?
- how does not only "the company" (board of directors, PR department) position itself, butAre your department head, including your direct superior, particularly demanding part-time work in general and "part-time for managers" in particular?

what is the economic situation of your company at that time,does it have the time, money and will to create a modern image in the direction of "We are at the forefront of progress also on the issue of Part-time for female managers" or is it fighting for its existence and has completely different problems?

how are you changing, including your goals and values,

through partnercommunity, pregnancy, parental status?
 It is one of the problems of A-candidates that they are used to finding a conclusive answer with the predicate "correct" to all questions, at least those of a scientific or technical nature. Who
"knew everything correctly" got his 1. But this oneis the full human life, determined by sheer imponderables, human weaknesses, medical aspects, etc. If the often not so extremely clever voters make a decision at the wrong time, arising out of some heated situation, you suddenly get a law, that throws all your planning upside down. Dealing with it as calmly as possible, planning some things, but not planning others at all and simply letting things come to you, that is the great challenge we are faced with.

Many large companies B. do not plan specific personnel developments for their employees more than two years in advance. I wonder why?

*
*

2.3.2.5 To the team leader abroad?

Ask

I am a graduate industrial engineer, in my early 30s and have been with them for several years
working for a German group. After an internal transfer, I now work for a subsidiary, I like the tasks and my boss is happy with me. However, the group has meanwhile gotten into lasting economic difficulties. Everything indicates that there will be cutbacks in staff. Although I'm working in a growing area, I see fewer opportunities to achieve the position I'm aiming for as a team leader.

So I came up with the idea of looking for a new job abroad for about three years. After that, I aim to return with the aim of working as a team leader. I hope to escape the uncertain situation in the industry and in the current company until the situation has calmed down.
As an advantage of this plan I see the opportunity to gain new experience and better job opportunities with the experience gained abroad. A disadvantage would be the lower protection against dismissal abroad and possibly worse pay. Since my current employer practically no longer offers foreign postings, I would have to find a job myself.

Do you think my plan makes sense? How could I be meaningfulReferences that are often required when applying for jobs abroad?

Answer

You spent a year at a foreign university during your studies, so you have a certain amount of basic experience. You are therefore immune to the accusation that you have never stuck your nose out professionally beyond national borders. You're also single – with a wife and two school-age children and the usual mortgage payments to deal with, it would all be much more difficult.

So you didn't go abroad with your German employer, but started out in the foreign country as a self-reliant "foreigner" – that's quite a big difference. Get advice on pension and health insurance issues beforehand so that there are no surprises on these important issues.

Let's talk about your motive for the project: I have the suspicion that you simply want to go to a very specific country and simply add the reason here. That would of course also be allowed, but then it would be advisable for you to admit it openly. It could even be that the same applies here: If a man does something unusual, then you only have to dig until you come across the woman who is to be regarded as the root cause. But that's beyond our scope.

I see the following aspects youhave to weigh for themselves:

1. In our world shaped by globalization, professionally relevant experience abroad is becoming more and more important. It is often a prerequisite for certain career stages, forms the personality in any case and imparts valuable experience. Incidentally, it is a value in and of

itself, and it hardly depends on the country: anyone who knows Poland "can also do China" (a bit of an exaggeration, of course this also applies vice versa).

2. It sounds a bit twisted, but it is actually taken from practice: experience abroad is good for a career and usually increases the value of an application – but only once the reintegration into the German labor market has been successfully completed. So about two years after returning.

3. The time spent abroad should not exceed three years, at most (!) five years, otherwise one is quickly considered "spoiled abroad", whereby some countries weigh more heavily than others (neighboring European countries are less critical than "exotic" regions).

4. The value of experience abroad lies in "functioning" abroad; the demands on the type of activity, on the position in the hierarchy and on the extent of the responsibility held are not quite as great as when looking at a career in Germany (although you should be able to see a "red thread" in the career overall , but the thread may be thinner or even "knotted").

5. Basically, your plan violates two basic rules of career planning:

a. In the course of your career, you should only strive for a position because of its factual content or its position in the hierarchy - not because of the "place" at which it is located. "Abroad" is also a kind "Location".

b. In the middle of your career you start something that you know you will have to finish in the foreseeable future. You are thus exposing yourself to the completely unpredictable situation that will prevail on the German labor market in about three years. In the recent past we have had rigorous hiring freezes, even in the most well-known houses. Anyone who starts studying also exposes themselves to this risk – but cannot act differently and therefore need not blame themselves. In addition, there would be no job market for him as a high school graduate without training. But you are already trained and have a job that is not even threatened.

1. If you want to return one day, you have two problems ahead of you:

a. You are applying from another country. Depending on the region, this can pose different problems. i.a. how expensive it will be to travel to an interview (usually there are several) and who will pay for it.

b. At the moment of the application, it is difficult for you to fit into one of those patterns that the potential employer you are writing to works with. You then did something for about three years that might have an unfamiliar name and is structured differently than in Germany, and that is difficult to classify and compare. You also have to get used to German office habits first. That's not too much of a problem if you don't want to get in as a leader here again. But in the eyes of the decision-maker, do you really have an advantage over the 30 competitors who all want to be team leaders, but who have worked here in comparable companies for the last few years? have worked in easily assessable positions? Does the internship abroad help you specifically in leading a German team?

2. Eventually you will be in theAs a rule, you will not receive a job reference from the foreign employer according to our standard. This is particularly

important if you want or have to apply again later (after your return).

This is not a blanket warning against professional engagements abroad. But it is an indication that being posted abroad by an employer based in the home country with a return to Germany guaranteed in the contract has its advantages. In the liberalized labor market within the EU, going abroad "on your own" generally presents few problems. But a blanket recommendation in terms of your planning is not possible.

As far as references are concerned: There is no such thing as "abroad" across the board, every country or large region has its own customs. Something will be seen differently in Hungary than in Egypt, for example. We also know references in addition to job references for management positions. If something like this is required, think of former bosses (also retired, left), former university teachers (if your studies were only a few years ago), if necessary, friend friends of lawyers or external business partners. Some things are different abroad - it's all about proving that you've mastered it on your own.

2.3.2.6   From skilled workers to board members

I'm hoping for your advice on what strategy I should pursue in around ten years' time
to achieve my long-term goal of sales manager or even better sales director/managing director in a large medium-sized company (approx. 2,000 to 10,000 employees) and how I can best deal with my plan to achieve an MBA.

After training as a skilled worker, I had successfully completed several specialist training courses. After that my thirst for knowledge was really awakened. When my boss at the time said: "You won't get anywhere like this. If you want to pursue a career with us or elsewhere, you must have a degree. So you'd better be content with what you have", that's what prompted me to start studying mechanical engineering at a university of applied sciences. Despite certain initial difficulties (math, physics, etc.)
was able to achieve very good results and was even able to acquire an additional foreign degree during this time.

I started my career at a small, medium-sized automotive supplier (fewer than 300 employees), where I was soon able to succeed the sales manager. Unfortunately, the company "slid" into insolvency. Since a change was almost impossible during the general financial and automotive crisis, I "decided" to stay there. I played a key role in finding investors, had to conduct appraisal interviews, keep top performers in the company, but also initiate separations. And I worked very closely(!) with the managing director/owner.

After just a few months, we managed to find a suitable investor. Because I got on well with the new owners, there was a lot of tension between the former managing partner, who had remained managing director, and myself. This smoldering struggle became more and more extreme and obvious, I took my consequences and switched to my current employer.

I'm now in a much larger company that corresponds to the target size I mentioned at the beginning, instead of being a sales manager, I'm just an account manager. But I have a much greater responsibility for sales and look after an OEM (instead of previous suppliers of the subsequent levels).
I

The new company is ambitious and has enormous growth potential. I just don't find the product as interesting as the one previously represented. Although the workload is relatively high, I no longer really feel challenged. They took note of my wish to further develop myself, but I was put off: I should "not be impatient". I understand that, since I've only been here for a year.

My boss and his boss have sworn me to my current job that I should concentrate on it for about three years, the upcoming project is too important. There will hardly be any new challenges for me there in the next two years (apart from a conceivable nominal promotion).

In order to improve my holistic understanding of a company, I have been toying with the idea of doing an MBA ever since I studied mechanical engineering. This thought has now developed into a heart's desire. So far, no employer has supported this and my current boss attaches little importance to this wish. I can understand that too (costs + loss of work).

Nevertheless, I am seriously pursuing the idea of financing the MBA on my own and doing it part-time.

1. What do you make of it?
2. How can I persuade my employer to at least approve it?
3. Is there a common thread in my career?
4. Does my long-term goal seem achievable?
5. What can I do/improve in the future to achieve this goal?

Answer

So you know very well where your professional journey should go. measured onaverage young graduates even extremely accurate. The advantage: you can plan the further path quite precisely (the realization then has its own pitfalls). The disadvantage: If you narrow down the goal too much, it can block your view of alternatives, of opportunities that suddenly arise along the way. With this we can already locate your first mistake: If one day you start your career in companies with 2,000 to 10,000 employees

If you want to "crown", then it is very wise to start out in even larger companies and follow the motto: when changing companies, go down one level in company size and go up one level in the hierarchy. Or you can at least get in on the target size and stay true to it with every change.

Or you start "small" and eventually have to grow in size "high", however, this usually crunches in the hierarchy gear (we will see it in a moment).

With regard to your "roots" it is permissible to

speculate that you came from a non-academic family where nobody recognized your talent. Now you had to work your way up. This has consequences, e.g. B. Age on graduation day. And, please never forget that, personality formation also takes a completely "different" path than that of those engineers who graduated from high school at the age of 19 and their technical college exam at the age of 23 or 24. I say "different", not "better" and not

"worse". Of course you bring your specialIt also takes away some advantages, but also some special features that can lead to problems one day. An indication: Nobody would think of raising your path to the "standard for everyone". Even if it's because you always lack six to seven years of professional experience as an engineer. Of course you deserve recognition for your special achievements. But keep in mind: The "others"
who grew up in the usual framework form the standard by which you are also measured.

So that you have an example for statements of this kind: According to my observations, people with your background tend to overestimate the details of education (another degree). "If I still had an MBA, then..." - the other type, on the other hand, has a degree from which he can apply 5 to 10% in practice, then sees that bosses and colleagues with different degrees achieve different things that are independent of training rolls up his sleeves, makes "heaps" of sales (in sales) and is constantly promoted.

Let's put it this way: you have a degree. To become Sales Directorden, you need sales talent, success, the right personality, ambition and the willingness to pay the price that is demanded of this goal. I'm not saying that the MBA would bother me. But if one of the above requirements is missing, the MBA is of no use. That's fine, you need business and economics knowledge, but you can acquire it in different ways. Weren't you allowed to play a key role in the search for investors at your old employer, without an MBA? I mean that. Without a degree, as the former boss was right, you hardly get anything today. Especially not via external

applications. But with a(!) exam in your pocket, all doors are open to you, you just have to pass them through. And, check it out so terribly often an MBA is not required in job advertisements. A private search in a large Internet job exchange in November 2011 revealed: 16,000 advertised positions in "Engineering and technical professions", including 95(!) positions in which the requirements stated an MBA (sometimes mandatory, some only desirable, some
only under "z. B.").
What remains is your anger with the former owner, who continued to work as managing director after insolvency and the investor's entry: Such an owner suffers one of the greatest conceivable defeats with the insolvency of his company. This will usually shake his personality to the core. After that, he can hardly be the same person. If he previously ruled with a kind of omnipotence, he is now only an employed managing director by the grace of the investor. He tends to hate this one. And internally, whoever is for the new masters is against them. You had worked very closely (with exclamation marks) with him - and then defected to the "enemy" (the new know-it-all master). So he hates you too. Well, at that time you had 1 (one) year of

professional practice after your studies. your special Weg had made you personally mature, but not relevantly experienced in tactical contexts.

Luckily, the very factually formulated "good" (not very good) report card from that time does not reveal anything about the problems there. If you don't talk about it, there are no charges from this corner.

Let's take a look at your further path (we'll save the one to the Sales Director until the end):

The hierarchical "descent" when changingis the price of your move from a much smaller to a much larger company. You have each taken special paths with your training and your career path. Let that be enough.

You are now in the target company size that is right for you. Stick with it and don't experiment with it, certainly not down the size of your company. You have about five years of professional experience as an engineer, so your current job is great! But: If you take a path in the wrong direction, one or the other aspect can seem incomprehensible. And the usual path in the profession is the one from the larger to the smaller company. There's no use wasting your energy trying to figure out something that's already been

"State oftechnology" applies. And another very important argument: A company that hires a new employee has a "moral" right to having them do the job for five (well, let's say at least three) years without complaint, with commitment and with the greatest success, for which he was hired. Then maybe it's time to talk about a promotion. And the principle ranges casually from clerks at 23 or 25 to board members at 45. If you think otherwise, you shouldn't have signed there. Your bosses are absolutely right when they say you should "don't be impatient." Your standards are a little off, everything else is fine.

Make sure this MBA project doesn't turn into what you call an "idea obsession"! You argue wrongly, namely not "I need this here", but "I want this". A convincing argument would be: "I've found that 80% of all sales executives are MBAs. Now I want to be a board member too. So, to be on the safe side, I would also like to do an MBA." You are a long way from that with your "heart's desire".

To 1: Little. Rather make sales, read specialist books and please your bosses. That will definitely help, the MBA might just help you.

To 2: Not at all. First you divert 20% of your mental capacity toto acquire something that you do not necessarily need according to your bosses. In their eyes(!), you go to 80% of your performance in your main job.

down (bad). Then, as soon as the stamp under your MBA exam is dry, you will loudly and insistently demand a promotion – or you will leave (very badly). Most of the other second-degree graduates did the same – why not you too. So the bosses don't love your project. To 3: Yes, definitely. Sales in the automotive supply sector with increasing sales responsibility.

To 4: Yes, if you don't make any mistakes now. For example: irritate or annoy your bosses by constantly peddling your "fixed idea" or by changing after just one year of service instead of five (at least three) years of "going on" successfully work.

To 5: Read my answers carefully, feel free to get

angry, then read them again two days later. Above all, think about origin-related "other" characteristics, about the standard majority and your age: You are in your mid-30s, according to the standard you would have had ten or twelve years as an engineer, you would be in a managerial position and you wouldn't either put all your energy into a second degree.

And: Further training in itself hardly ever hurts. But the expense/disadvantage involved can outweigh the benefit.

2.3.2.7 Change against the will of the boss?

Ask

As a mechanical engineer with a doctorate, I first became a technical specialist for a
Specialist area, then group leader for quality assurance with disciplinary leadership of a "handful" of employees in a large company. My responsibility was initially limited to one plant, but was then extended to several plants more than five years ago. Now I think a change in the field of activity makes sense and is overdue, as I am curious and not married to the subject.

I am interested in the product development process and comprehensive disciplinary management. I'm aware that I have to bring the right skills with me when I move. After a few unsuccessful attempts, this is how I see it for our house:

a. When it comes to quality, people are perceived as neutral (if everything is going well) or negative (there are quality problems).
b. Vacancies are primarily filled from within the department.
c. The area of responsibility does not offer any opportunities for advancement, especially since it is narrow
"Guard rails" no special projectsallow.
Despite repeated requests, my supervisor does not agree to any changes (change of department) because this would cause unrest in the system and it would be difficult to find a replacement for my qualifications in the company (I have good to very good ratings and receive additional benefits). What is the best way to

change in the company against the will of your superior if you are only "visible" to a limited extent outside of your own area?

Answer

I hope I understood you correctly on every point: you have been for about
ten years in Q, want to move up the ladder, are fed up with the quality, but want to stay with the company, your boss doesn't want to let you go. This raises several problem areas:

1. After ten years in Q and disciplinary management there, a change of department with a growing scope of management is very difficult internally, and practically impossible when changing to another company (change of employer). Background: A group leader is generally a kind of "leading senior expert" in his field. You wouldn't be able to present that in a foreign subject area, you were starting again from scratch and "at the bottom".

2. Q is no less interesting than other areas, only you are now bored with it. That's your right, but not exactly original after such a long time. If you notice something like that, you push to new shores much faster, for example after two to three years of corresponding activity.

3. Managers who are permanently satisfied with themselves and their professional world, who do not strive for more and do not want any unrest (ie change), neither above nor below themselves, are the terror of both their bosses and their aspiring subordinates. This perseverance is a question of personality, you as an

employee cannot generally change that.
I see two possible solutions for you:

I. You're changing employers. In doing so, you will largely remain fixated on Q. You can try to join another large company in your industry in a comparable or higher Q function. Or, that is the normal case, you switch with a clear jump in the hierarchy to a supplier or to a large medium-sized company in a similar branch. You do not need the approval of your current boss for this change. They also let others
"In-house" burdens (such as the majority of vacancies being filled with applicants from within the department) behind you.

But you need the courage to start over. It's not without risk – but where else is there a chance to win something without betting anything? For situations like this, there is the labor market.
II. You stay with the company but want to change tasks/departments – knowing that your boss is against it.
First of all, you need information: how does something like this work in your company (the regulations are very different)? The central question for you is: Is an internal change possible without the consent of your boss, is it planned in the system, is it wanted by the company? Your HR department has the answer, and there may even be a Group-wide HR development department. Be prepared: In many large companies, the difficulties are so great that changing employers is easier than changing departments.
If the information is positive, you have to look for a new

potential boss internally who has a position that interests you – and you would take it. Another piece of information you need to know is: Is this potential new boss even seriously negotiating with you without informing your current manager?

Then you have to decide. To be on the safe side, I say that changing employers is a perfectly normal process that thousands of employees go through every day. You just have to know what goals you have and what priorities you give them.

A future manager must not be too thin-skinned

Ask

After studying at the Technical University, I worked as a research assistant at an institute and did my doctorate.

I've been working for a large company as an "engineer" for about three years now.nieur + specialist" (I paraphrasethe correct designation for reasons of discretion; H. Mell). I am currently working in department A, but on the basis of special experience from the institute I also support department B in my area of activity.

For me, after this time, the question of personal development arises. One reason for this consideration is that I am not completely satisfied in my current position.

My dissatisfaction is partly due to conflicts that arise from working in the two specialist departments, but mainly because independent work is not encouraged in my main department A. The team leader who is in charge of me (without disciplinary responsibility) is behind I prefer to say that I am a specialist engineer and not a manager. His de facto deputy, a colleague of mine, is very well connected in the company and is accepted as a contact person by the other departments. Unfortunately, neither my team leader nor this colleague communicate and distribute the work in such a way that sufficient information reaches me or the other colleagues. Likewise, I can't find any answers to the technical questions about my projects in these two.

I am virtually invisible to other departments. In department B, the situation is exactly the opposite.

There I can work independently and I am perceived as a contact person by the neighboring departments.
There are three options for my further development:

a. I am applying externally.
b. I could apply for the position of a corresponding specialist engineer in specialist department B. I work there in an area that I am very familiar with and could possibly take on the role of deputy head of department in a smaller area of the site.
c. i stay where i am The team leader will retire in a year due to age. He indicated that he could see me as his successor. However, he is not sure that his superior will ask him.

My review:

Possibility a is out of the question, since my period of service is not so long that there is already a need for action.

With option b, I would practically be back where I was at the end of my time as a research assistant at the institute.

In addition, this department basically had three years to make me a good offer. This was only done when the position had to be officially filled.

This leaves only option c: to wait and see how the situation develops whenafter the departure of my team leader and, if there is no chance for me, after four years of service, I look for a job in a completely different department or with a different employer.

I can't imagine working "under" my current colleague, who is actually my team leader's deputy today and could also become his successor.

In the next step, my goal is to achieve a management position, although I would initially consider professional management to be sufficient. The

The lowest disciplinary management level in my area has more than 100 employees and is therefore a project for the future, but not for the first step.

There is one more point of view that I cannot clearly evaluate. Working in department B often leads to contacts with customers, suppliers and competitors. In my current main function in department A, the contacts are more internal. Such in-house contacts could be helpful for my further development in the group. The external contacts that you have in B would be important for development outside the group.

Answer

Don't take me for particularly petty, but if you think through and present problems systematically, the solution is easier. However, they construct a mixture of problems that unnecessarily obscures our view of connections and backgrounds. The thing is this:

a. You are a young, ambitious engineer with a thirst for action with an elite education, even if according to the attached CV it took you a little long to get there at some stations, but not at others. It is completely normal that after the first three years of practice you are now interested in your "personal development".

b. You are a little unsatisfied. This is also normal in the sense of usual, especially for one of the "A candidates" like you, who are often the focus of attention here.

But: "Personal development" is not a therapy against burgeoning dissatisfaction in the previous job. Advancement is a way to achieve a professional (career) goal. The therapy against frustration is frustration reduction, e.g. B. through special measures up to the change. But not advancement. When asked why he sits where he sits, the CEO of your company will usually answer because he wanted to be there

– not because he was "not entirely satisfied" in the levels below and always sought further development as a solution. I'm sure you understand the difference.

Now let's talk specifically about you. Anyone who writes a lot as an amateur writer reveals a lot about himself, there's hardly any other way. As an experienced reader, one often has the feeling of encountering individual key

sentences that allow conclusions to be drawn about the peculiarities of the writer's personality. And there are facts
that allow for interpretation. Both together create a picture. Let's try it once:

You don't name your Abitur grades, but I know your age at that point in time and I know the (detour) path that you took to get there. And if I put that in relation to the man who will one day have his TU diploma with
"1", talks about it happily and only needs a little time for this diploma, then the way to school was not talented. Either you used to be lazy or you come from a family that didn't have much to give you in terms of training/occupational design. That would not be viewed critically, but it is likely to have had a personality-forming effect in early youth.

We are all the result of some imprint, maybe that was yours.

I need this aspect when I now give an impression that I got from you. I could be wrong, but if not, you have a problem that you should do something about—and factor into all of your planning and decision-making. It goes without saying that I don't want to criticize you with this either - but if I'm to help, you also have to know what I'm assuming:

I believe you fromare characterized by a special sensitivity that you react to your environment much more thin-skinned than robust. Your self-confidence is not as strong as it should be after the very successful completion of your training phase. Or maybe your need for recognition is quite strong, which would make you vulnerable (but is by no means uncommon in

managers). Starting points for this assessment are sentences from you such as "I'm practically not visible to other departments" and "In addition, this department (B) basically had three years to make me a good offer". You show an almost mimosa-like sensitivity, feel "under worth"
used and treated, but above all far too little recognized.

I understand that, but you have to look for the cause within yourself.Perhaps you are too introverted, don't sell yourself well, present yourself too reservedly. This world belongs to the rather "loud" people; just being able to do something is not enough. Or as we consultants say: "Do a little good – and then talk about it in detail." You have to present yourself a little like companies present their products.

In addition, you are still attached to your time at the university institute: "With option b, I would practically be back to where I was at the end of my time as a research assistant at the institute." The option mentioned there b is moving over to the neighboring department for which you already work today – in which you can work well and in which you have hopes of partially deputizing for the head of department. You could say that moving to this department would keep you where you are (but have all the benefits of working in Department B, which you vaunt). But the comparison with the world of the university - which is done for you - doesn't help you any further.

Let's put it this way (exaggerated a bit): In university and institute you were a kind of "king" with an A degree and an A PhD, but now in practice you feel treated like an average person who is threatened having to work under a colleague in the future who the current team leader currently prefers to you. This is part of what is

called "practice shock". This practice is not the continuation of university operations by other means, it is diverse and profoundly different.
About your options:

Regarding a (external): From the point of view of the market, two years per employer are already sufficient for such a step (in the first position). But you are currently stuck in such a "mixture of small problems" that you would simply run away from an unclear situation if you gave notice. You also never find out what actually happened in your current environment, what chances you had, etc. And: there is no pressure to find an immediate solution. Regarding b (switching to department B at first at the same level): That would resolve your current frustration, you could be happier there, you would have a chance (deputy head of department), you could set up an external network and get in touch with neighboring departments (and thus throughout the house). If you stay there for two more years, sound out opportunities and haven't missed anything yet. Enjoying your work would be nice too
a progress. Regarding c (staying in today's Department A): In the event that you should be a bit indecisive (I have no clues for that), this would have a special charm: you don't have to do anything at first, so you don't actively do anything wrong. You officially throw your hat in the ring for the upcoming successor to your team leader with his superior – and wait for the decision. From this you could learn a lot about how management there judges you.

If your colleague becomes a team leader, you have a good reason for yourself to change, but then the company. No one outside would find out about the "defeat" that you would then have suffered, you would have the chance for an unencumbered new beginning.

So I recommend b or c. Forget arguments like the one that Department B let three years go by in which they should have had your recognize talent and poach you. Being offended is not good for future managers.

The professional life is in many areaswith the surrounding, everythingcomparable to the prevailing business world. And that is where success is required. The following applies: success is an "event in itself", hardly anyone asks about the reasons or even the background. Whether the market is suddenly buying what it didn't want yesterday, whether you were "only" promoted because your boss suddenly died

– no one examines what success counts (on the other hand, no one wants to hear reasons for failure). In this environment there is no room for offended reactions, because B did not offer you something three years ago, but only now (you always need a vacant position in this category for such an offer).

Read my analysis (which could well be correct), wait two to three days to get angry about it, decide on one variant, then let off steam: revolutionize the professional world by developing completely new methods Your area, work – if it helps and is seen – occasionally late into the night, make yourself indispensable to your team leader and make department B happy with tremendous commitment and unimagined results. They sparkle with enthusiasm for work and creativity, erase the epithet from the "misunderstood genius" and live the rest. What is a top candidate for?

And remember (A-candidates need this hint): It's hardly ever just about the thing, it's always about tactics, about selling, about the right time - and always especially about fortune. I wish you that.

2.3.2.8 "Change faster" or "stay longer"?

It is no longer mandatory to stay with every employer for at least five years. Many entrepreneurial decisions today, depending on the industry, are aimed at a much shorter period of time. Accordingly, we are looking for employees and executives who have proven in the past that they can quickly familiarize themselves with new topics. I can name various companies in the computer industry and telecommunications as examples. I don't want to claim that all companies in these sectors are short-term oriented, but an ever increasing proportion and more and more business areas, especially in the international environment. The higher your career level, the more you are personally exposed to this short-term nature.

Before you speculate in the usual way and now assess me: Yes, I have worked for a great many employers (five in eighteen years of my career after studying industrial engineering at the Technical University...). The change was not to my disadvantage 80% of the time.

Nevertheless, I'm slowly starting to feel a form of "burning out" and I'm looking for a position in the level of responsibility I've reached as a division manager that I can really hold for a long time - "if possible until retirement". I have now found the position.

Conclusion: The rules you set up for aSuccessful professional and career paths are definitely correct in the past and in traditionally shaped companies, but not necessarily in a large number of other companies.

Based on your solid facts, I can also make another statement about the statistics of your CV: In the last twelve years (before that there was a phase that is not entirely clear to me according to the data available to me) you currently have your sixth employer – and there it is Your tenure is very short. It would not be good for you if you had to start looking for a job again now, particularly stressed by this much too short period of employment with the current company. And as we both know: A manager can lose his job very suddenly and through no fault of his own – no business enterprise is immune to this.

The companies always work according to the principle: Anything that is useful to us is allowed. They don't like people who change frequently - but if they urgently need to fill a pressing personnel gap, there is no comparable competitor and this one candidate could bring the technical solution, then if necessary they will also make compromises that violate elementary principles. The next recipient of an application can react much more severely – or this tolerant company in its next, slightly different procurement case.

The reference to the increasing number of short-term projects in certain sectors is absolutely justified. But for that you need flexible managers and employees, not necessarily constantly new ones.

In principle, every established rule must always be applicable across the board. And this makes it clear: a classic industrial company cannot live with a workforce of qualified employees who change companies every two years. As always, exceptions are possible in individual cases. But no applicant can rely on the fact that he will always and permanently pass as such. In your case, too, there is a certain probability to the effect that you didn't get your current (very good) management position because of, but in spite of, your previous short periods of service.

Perhaps (and why not) you will appear so convincing in the interview that you will cover up any concerns you may have. Anyone who is a little weaker than you could fail in the first round. At the end I'll go back to the problem in principle. But first comes a reader who wants exactly the opposite from me: one should do not "stay" shorter than mesay it, but longer.

questionerB

I read your advice mainly for its entertainment value. It's almost touching when you stand by the side of many a newcomer like a fatherly friend during their first steps into the oh-so-tough world of work. But I really enjoy it when you take one of these very clever high-flyers out of the sky and ground him in the normality that surrounds us all with your almost superhuman professional experience. Thank you for the short weekend entertainment.

I mostly agree with your views and have often found the laws you describe confirmed in more than twenty years of everyday work. There is no question that your principles such as: local flexibility, concern for the favor of the superior, respect for the usual working practices... are conducive to a positive career. But haven't you found in your many years of work as a personnel consultant that there is more to a fulfilling professional life?

Isn't sticking to one's home town with its social networks, one's own family, the familiar surroundings and landscape and the perhaps higher recreational value of a rural community - compared to a big city - a valuable basis and source of strength for a demanding and demanding task in a regional one Company? (By the way, I consider the "standard length of stay" per company of three to five years to be avoidable damage to the economy).

I therefore advocate longer residence times per employer - although I would like to differentiate this somewhat. After two six-month internships at two corporations, I sought my professional fortune at two classic medium-sized companies (one for seven and one for thirteen years). Experiences in different companies are extremely important, otherwise there is a risk of fatal "stable blindness".

Of course, career advancement can be significantly accelerated with planned changes of employer. However, this is exactly what needs to be questioned! In the classic engineering professions, this follows after a change of companya one-year learning phase (in some cases even longer if you change industries). After two to three years in the company you become really comfortable – only then, I claim, does an engineer really work "profitably". If he then looks again for the next challenge at the next company, that's the avoidable economic damage I'm talking about. Of course, the responsibility lies primarily with the companies, which have to offer internal development opportunities in order to keep performance-oriented employees in the company in the long term.

Answer to B

One could argue about the advantages of the rural environment compared to the big city, we want to give that to ourselves. Both have something for and from another point of view just as much against themselves, it's about home and the "grace of the randomly given birth region". Even the most convinced Bavarian, for example, has to admit that his country of origin is not based on a carefully considered selection from all German offers and possibilities, but on the "geo-strategic" randomness of his place of birth: If his parents had moved to Berlin before his birth and stayed there, he would have become a lowland cosmopolitan with a dialect that horrifies him today.

First of all, let's note: Reader A pleads for more frequent employer changes, B for less frequent ones. And me? I declare that one
"big topic" and will always:

Answer to A + B:

Looking at resumes, length of service per employer is one of several ways to make critical mistakes. Of course, I cannot do justice to every conceivable individual and special case. But the basic orientation can be:

1. The fact that there is a change of employer at all is absolutely indispensable from an economic and business point of view. The individual company must be able to lay off or recruit workers; unemployment as the only buffer in between is not desirable. And the individual employee must also be able to be a free

person who can and may look for a new job at certain intervals. I also agree that the graduate workforce called upon to be creative should certainly have experienced more than one company, at least a large proportion of them.

Conclusion to 1: In principle, it must be possible to change employers without restrictions. This is essential.

2. If very large parts of the workforce in a company were to be replaced very often, about every six months or every whole year, there would no longer be any know-how worth mentioning, no one would be solidly trained and chaos would break out.

Conclusion on 2: The change of employer of the individual employee must be limited by rules and/or empirical values, the change may only take place "in moderation".

3. As an important marginal aspect: The security that was still widespread fifty or even thirty years ago, which some corporations as well as some private medium-sized companies in the provinces seemed to offer against job loss (whereby changing employers in life planning often

classified as "not relevant"), there is no longer a general rule. Every employer today has to reckon with constant changes between increasing and reducing staff, every employee has to adjust to the need to change companies.

Conclusion on 3: Every company and every employee must assume that periods of service of 35 or 40 years per employer (i.e. without a change from starting a career to retiring) can no longer be expected.

4. If every worker has to deal with both involuntary and

voluntary changes, then it is good to be prepared. The key element to this is practice. If this is missing, failures are very likely.

Conclusion to 4: It is better to plan at certain intervalsto change - and not to be completely surprised by the need to make the first change after twenty years of service.

5. What can now be regarded as the standard (which of course can also be deviated from in individual cases)? There are four phases between the start of work and the last working day of an experienced academic/manager in a company:

a. familiarization phase;

b. Frustration phase (perceived burdens are getting bigger, the desire to change is getting stronger, doubts about leaving the employer are fading, the decision is made);

c. Job search phase (anyone who decides to change must first come to the new contract via applications);

Notice period (contractually defined periods elapse before the employee leaves, e.g. six months or three months at the end of the quarter Now, for the sake of simplicity, set six months for each phase- Sometimes it's a little more with the induction, then a little less with the notice period, it balances out.

Between the day of entry and the day of departure there are four phases of about six months each, in which the employee practically never shows the full, committed, joyful performance for a single day. That's about two years together. The total length of service should now be so long that those two years are surpassed by the proportionate time, which is to be seen as unreservedly positive. If we assume three years for this, then that results in five years of service per employer as an average value. This is supported by the experience growth curve, which then bends, as well as by the recommendation to be promoted about every five years if there is a corresponding interest (if necessary by changing companies).

Conclusion on 5: It is desirable to stay with a company for five years (ten years are no problem, fifteen years can be critical if you then have to change). Changing too often is more critical than too seldom, and job entrants are allowed to leave once after two years (from the perspective of the applicant, not the "old" employer!).

d.).

2.3.2.9   promotion desired

I've been an engineer for more than five years, more than three of those years
with the second employer. I'm listed as an "engineer" there, the next higher designation is "senior engineer".

My annual personal rating is usually slightly above average (3+ on a scale of 1/excellent to 5/inadequate), although I have to say that the company takes care that the department average should be pretty much a "3".

Now I'm wondering if I can expect a promotion in the near future. Should I perhaps even demand this or should I just wait and see? If I change employers before I get a promotion, can I ask the new employer to be a senior engineer without coming across as arrogant?

1. Presentation and question touch on several aspects: Engineer" and "Senior Engineer" are by no means standard industrial designations that are used everywhere or even predominantly. It is therefore possible that your problem does not exist at the next employer and is not understood there either. If you apply, pay attention to how the new position is described in the job advertisement.
The two "stages" mentioned are probably company-specific designations. I also suspect that the "senior" differs from the "engineer" less by a real personnel management component, but rather by the particularly experienced, proven clerk without management but with a better salary. In the past, something like this was

usually called "main clerk" or "head of department".

2. "Real" promotion levels, on the other hand, are e.g. B. Team leader or group leader – with a technical but not yet a disciplinary management function.

It depends on your objective: In your company it can be interesting, for further promotions it can even be recommended or absolutely necessary,

to become "senior". an externalIt's actually not worth applying just because of this level. On the other hand, it is worthwhile if you want to become a project, team or group leader.

Of course, a new employer wouldn't consider you for this "real" level if they knew you were "not even a senior" with the "old" employer. However, he probably doesn't know this "high clerk level" at all and doesn't miss anything from you. So he will examine your application without prejudice.

3. But Iin the position of your current boss would not promote a "3 +" man! That would only be a little above"

4. average; something like that is enough to protect against dismissal, but not for promotion. For this you normally need a 2+. So it's a matter of fighting for it - not through discussions (bosses hate that), but through performance that is well above average.

5. On that basis (they try to do so much that a rating of 2+conceivable) then also applies:

You don't ask for a promotion, it gets you nowhere. On the other hand, one is such a high performer in the department that the boss is afraid that this top employee could leave - and e.g. B. promoted to keep him as possible.

This strategy can be accompanied by "registering the

claim". You don't make any demands, but you make it clear that you are definitely striving for the next level. The best way to start this is with a question.

Employee: "How do you see my possibilities with regard to further development to the next step/level?" Boss: "Wait a minute, we'll see, one day, just right now..." Employee : "Is there anything I could or should do differently in terms of my appearance, my performance, my way of working?" Boss says something. Employee: "That is very interesting for me, thank you for that. I will take all this into account and make an effort accordingly. This is very important for me because I really want to qualify for the next level."

The claim is thus registered. Bosses have a keen ear for it and now know: If he doesn't become a senior soon, he'll be gone one day. And that's exactly what he doesn't have to shrug off, but fear.

I would like to take this opportunity to repeat the warning that has often been voiced: You can ask for promotions/development, you can ask for it if necessary, but you must never threaten: "Otherwise I'll quit." Bosses note this as "blackmail" – not legally correct , but will stay in your memory forever. If you ever want to quit, just do it, but don't talk about it beforehand.

2.3.2.10 down downmid 40s

Ask

I'm 48, a manager in the technical management of larger medium-sized
shear company. When I attempted a self-critical look at my CV, I was somewhat shocked to discover that although there has been an upward trend in terms of hierarchy/scope of responsibility when changing employers in recent years, the length of service and – in my opinion – the tenor of my service references have recently shown a trend that could well be called critical. In short: The times per company are getting shorter, the testimonials in the statement more reserved.

I have absolutely convincing explanations for each individual case, but I'm not sure whether a suspicious application reader will believe me or whether they even want to hear my explanations. Is that because of the economic crisis – and above all, how do I deal with it?

Answer

There are two very typical developments that lead to such appearances:

a. It starts with missing out on a development: around the end of your 30s you have your first real managerial position, everything is going great, including in your private life. The house, the children, the teething troubles have been overcome everywhere – things "make themselves" on all fronts.

Maybe you can see that the next promotion should come around 43. But nothing is happening internally at the moment and a move would be particularly inconvenient due to the school situation of the children. So you miss the optimal time for the next step that is due. You don't bury further career ambitions (which could have been a real solution to the problem), you just suppress them. One day you wake up: you are in your mid/late 40s and for ten years nothing has happened that could have been seen as the fulfillment of further career dreams. But the clock is ticking relentlessly, now it's time to act quickly, you'll soon be 50, then hardly anything will work.

Now it turns outa special dilemma: you have missed a promotion step, now the next one is due. So you look for the super dream position and hope to be able to take the boisterous step from five years ago with you. Somehow. In practice, however, "high-flyer applicants" are not very fond of them. If you simply didn't find what you were looking for in the search for the super position, which is now being carried out with high pressure, this would be the lesser evil: nothing bad would happen. But there is the market with its laws. And just as there are of course used cars if you can only pay EUR 1,000 (they just don't last long), there are also items that seem to offer everything that was desired. And just as things are not all right with this applicant (ten years of pause in promotion were far too long and the leap they are now looking for is far too big), the contract offer that was finally found also has its "quirks": The internal constellation is extremely difficult ; Solid candidates for promotion who can choose look for other jobs – so one partner each remains on the employer and applicant side, who no longer have a large selection.

But neither of them realizes that what they offer has pitfalls – and that, according to the laws of the market, what they get is also problematic. And shortly after starting work, there is a "bang" for the manager, a new change is due. There is time pressure (risk of unemployment).

Or it doesn't "bang" but disillusionment spreads among the newly hired manager. It must not have been "that" by any means, that doesn't last until 67, that was a failure, it has to be looked for again.

However, the search carried out under difficult conditions under the strain of too short a service period (which raises various questions).

after a replacement solution is even less promising than the first one after the quiet ten years. The new position that was finally found is more problematic than the previous one, and here too the period of service is consistently short. Then we come to the observation you made on your resume.

And just in case you don't like these examples because they don't quite fit you, I have another explanation: A manager who really and undeniably had significant potential for further advancement would not have lasted ten years let years stay in that lower position. The combination of ambition and talent would not have allowed that. Perhaps this too long a wait was a sign that one's own limits had been exceeded - and that the game is simply overwhelmed.

If you already recognize these symptoms in your CV, then you can only act cautiously. A solution could be to lower the current/last position in a new application and, on this basis, to aim for a "smaller" job that you are better able to cope with. You can still help someone who has completed ten years in the old position and has just "woken up". He must realize that lost time cannot be recaptured. The step that was due five years ago cannot be skipped, it must be completed now. The "sacrifice" was brought to a harmonious family life, which can be quite meaningful and rewarding. But you mustn't try now"in one fell swoop" to catch up on the step that was missed at the time.

And anyone who has just passed the first half of those "happy ten years" has to make a conscious decision. But just as you can only spend money once, you can only invest time once, e.g. B. just in family life. At some point, "making things right" again with a violent attack, that works just as little in professional life as it does in gambling.

This variant is simpler and more brutal at the same time: the potential of each of us is limited, somewhere. The resulting individual development limit is fluid, it lies within a certain range, it depends on the circumstances of the work environment, it is difficult to recognize in advance - but it is there! And it shows itself through warning signals when you approach it: the periods of employment are getting shorter, the certificates are weaker. What is needed is the insight of the person concerned, to recognize the signals, to interpret them and not to want to iron out "further up" what was already unsuccessful "down below". Not every priest is born to be an archbishop, not every career officer to be a general, and not every operational executive to be a general division manager or managing director; Self-restraint is required. what youdescribe are symptoms. Do not overlook the suspected illness behind it.

So: Your guess, dearThe sender that there could be a crisis behind it was correct. Only it wasn't that of the economy, but your very personal one. Accept the problem and don't try to solve it in one fell swoop.

PS: As you can read about me elsewhere, I like to uphold the principle: get out of yourself what is inside. This relates to training levels as well as to a career path to success. But how do we define this "pulling out"? Do we demand 110% of the given capacity? Certainly not, there is a risk of being overwhelmed and overloaded. If we go to 100%, there are no reserves for onerous special cases, extra assignments, sudden project requirements. If we cope with everyday life with around 85-90% of our existing capacity, there are solid reserves for special cases, 110% is also possible for a limited time - we then rest again.

But those employees who do their day-to-day business with 85-90% make,are sovereign, relaxed, are still far enough away from "full throttle driving".

You, dear sender, are showing clear symptoms of 100% of your capacityity requirement. And that doesn't get better with age.

b.

2.3.2.11   Up is clear - but how does it go down?

I have been reading practically since the beginning of my studies more than 30 years ago
weekly your career advice. I found the tips and hints to be consistently practical and helpful.

My own career has been gratifyingly smooth and straight forwarddeveloped. I have been Vice President at XY AG for a number of years and, with my more than 50 years of experience, I am responsible for an area of almost 1,000 employees.

Performance demands and workload are naturally high. The work is still fun, with the usual limitations. Where is the problem then?

It's in the word "yet". I would like to slowly but surely reduce the speed and time required for professional work. A new
The solution could be a task with much more modest financial resources.

But exactly this request does not seem to be provided for in the system. Externally, the question of the reason for the change immediately arises. An honest answer is simply not believed, internally I prefer the variant of not even addressing this question.

So how do I get down the career ladder a bit in a planned and controlled process? Which procedure is recommended?

Unfortunately, I have to point out the dislike of many companies here again and again
to applicants aged 50 and over. Precisely because it is

assumed that these candidates have, let's put it that way, already passed their performance/career/dynamic/ambition peak. At least there is a suspicion.

You, dear sender, not only confirm that such a development does occur and is conceivable, you go a whole step further: you show us that there are even managers in this age group who "go back" actively seek. Because they recognize that a reduction in the overall burden at that age is due to a reduced willingness to perform or
– wealth could well be appropriate.

Of course, this restriction must be mentioned, you are initially only an individual case from which no general knowledge can be derived. Other members of your age group may protest that they are not just "hungry" but are quite consciously on their way towards "better, bigger, nicer, more" or at least interested (if they would just be allowed to). But I know with 100% certainty that you are not alone - and that if there were a regulated path of this kind, it would be welcomed by managers who share the same experience as you.

And I am convinced that employers would be well advised to at least consider such a path. In an earlier post in this series, I even suggested such an arrangement for older applicants—with the usual success of the individual setting out to change the world.

First of all, let's set out what an "orderly withdrawal" could or would mean for everyone involved:

1. Today, the employee is promoted or promoted as long as it proves useful to his employer. If the bosses are no

longer satisfied with him or her, the last professional step turned out to be unsuccessful, or the employee will be dismissed due to organizational changes.

gene in his environment in thislevel is no longer needed, the following applies: There is no going back behind the current line, there is only total separation. Instead of demoting a division head who yesterday was a department head back to department head, you completely forego his qualifications. The man no longer has the value of a lower level executive to the house, he has no value at all. That makes no business sense.

2. If an employee affected by this is over 50 and interested in going backwards, he is threatened with unemployment on the inevitably necessary way to the market, because external (potential) employers do not hire an ex-head of department as head of department. This is economically questionable.

3. If an employee comes up with the idea of wanting to go back to a preliminary stage of his current hierarchical level – which he has already successfully completed before – without external pressure, he is met with the same rigid rejection both internally and externally as those candidates who open themselves have to "change" the initiative of the employer and would also be willing to go backwards in order to secure their existence.

4. A person's performance curve doesn't always go up and then suddenly breaks off at 65 or 67 years of age. It also doesn't increase to about 50, then stays at a level until 65 or 67 and then breaks off brutally.

It develops - differently for each person - initially upwards, stays there for a while or changes slightly and then falls with varying degrees. It drops in any case, even with the highest position holders (except consultants + series authors). The way our system deals with this is absolutely illogical: We react positively to that part of the performance curve that rises - and promote the employee accordingly. We can also cope with the peak of the curve or with the plateau that it represents for a few years: The employee is now "up" by his standards, we keep him there for a few years.

But then comesthe waste, a gradual waste mind you - and we have no recipe for dealing with it. We only know of two extreme reactions to this: the man stays where he is (or is even promoted further) or he is shot".

Since the system reacts so helplessly and inflexibly when it takes the destiny of an employee into its own hands, it also reacts in exactly the same way when an employee himself, having his performance and/or motivation curve in mind as a trigger and argument, in or applied externally (sa 3.).

Conclusion: With regard to the hierarchical development of a manager, the system only knows the "all or nothing" principle: the candidate remains what he is (or becomes what he was before) or he loses everything. A way that going down as gradually as it went up at the time is not foreseen, in fact hardly conceivable at the moment.

We agree, dear sender, that this regulation in the system of industrial management is unsatisfactory. Maybe I can also get a reason why it – supposedly – has to be like this:

a. The principle explained not only applies to industrial management, it also applies to many other areas of life:

– A former federal chancellor cannot then become

minister of a federal state or mayor of a city. Sometimes there is still a job for him somewhere, but on the ladder he was at the top of, a position three steps down is unthinkable.

– Our entire management structure goes back to military organizations: Caesar already had legions before the word industry even existed, at least not in its current meaning. And nobody would think of reinstating a former colonel as a captain – in a position that he once held.

– A sporting great tends to build their career along their performance curve as they age, eventually get up (perhaps missing the point where their curve falls) and then retire. As a rule, there is no way back from the German champion to the new district champion Posemuckel.

– A corporation can report sales of three or thirty billion. But woe to him, it's a paltry 8% down year-on-year or the industry trend. We are a successful company: always forwards, never backwards. Maybe it's in our genes.

b. In practice, stepping back down the career ladder would encounter some real and/or perceived problems, psychological barriers, or deep-rooted fears:

5. A department head who is appointing a new department head in his area usually wants a young, upward-oriented, dynamic person who strives for top performance out of ambition, who will do everything to achieve a good evaluation and to satisfy his boss (otherwise he will never become a department head). On the other hand, he does not want an older gentleman who no longer wants to prove anything, who no longer

has to "show" anyone, who replaces dynamism and

commitment with wisdom of age and, due to a lack of professional (promotional) ambition, is only very conditionally concerned with the good assessment by his boss fights. As an extreme case: An ex-head of department as a clerk is a horror vision for every manager. "Among other things, we use money as a motivating factora. EUR 180,000 definitely motivates someone who has previously earned EUR 140,000. But as a motivational element, they are not good for someone who has already
had 250,000 EUR.

- The toughest argument: A department manager (you see, I deliberately avoid examples with vice presidents) who puts an ex-department manager or even ex-MD in one of his department manager positions will always(!) fear that his new "subordinates" will miss it " of respect for department heads. The new guy could tell his wife in the evenings: "My boss shouldn't puff himself up like that; as much as that is, I've been for a long time. And I deserve more than he does."

c. There is a solution for you that comes from a completely different task, but could fit here: Applicants who are already under (time) pressure, are already unemployed and/or have to deal with limited attractiveness on the job market, are often forced to lower their claims below what they (still) have today or had in the past. For them, the motto is: readiness for a downward trend - but nobody should notice that because it would be "suspicious".

In order for the new, smaller job not to be a relegation,

you too (just like the "problem applicants" mentioned) would have to be "smaller" today than you actually are. That wouldn't be entirely accurate, but it would be relatively harmless - and there are no convicted crooks in prisons. The alternative is: no chance.
It would look like this for you on the occasion of external applications:
You are not a "Vice President" in your CV and cover letter today,but merely a "leader" of your department. From me one with power of attorney (which you actually have).
Leave out the number of your subordinates in your CV. In the job interview, when asked about a hard core of subordinate employees of perhaps 100-200, there would then be "further, primarily professionally assigned employees in a plant". You always say modestly: "The number of subordinates is never important to me." You give your income as a tightly calculated fixed amount, but forget the term "fixed" ("My income is around EUR 120,000 , but what is decisive for me is the task"). Then you need a reason for the application, which must be stated in the cover letter. Note: A manager your age never leaves without reason, it must not lie in your person (decreasing willingness to perform or reduced performance), not in professional mistakes, not in trouble with the boss and certainly not where it really lies with you. Example: "My application is related to a situation in our market that is gradually becoming more difficult; As a result of this trend, various internal restructurings etc. are under discussion. I am applying for a new, challenging job from an absolutely unencumbered, non-terminated position before I could be subject to any internal

restrictions of various kinds." And with that you are invoking a principle that you are actually specifically questioning: none should give regression. The world is already pretty crazy.

2.3.2.12 Here I stand and must not do otherwise

Ask

I work at XY AG, a large company whose values and corporate culture I believe in. Unfortunately, I maneuvered myself into a very uncomfortable situation last year.

I'm in my early 30s; I started my career there about six years ago in a large-scale research project in central corporate research. After two years, I got the deputy sub-project manager in a corresponding project area.

My superiors attest that I have strong analytical and technical skills as well as patience and perseverance in pursuing the goals that have been set for me. I enjoy dealing with intellectually demanding tasks and I like it when my solutions are implemented in products.

In the future I would like to take responsibility for this implementation myself. That's why I want to lead a development project and, if I stay in the private sector, I'm aiming for a group or department head in development in the long term.

For this reason, I recently accepted an internal offer and switched to a newly established Department A in Division I. After a few months, I was supposed to take over the management of a development project. Even before this happened, a new top manager dissolved "my" department and canceled the development project I had promised. Despite considerable protests on my part, I was then transferred to a clerk position in another development department (B).

I wanted this position as soon as possibleleft as possible and after a short search found an interesting position as a team leader in development in department C in the growing business area II. Unfortunately, my department head from B prevented this change by vetoing it and blocking me for two years. As a "consolation" he appointed me as team leader for the series support of a component of a product. Significantly, this position had become vacant because my predecessor, who was also tied to this position for a two-year blocking period, left the department immediately after this period had expired.

I'm very worried that my current series support team leader position doesn't match my professional goals (responsible tasks in the development of new products):

- My job consists of routine activities and fire brigade tasksworking on a very special, rather "old" product. I am not challenged professionally and I hardly develop myself professionally.
- This series support is to be relocated abroad, the correspondingjobs in Germany are to be cut in a socially responsible manner. So, in the long term, my position will be eliminated.
- There are hardly any new projects in my development department.From this
  Because of this, numerous top performers are leaving the area.
- After my two-year transfer ban expired, I would bealready 35 andwould only have limited time to move up another level in the hierarchy (our general rule is that no significant career advances are possible after the age of 40).
-

- Since I'm not allowed to change internally, I only see the option to remain "team leader in series support" and make the best of it or "change to another company". What do you advise?

Answer

-
- Submission is informative and valuable. Everything that is described there is there

it like that everywhere. And despite the negative experiences of our questioner, it is a company "of whose values and corporate culture I am convinced". I find that brave (that with conviction). So what have we learned so far from the environment of this man who – of course, you guessed it – is one of the top candidates? It is as if many of these people drive a sports car when they use their special skills in classic commercial companies excellent performance data on a field-woods-and-meadows race track and would find it difficult to get the ideal line in every corner, to say the least.

So now to the touched-on aspects:

1. There is the start in the corporate research of a highly renowned large company. This is undeniably fascinating for a young, gifted and ambitious achiever. That sounds incomparably nicer than "series support for left rear wheels". The sender likes it there. And he "enjoys dealing with intellectually demanding tasks". That's research – but the money is earned with "left rear wheels". They also have demanding tasks, but these are not generally classified as "intellectually challenging" and certainly not on a daily basis. And if they were, it wouldn't be called that.

But the candidate knows that at some point he has to get out of the ivory tower; if you want to have a broad career, you have to go where the music is playing. And that is where you sell customers concrete solutions or products for money. The company is there to do that: Research is fascinating and of course also important because it creates the basis for concrete product development, but it has more of a supporting function. If you want to find your work reflected in tangible and salable products, you have to "go to the front" at some point.

And then there is the question of whether going straight into product-related development after completing your studies, in which you would now have about seven years of professional experience and would be firmly anchored, would not have had its advantages.

2. Now the story with the intended management of a development project in a newly founded department:
No one could have known that a new department would be dissolved so quickly and that the development project would be canceled – but behind "new" there are not only opportunities, but also risks. Normally they are balanced against each other (big chances mean big risks). Whether the new top manager was the cause of this radical change of course or whether he was brought in and used to initiate exactly this process is open (and irrelevant to the point).
Conclusion: Every job change, both internally and externally, is a risk that can end in disaster. So do you have to avoid him? no way. Anyone who moves wants to do a "business", make professional progress, etc. And the old principle applies: no business without risk. That

is simply part of (professional) life.

3. Now it was getting tight in terms of career for our sender: He was out of research, there they had meanwhile orientated themselves differently and his old job (which he no longer wanted to do anyway) was filled again. In his new professional environment, however, he was still "nothing" (he was less than before), he would only become so after a few months of working there. But the department was dissolved and the development project was canceled when the sender was already operating in the new environment, but before it had "become" anything. When there is a "crisis", only facts count, no expectations or promises "for later".
The clerk, who he was at the time, became superfluous there – and was transferred to a vacant clerk position somewhere else. That was formally correct, but disappointing for those affected.
He protested against this transfer. All right, it didn't do anything.
4. This was not how the change from research was intended, so our sender tried to get a promotion in a completely different area. That was logical from his point of view, but unsatisfactory for the new boss he now had. He had done what is popularly known as a "bargain": to fill a standard clerk position, an excellently trained man with many years of corporate experience with experience as – after all – deputy sub-project manager and certified project manager potential snowed into the house. A stroke of luck for this boss. The new employee just wants to leave as soon as possible, which is understandable. So this boss uses an

extremely effective "weapon" - which many readers don't even know can exist: He blocked the internal change of his employee for two years. This possibility is not standard in all companies, but it underlines the basic principle: an internal change against the will of the previous boss is not welcomed, is made more difficult or - as here

– made almost impossible. You, dear reader, have to find out for yourself whether and which restrictions of this type apply in your company. HR knows that.

Now our sender is as follows: A-level exams, employer with a great image, first partial career successes, then chaos all along the line, today employed "below value" on a job that he never wanted. But now he was appointed team leader after all – although "series support" is quite a long way from the original area of "research". And the sender is locked up there and cannot change internally for two years. This coercive measure makes a person nervous even if he likes the job as such. After all: he can of course quit and switch externally, that can't be forbidden (but maybe with the unspoken threat with a weak testimony at least make it more difficult. Because that's the disadvantage of working for a No. 1 corporation: What you are there, will, won't be, or what you have in your testimony from that time is "like it's carved in marble". Having an unsatisfactory career at XY AG is worse than if it happened to you at Müller & Sohn KG).

Conclusion: Our sender at least operated unsuccessfully. Guilty or not guilty is secondary. Did you, dear readers, find the possible key phrase for many things in his submission? "... and if I stay in the private sector, I'm aiming for the long term..." Anyone who also has other goals in mind always exposes himself to the suspicion of not fully meeting the requirements of his current goal. But there are examples of people who "changed horses in the middle of a (professional) race" and became successful + happy in the new profession after they were absolutely not successful + happy in the "old" system before the change. Perhaps such a change would be the solution here?

You've been badly played with lately - presumably completely unintentionally and not directed against you. The elimination of the project manager position in department A and the cramming into the clerk position in department B was bad enough. The company allowed you to be banned from further changes in this unloved, undeserved position in B and have to stay there for two years. The team leader in the area of series support that doesn't suit you is little consolation. The company has thus cut the "bond of basic trust" between you. You weren't treated the way you would be treated

"bearers of hope" would and should treat. I would think about a general change of employer.

The chaos in your career since you leftResearch shows that your expectations - and perhaps your skills and any handicaps - on the one hand and the company on the other no longer match. This statement is meant to be non-judgemental, it is not intended to criticize either the company or you. But you had to take note of so many indications for this assumption that it would be negligent not to draw conclusions from them in good time.

By the way I understandalso your current head of

department: Under the circumstances you describe, he will hardly find anyone with convincing qualifications who would like to do your job – but that doesn't mean you have to be happy about being tied to the unloved chair.

Maybe wereYou are cautious enough to let research give you an interim report. Then that determines the tenor of the later final document. hp I would think it is conceivable that your gifts and perhaps your talents lie more on the technical side than on the managerial side. Check this and, if necessary, take it into account when selecting a new position.

2.3.2.13 priorities

Ask

After completing my doctorate at a very renowned institute, I got one
Entry position as a development engineer in a large corporation. After a short time, I was accepted into their support program for young managers. In the period that followed, I successfully managed various projects of increasing scope and also had some, e.g. T. "highly hung" cross-sectional tasks. Even before the actual promotion, however, I was forced for personal reasons to look for a new job at a more favorable location with the possibility of part-time work.

Of course, with my previous position, I also had to give up the youth development program. After some searching, I found a suitable position, which was more commercially oriented, in another area of the group.

After five years in the non-developmentWorking part-time gave me the opportunity to return to development in another, newly established division of the group. I gladly grabbed. After a short time I was asked if I would be interested in taking on a managerial position. I signaled readiness. Shortly thereafter, the area was dissolved and the fragments were assigned to other units. Now I find myself in a situation in which not only has the potential managerial position been eliminated, but my job has also changed in such a way that it has become undemanding and unattractive.

So a new change is imminent. I'll take the mortgage with me (no real promotion in the meantime in several years of work), I leave the successes behind. How do

you assess the situation? Should I try another type of employer or is another internal one despite bad experiences
change preferable?

Your analysis in the penultimate paragraph is somehow correct, but far from it
everything. In order to see what you've done, we need to dig deeper into the details: It starts with the fact that you're not a "dyed-in-the-wool" engineer. You have a different one, actually a little less for the engineer ger studied related natural sciences, so are "Dipl.-XY" and then probably became a Dr.-Ing. PhD in a specialty. I don't even want to speculate whether someone with this non-specialist basic training now has a Dr.-Ing. at all to become an "engineer" or, as it is called in advertisements, "dipl.

Then it's simply not true when you say: "After my doctorate ... I got an entry-level position ... in a ... group." Nice, at some point you had a doctorate and at some point later you got this entry, but in between there were four whole years in which you remained at the institute as a doctoral researcher. Perhaps it was your work there that persuaded the group to accept you despite the unusual "basic training" (I estimate that for every 1,000 engineers in the company there is one Dipl.-XY who has a degree like yours).

But the basic rule is: leave the world of university after graduationor institute, unless you are doing a doctorate. And after the doctorate away from the world of university or institute and into industry or suitable companies. Always assuming that this industrial world is the career goal.

Due to the combination of your two peculiarities, your professional basis was somewhat outside the norm, the "foundation" of your "house" showed - depending on the observer - weak points; it wasn't, you could call it, 100% resilient. That means: If possible, do not justify any other abnormalities in your CV, these here are completely sufficient.

Then you've made it, despite - in individual cases maybe even because of, butthat doesn't count - these special features to get a great job at a top company and to get multiple "awards" there. The "actual promotion" was coming up, you were there for more than five years, things were going great – and everything was fine. No one would have looked more critically at your slightly out-of-the-ordinary "foundations." They had "done it" (whatever that is)! Technically, you now lead development teams; the products had to do with electronics, far away from your Dipl.-XY.

Then came the "personal reasons" thing. I have to go into some detail here, otherwise no reader will understand. No, it wasn't the new girlfriend in Hamburg that didn't suit the old job in Munich. They felt obliged to look after relatives in need of care elsewhere. This is absolutely honorable, deserves great recognition, no one has the right to judge this step, including me, of course. But: Now you had - for the noblest motives, but still - the solid one shoveled the "ground floor" of your house (standing on the not-so-problematic foundation) until it fell into rubble. Her new job, found with difficulty in the group and dominated by the two mandatory conditions "special location" and "must

allow part-time work", looked exactly as it was to be expected under these conditions and lasted five years. The previous development activity was dead, your new field of activity is still charmingly described as "more commercial oriented".
Consequence: Nobody who reads the CV now understands it.

I have resolved not to criticize you. But I can say that you paid a damn high price. I don't know if there was another way to solve your personal problems – but the professional future of a (relatively) young person is an extremely high stake. "Only" giving up a promotion level and accepting salary cuts because of part-time work would have been "checked off" and considered reasonable and appropriate. But you went beyond that. And we don't know whether that was all the "price" paid or what is to come and how long it will take.

To put it this way: Perhaps the price to be paid would have been lower overall if you had brought the relatives to be cared for at your old location and somehow settled there.

Let me conclude this aspect like this: If I were in the situation of the relatives, I would be happy, one of my sons would be willing to make this sacrifice. But I would never want him to actually bring it because of me – indefinitely, with unknown consequences.

Your latest job has been on your resume for 1.5 years now, outlines a technical product area that is new to you and is technically a new, now the third, job orientation.

They wanted to hear my opinion, read my recommendation. As a consolation: You don't have to do what I say. My advice is:

1. You can't go on like this. You'll break it. One day your self-imposed care assignment has been completed and you are there as "used + embittered". That doesn't help anyone.

   You have done enough for your relatives, at least in this radical form. Now put "my job" at No. 1 on your priority scale and align your support with the options that you still have. You can be asked to make sacrifices, but not total self-abandonment. Your concept is standing on shaky ground anyway: If something happens to you tomorrow, your relatives also need solutions that You should already consider today - with you as the existing person in the background who can take care of it.
   Of course, you have to make this decision all by yourself.
2. From today's unloved jobyou have to go, absolutely and as soon as possible.
3. Anyone who only sees the CV shrugs their shoulders. He must think of you as someone who makes an incomprehensible decision every few years and then makes a sensible decision again, whose qualifications and ambitions come and go like the ebb and flow of the river.
a. Shethe backgrounds and motifs that have been yourdetermine professional life, explain it openly. This is the only way you can justify that you are not already "broken" or something.
b. A far-reaching solution (attaining a reasonably satisfying position that corresponds to your previous qualifications) requires that you assure your potential bosses: "It's over, I've been able to solve my private problem, I want and can now go back to freely and I

dedicate myself to my professional work with full commitment." That really has to be the case, otherwise it won't stand up to scrutiny in the job interview. This aspect is mandatory.

4. People only leave a company like yours for good reasons. So far, you can't blame him for anything - you alone "dropped out" from the usual employer/employee partnership. Everything that happened after that depends on your unilateral step. Internally, you have something to show "from the past", you knowold sponsors, do you have contacts, are there people who are not (anymore) bothered by your seemingly unmotivated Dipl.-XY. Externally, you're a blank slate with highly odd facts and a not-everything-satisfying (never forget that) explanation. There will be people who think you shouldn't have done it "that way". So I would try it internally first (group-wide).

5. I recall points 2 and 4 again. Otherwise nothing works. Don't try to work part-time again (don't say you can't; if you drop dead tomorrow, you have to).

6.

2.3.2.14 Why don't I choose theBoard own

Ask

I am Dr. Ing. and arrived at the management level below the board of directors of our AG. I recently underwent a multi-stage, very comprehensive and thoroughly convincing selection process for a possible promotion to the board level.

It was a very inspiring and challenging experience for me. Ultimately, I came to the conclusion that the target profile offered for a board position did not suit me and I decided to withdraw from the selection process. The main reasons for this were:

1. According to my assessment, which I gained in the assessment and from the discussions, the target profile is more in the direction of short-term, spontaneous and intuitively acting troubleshooters. My strategy, data and fact-oriented approach tends to be a hindrance.
2. I'm a militant efficiency fetishist and, after getting to know many board and supervisory board meetings, I have to realize that my idea of effort and benefit (in terms of content) cannot be realized in such a position.
3. The package of tasks for a board member with us contains too many topics that cost me a lot of energy, e.g. B. Networking at the highest level.
4. I amconvinced that I can do more for the future of the Group with my current tasks and opportunities – as long as I'm allowed, of course.

Answer

Some of your observations and analyzes are surprising,

others make sense or are questionable - my eyes almost light up at the thought of dealing with your individual points:

To 1: First of all, your conclusion is amazing,it even seems wrong. "Up" is no longer thought strategically, but only played intuitively troubleshooting? This can not be!

You have to let your observation sink in for a few minutes, then you understand better what you mean - and you can imagine that you are largely correct from a certain point of view:

In a well-ordered large company there are staff and staff-like departments (from corporate planning to business development). Their task is the strategy and fact-oriented, conceptual approach. Either the employees there have useful ideas themselves or they work out corresponding rough concepts, food for thought or even

crazy ideas of the board of directors in a detailed and time-consuming manner. The board listens, corrects, deletes, confirms, rejects - and decides (or adjourns). But he doesn't have time to work out all the details himself.

The troubleshooting thing is also correct. Sooner or later, every difficulty that is halfway serious ends up on the executive board's desk

- from the individual personnel case to quality or sales problems or even a plan deviation in the area of earnings. Very quick decisions are often required without a solid background of information.

After all, a central motto when running a company is:

"Something has to happen!" The supervisory board wants measures, the shareholders want them too, and the powerful business press also demands actions – they always want to see decisions that appear sovereign. After all, the motto mentioned is not: "Something has to be done – as soon as we know the entire background of the problem, have analyzed everything calmly and have been able to weigh up possible risks carefully and without time pressure." After all, anyone could do that.

Let's put it this way: Top managers have to make decisions. In this area, making a decision means having to choose between different options for action without being able to overview all aspects. A lot of what you call "intuitively acting troubleshooting" then comes out of it.

But the following also applies: the Executive Board must still have visions, must be long-term oriented when thinking and acting. He does that too! You see, in extreme cases the following is possible: A staff department with several people works for months on a concept, the board reads it through (2 hours), asks three questions (1/2 hour), wants two corrections (2.5 hours) and decides in a meeting of 5 hours. Do 10 board hours for a concept that defines the main activities of the house for the next few years. But at this very meeting, the next item on the agenda can be pure troubleshooting; the problems that arise there would be made known to a broad public, e.g. T. seem frighteningly banal ...

Conclusion: anyone who refuses to make spontaneous decisions based on gut feeling and only wants to work the way you claim to be, would not be the right person to be employed there. A board of directors must have many very different arrows in their quiver, shoot them unperturbed if necessary - and immediately move on to the next topic.

To 2: The "militant efficiency fetishist"I like. But I tend not to see the term in – fictitious – job descriptions for board members.

Let's start very carefully: board members are people. And when they are among themselves, some become little boys again who have been arguing about sand cake in the sandbox: "Do you cut my mold, I will cut your mold." Only today that means: "Are you against my new work in Brazil, I'm against appointing your general manager as director." So not im-
it's always like that, butit happens. Just like in the municipal council, in the leadership of the golf club or on the board of the rabbit breeding club.

Then it's one of those things with the question of the effort and benefit of the activity of a board member. Let's assume that such a top manager has to decide on the appointment of a new sales manager for Europe, who will ultimately be responsible for sales of EUR 800 million. Someone has to make this decision, it is extremely important: the wrong sales manager will result in lost sales, the right one will consistently build the company into No. 1 in the market. The board may need 2 hours for the decision; then he could read the newspaper for three weeks – if the decision was right.

You are a very typical engineer: shaped by permanent professional activities. You hate suddenly having to make extremely important decisions and then spend days doing things that don't impress you. But you can tell from the salary: the company considers this special work of the top management to be more valuable (and therefore more expensive) than what is done at the levels below.

Conclusion: No, it is better not for a militant efficiency fetishist to join the board. That's not to say boards aren't efficient, but it's a different kind of effectiveness and economy.

To 3: A board must be very well networked. In his field anyway, but also in politics, in the social sphere. Establishing and maintaining these networks, which are indispensable today, is pure elixir for those with the appropriate disposition, others consider "something like that" to be annoying. What's more: Networks are maintained across the board - in the certainty that they will eventually prove useful (even if it's only 10% of contacts). For the "militant efficiency fetishist" the efficiency of the corresponding action would be too low.

Conclusion: No matter how capable a specialist and manager at the levels below the board of directors could reach their limits with a climb to the "Olympus" or have already exceeded them.

In the first few years of my career, I was assigned to the project group in a group that no longer exists that was responsible for the "settlement" of a newly built administration building. In doing so, I had almost fantastic experiences: the higher up the managerial hierarchy, the more sensitivities, vanity and mutual distrust became evident. The highlight was a special meeting of the board of directors to decide which faucets should be installed in top management's washrooms. Otherwise an agreement could not be reached. At that time I was about 21 or 22 years old, so I had these experiences in one"early professional formation phase". The advantage: later on, almost nothing amazed or surprised me anymore...

To 4: Nicely said. A view that is widespread in middle management circles – which can be interpreted in two different directions:

a. "In my current position, I can do more for the future of the Group than I could on the Executive Board, with my special and somewhat limited qualities and skills." That is noble, self-critical and sounds convincing.
b. "In my current position, someone like me (which stands for a "reasonable" person here) can generally do more for the future of the group
– because the board job is so strange."
No one can provably interpret your statement in the direction of b - I'm just pointing out this dangerous possibility of interpretation.
And your "if you let me" is a classic sigh of dedicated, capable employees. If it's any consolation, you have bosses, I have customers. The race for the answer to the question of which group has a larger proportion of unreasonable personalities who consistently oppose a convincing solution must be viewed as completely open. Thank you for the valuable suggestions you have given us here. And even if not all of our readers want to become a board member (fortunately): If you want to understand a system, you have to look at the place where the decisions are made. That's exactly what we've done here (and of course the demands on executive boards are as different as companies).

2.3.2.15   Notes from practice

Answers that were important to me, even if there was no suitable question at the time

And what do you do afterwards?

Let's say you have a great job. Or you have a prospect. All your professional problems seem to be solved with it; unless something catastrophic happens, nothing can go wrong. They think.

No, for once I am not talking about the classic risks of working life, which of course still exist. I noticed how fatal a circumstance often is that hardly anyone takes into account in their planning:

No matter how unique, fulfilling, and all-around satisfying your new or current position may seem to you, in about five years it will bore you. Nice, so as not to provoke a predictable contradiction, I have to admit: There are people who are still not bored even after twenty years of happily "carrying boxes" – and there are those who are bored after months. But five years is a realistic average.

Why it is like that? Well, the allure of the new eventually wears off, routine dulls - and you change. You grow with your tasks; the demands on what you classify as a challenge are constantly increasing. And even if your later ambitions are not aimed at "higher" positions, "I would like to do something completely new" is a popular motive for change. However, you will, if you are young enough, after about five
want a new job that you think is simply "even better".

And then you have to give the "old" one "in payment". Kind of like in the car market. The old job qualifies you for the new one (just as the proceeds from the old car are often the main funding base for the new one).

No matter how "dreamy" your new or current position may be: one day it will only be the central foundation of your later application. And such an applicant checks very soberly: Does what the applicant is doing match our vacant position, our requirement profile? He is not interested in what seemed fantastic about it "back then", he does not enjoy a particularly exotic job from which you come.

Therefore, the requirement for a "dream job" that should make you completely happy (well, reasonably happy) is:

a. I must really like it now and it should look like my passion for it will last about five years as well.
b. After that period, it must lead to other existing(!) positions that I then regard as progress. Job offers published today provide examples of this.
c. So I always have to have an answer to the question: "What do I do afterwards?" And if I can't find one, the new job is not suitable as an employee's "dream job". Or: Mandon't buy a new car that can't be traded in later. I once had one like that...

Appropriate career choice

It is generally agreed that true universal geniuses are rare, almost "extinct". The modern employee and the corresponding manager "can" do a specialist area, maybe even a second oneIn exceptional cases, a third and also fits into the professional environment of his profession. More is usually not possible.

Now the human being is constructed in such a way that – see also the universal geniuses that can no longer be found – a particularly pronounced talent on the one hand entails various missing skills on the other. In fact, it seems that the level of ability is quite proportional to the level of ability (or several of them). The observation that there are numerous people who are "quite good" at many things, i.e. who can be used almost universally, fits in well with this: Their solid "versatile" talent is offset by the lack of in-depth development in a narrower specialist area.

If you accept these connections, then the next step for you is: I have to recognize my talent(s). It can't be that difficult. The yardstick is the others with whom you are together almost every day from the age of six (school at different levels, possibly training/apprenticeships, possibly army/civilian service, studies, professional practice). Anyone who stumbles through life with halfway attention can hardly avoid realizing what he can do better than others or where he at least belongs to the top group (it can also be pronounced versatility at a medium level). Your professional orientation should be based on this talent, supported by an interest in the profession. You can get along with it quite well, even though many people tend to overestimate rather than underestimate themselves.

My concern today is more about talent. The following applies here: recognize – and keep your hands off this area.

Unfortunately, all too often you meet people who are unsuccessfully romping around in areas for which they have absolutely no convincing talent. Sometimes things are so close together that extreme care is required in observing.

I'll give you an example of mine (hardly any reader can feel personally affected by this): Let's assume that in competition with other specialists it is important to analyze individual extremely important applications in detail. Whoever you choose as a competitor for me, I would optimistically face the challenge of delivering a performance worthy of discussion.

But put three hundred applications in one pile and set ten candidates loose on the task of working through them all in the shortest amount of time. If I were there, I would perish miserably: I just don't like a routine with little variety. Both are important in different places, so that's not the point here. But, and with that you still have a target group-oriented example: If you can brilliantly analyze and efficiently optimize production processes, you don't have to be able to successfully manage a production facility with three hundred people.

If he fails, the following applies: he should have recognized the risk (for him) and stayed away from it.

By the way: It is also advisable not to choose a

professional direction in which one does not correspond to the "type class" in terms of appearance or appearance ("first impression"). This is not so important when it comes to internal career planning, since the real personality – known to the bosses – outshines external appearances. But with every external application, the decision-makers only have that first impression when they have to judge. In concrete terms: It is helpful if a production manager applicant does not look like the author of a volume of lyrical outpourings ("Taubmurär Geist am Musenhain", Loriot).

No experiments!

For the younger ones among us, the headline will probably have to be explained: it is the slogan with which the CDU went into the 1957 federal election campaign. It is still relevant in important areas of (professional) life. If you want to formulate the maxim positively, it should say at this point: Pay attention to the
"red thread"in career.

I have just encountered another specific case that underscores the recommendation and gives a "face" to many other observations on the subject: A man is applying to be a managing director. He has the right education, is the right age, and has been doing the right job in the right industry environment for eight(!) years. Everything is actually fine. But my medium-sized client complains about the candidate: Eight years ago, that man was in industry X. Just think: X! "What do our employees think of a man who comes from X?" If you are looking for reasons for "inexplicable" rejection: Search here too!

You know those X industries yourself from the point of view of your current environment. The actual activity during this time may still fit the topic to some extent, but if the industry is seen as "outlandish", an application can still fail years later.

This one was just one particularly glaring example. There are standard violations of the "red thread law" in many CVs. They arise as follows:

a. at the request of the employer in pursuing the goal of training universally trained and experienced group managers. But: It's about this one company where the candidate is currently working – for other employers, an applicant who, after three years in the design office, first follows two years of personnel development, then two more years of internal sales management and has the goal of "internal top Management" has a "pattern without value"

be. "Generalists" are always hard to sell, "generalists in training" are poor devils if they suddenly want or have to apply before they have reached their internal development goal and have worked there successfully for a few years.

b. at the employer's request with the aim of plugging a personnel gap that had just opened up somewhere internally. And Mueller? Müller was so favorable, was asked "urgently", couldn't refuse - and now hangs around in a very special position that hardly exists anywhere else in the country.

c. at the employee's own request because the new job was so exciting or otherwise seemed particularly appealing to the person concerned. This also includes the executive assistant at 40, the representative for something for whom there is no logical "after" or the "versatile" who starts something new every two years.

The rule is: Always(!) expect to have to apply externally at least once or even several times. Before accepting a new job, check how it will look later in the eyes of an applicant, whether it fits in with your previous career and future career goals. And whether the "total work of art" in your CV looks as if it was based on at least an imaginable concept.

A job is a job – and private is private

Professional activity and private life are two of the central pillars that support our existence. They stand separately, but are connected to one another by many structural elements: if one falls, the other will be affected – your entire existence is in danger.

Both pillars are made of relatively sensitive material, exposed to constant attacks from the rigors of the struggle for life. They are sometimes more, sometimes less damaged and require our constant attention and also permanent repair efforts. We live with that.

But: We are not always sufficiently consistent when it comes to the renovation work that is due. And then we violate a "basic law" of this profession:
Solve the problemswhere they arise.

Take care of that pillar that has suddenly become problematic - and don't break stones from the healthy one to repair the weakened one. After that, your overall balance is just as bad as before, you just swapped the ailing column for the strong one.

No, if one of the supporting pillars has a problem, you have to leave the other one completely alone and tend to it more intensively. Because it will have to carry a higher load anyway until you have completed the repairs that are due.

Since it is high time to leave this picture, the urgent recommendation in plain language:
No professional change for private reasons.
If you don't feel at home at the new place of work at first: work on it, get involved locally, maybe move your apartment to the next town and drive a little further - but don't give up the job that is going well.

If two partners are temporarily forced to live separately due to their professional activities: look for e.g. B. by living in the middle or by a - temporary - weekend relationship to make the best of it
– but don't give up the job that's going well.

If your mother-in-law needs care, bring her over, don't move there. Of course, that brings problems - but the problems that arise with the other solution are greater in the long run.

Conversely, by the way, common sense prevents worse things from happening: only a few careerists get divorced and look for a new partner just because that would be more conducive to their own career or because their own boss likes it better. Why this partial inconsistency?

Do I think I have a chance of bringing about a profound change in behavior with this contribution?

Let's put it this way: I knowMeine Pappenheimer (loosely adapted from Schiller, Wallenstein's death). One of the key mistakes in career planning will not end overnight. But at least you've been warned.

2.3.3   The ascent also has its everyday life

Many issues are career specific. but even the climber

has to cope with the normal day-to-day business - or can fail at it.

2.3.3.1   What am I going to do now until I retire?

Ask

I'm 51, working my way up to the ranks in a larger companylead
management level below the Executive Board behind me, I continue to be successful and quite satisfied. But what am I going to do in the next fifteen years?

Answer

Summary: Same as today.

Because this statementis certainly perceived as unsatisfactory, a long version must follow:

1. In principle, all of the following points apply to executives as well as executive employees. Where there are differences, I will point them out.

2. Your personal development opportunities (promotion, more responsibility) are now considered to have been exhausted. So don't count on a further positive career development. It is true, however, that the chances of making another leap up the ladder are greater for executives. The age limit is a bit more flexible here.

3. Within the company, you can easily take everything with you that might still be useful in terms of positive further development. But with regard to external efforts, I recommend restraint (much more vigorously for non-executives than for managers).

The reason for this is not so much the question of

whether you could still achieve something with external applications - you would notice that. The problems only begin when you succeed. Because the existence of the employee rests on two pillars:

a) the current job and b) the certainty that if you lose your job at any time (!), you will be able to find an adequate position externally.

You, for example, are now largely satisfied with your position below the Executive Board. An external change was only worthwhile if it made you a member of the board. If you lost this job after one to three years, you wouldn't look "good" on the job market: 52 to 54 years old, too short a period of service in the then current position, was a board member for the first time and probably couldn't cope with it (too old?) . And nobody would want to hire an ex-CEO again as a manager below this level ("once a board member, always a board member").

4. So the urgent advice is to stay in your current position with your current employer and make your "peace" with it. The period of rapid professional development is or is coming to an end for you, just like so many other phases in life also have "their time" and will eventually be over. Because of #3, your strategic and tactical efforts on your own behalf must now focus primarily on maintaining what you have achieved. It is no longer important to qualify for the next step up, but to secure your current position. You come into this attitude if you accept my argument as logical, so to speak "automatically" in.

This is, with caution, one of the reasons for the possible differences between older, second-tier managers and younger, full-blooded dynamic CEOs. The latter want (have to?) conquer "the world", also in order to distinguish themselves, while the former also see the risk involved. So be careful: don't become a discernible skeptic, always help to conquer, but don't put everything on one card. Your approach will inevitably be more risk-minimizing.

And speaking of warnings, I see a disproportionate number of early fifties who have just lost their jobs. This phase seems to be a critical age for this. One feels quite unassailable due to extensive experience and long periods of service, and in particular dismisses the concerns of new (younger?) superiors as quirks that should not be taken seriously
– and is often "out there" very quickly.

5. The previous ones (1 to 4) didn't sound so terribly great - depending on the reader's attitude - now something calming to compensate:

You will not experience the next fifteen years with the dwindling (to put it mildly) professional opportunities with the personality of a young man in his best storm and stress times. That would be terrible though But people who are getting older are not only confronted with changed conditions in their professional environment, they also change themselves. (fight against this, at least partially: Don't let yourself be left behind by younger people when it comes to PC technology or the use of smartphones and navigation systems - that would only support the prejudice against older people). Some things just become less important, others take their place.

Of course, this develops differently from person to

person – but everyone is affected in some way. Then there is the health aspect. And one day you will no longer say "You have to be a member of the Management Board", but you will be proud of the fact that you still meet the requirements of your job at the level below in a first-class manner and that you can still hold your own against younger colleagues very well.

You have always or mostly done good, committed work and have recommended yourself to your bosses as an almost ideal person to fill the position with potential for "more". You will keep this working style, your commitment, etc. and will continue to recommend yourself to your bosses as an almost ideal person to fill the position. Just trying, potential for "more"

Replace showing with the goal of remaining a near-ideal position despite the beginning declines in many physical and mental abilities (which you don't have to admit to others).

I promise you, in the next few years this reasoning will start to make sense to you (by the time you are 55 at the latest).

The question remains: "Okay, no more advancement,.

6. but the same job for another fifteen years?" The consolation also applies to this: the desire for something new decreases with age. In addition, your board will come up with various restructuring measures that will successfully prevent monotony. And one day the changes that are characterized by new IT systems, new organizational processes, new employees and, above all, new bosses will be enough for you.

If you now ask me whether a company with more young or more old employees (especially in management) is better off, then I am convinced that there needs to be a balanced mix of all age groups, only that has a future. They need the young sky-stormers, believing in progress and idealistic, they also need the experienced, who slow down too much storm and stress. If the two groups, supported by a broad "middle" group in between, find a way to work together harmoniously, an optimum has been reached.

2.3.3.2   Alsoa GF has his problems

For many years I have been reading your articles in the VDI nachrichten carefully and with great personal benefit. As a manager, I consider your attitudes formulated there to be highly practical and relevant.

At my current employer, a medium-sized group, I initially set up and managed a central department that was very close to the operative business for several years. About two years ago I was appointed managing director of a group of companies within this group. The division manager who is responsible for me at the holding company is very satisfied with my performance, because I managed to get my department through the crisis much stronger and to achieve significant increases in sales, earnings, productivity, etc. I have a very good, trusting relationship with him and my colleagues.

In addition to (probably more "above"; H. Mell) the division managers, there is of course a CEO in the holding company who has held his position for a few years. He has spent his entire career almost exclusively in finance used to work in corporations, operations such as sales and production have remained alien to him. At first it had little effect. On the contrary, he has guided us through the crisis in a pleasant, prudent and intelligent manner.

The company is now growing very strongly again and he begins to reorganize the group to suit his needs. Since he has little connection to the operative business, he treats the management team with a certain distrust, which is reflected in excessive bureaucracy and condescension. As a result, I (and many GF colleagues) have spoiled the joy of my work.

I'm not in a position to criticize his actions and attitudes, the shareholder must have had something in mind. My job as an employed managing director is not to be happy, but to act in the interests of the holding company and thus the CEO. I do too and will continue to do so for a while.

But I stick to the motto "love it, change it or leave it". I can't love or change the circumstances, so I draw Mell's "invisible sword" and plan my departure.

However, I have only been in my position as Managing Director for almost two years and am afraid that an applicant will now instinctively assume that I am not applying as a successful achiever but as a failed manager. So I plan to only launch a few trial balloons next year, but then apply very seriously the following year (with three years of service as MD behind me).

1. Is the thesis correct that after only two (three?) years as a MD you are not attractive for a first-class company? I know a few managing directors who change companies every 2-3 years, but I was always skeptical.

2. If so, how do you sell that without badmouthing the current employer? How are secondary aspects such as B. Long-distance commuting included?

Answer

This isn't America! I feel, after some thought, literally pushes from this fundamental realization. Now the only question that remains is whether anyone has thought this far before me or whether I can claim an originality award for it.

I came to this conclusion because your motto "love it..." sounds strongly American to my ears. The internet did not help me with a short attempt. Google shows several million hits, I can't process them so quickly. So for me the creator remains in the dark, I'm guessing "American business wisdom" or a similarly named source. And that may well be good for America.

If it were also true for us here, thousands of higher or at least academically educated employees would have to be constantly on the run. Because that's the only thing they would have if they didn't love a situation or constellation in their environment, but couldn't change it either.

No, we say it differently here - and have been doing so for an amazingly long time: "Give me the serenity to accept things that I cannot change. Give me the courage to change the things I can change. And give me the wisdom to distinguish one from the other." (FC Oetinger, German Protestant theologian, 1702–1782). There's no talk of running away. More of persevering, trying to come to terms.

And also – in all modesty – JOSH DOUGLAS's sword isnot a weapon of attack, but the "only possibility with which an employee can defend himself in the struggle for existence". If he is attacked, if his professional existence is threatened, mind you.

Let's leave the quotes aside, ultimately you can't prove anything with them. But it's a nice intellectual gimmick to use other people's words to express what you're thinking. And in case a reader is not quite sure about the CEO: for the purposes of this article it is sufficient to compare the CEO with a chairman of the board.

Now to your situation: The shareholder determines the direction and sets goals. The main strategic direction in your case: "Numbers", i.e. business results, analyzes and planning. For the shareholder and his CEO, operational activities are more of a means to an end than an affair of the heart. Your bosses are allowed to see it that way. You are now required to move within the framework of these requirements ("The numbers dictate the procedure, not the needs of the operative business"). Luckily, there is a paragraph in the middle of your remarks, which you saw correctly ("I am not in the position..."). I couldn't have phrased that more clearly.

You don't like this new orientation of the company, you lose the joy of work. That's all! Does this threaten you so much in your struggle for existence that you have to draw the "sword" that says "dismissal"? I'm quite sure: No, that's not enough! Because we don't say "leave it" here if you don't love something you can't change. First of all, we struggle for the composure to be able to endure something like this - and we only draw our "sword" when we have to defend ourselves. Against a serious threat to our status.

But they don't exist! Of course I understand you: for you and your fellow managers, the attitude of the CEO is annoying, demotivating, you feel disregarded. But ultimately only because you define "from the bottom up" what would be best for the company in a way that you are not really entitled to, one could almost call it presumptuous. However, it is up to the shareholder alone to decide that. As you can already guess, the CEO only implements his will.

He's not attacking you yet, but he will if you continue to assert your view of "good and right". Only then would you have a reason to withdraw to "leave it".
Now I would like to present three more arguments to you:

1. I know my Pappenheimer (after Schiller, Wallenstein's death), meaning the sub-division managers like you. The group gets a new CEO, whom the shareholder takes from the finance department for good reason, because he expects the decisive battles there. This is how it actually happens in the crisis. And the decision in favor of this CEO was the right one, because he "led us through the crisis in a prudent and intelligent manner in a pleasant way". It almost sounds like gratitude, but in any case recognition. But then the crisis was over and things started to pick up again. Now, if you apply higher standards, the shareholder should have replaced the CEO ("reorganizer with a financial background"). But he didn't, it's not usual, would have seemed ungrateful. Factually, I agree with you, now is the time for the operatives.

That was preamble, now comes the crux: who "started" seeing the other side as misaligned and disruptive? Couldn't it be – and I wouldn't ask if I didn't think it was possible – that you and your colleagues first let the CEO know how little you think of his attitude? I don't mean direct confrontation at all, it's enough to resist his "excessive bureaucracy" etc., himself

"Lack of enthusiasm" on your part can already trigger reactions in him. A CEO is about ten times as sensitive to disregard or even a lack of following from below as a sub-business manager is to "trouble" from above. On that basis, is it possible that he thinks you "started" (an argument extremely important even to children in the sandbox)? Or from his point of view you are not involved enough? I ask you to think very carefully about this. For if his behavior is a reaction to your disagreement with his course of action, then you are doubly wrong.

2. Regardless of 1: With your dissenting opinion about right and wrong weighting of right and wrong priority (finances vs
Operatives) you can't be right at all, it's up to him to decide. If you allow yourself to be carried away to take ill-considered steps, it would be a great pity.
Try to take his point of view – and imagine that in his place you had to lead people like you and your colleagues. What would you feel, what would you do?

3. About "joy to work" isactually, you said so, nothing in your contract of employment. It's important to become and stay a GF, it's less important what you do as one. And yet what must be your main goal of staying a GF is not compromised - and your second main goal of making your bosses happy is still achievable.
Outlook: Of course you can and should leave at some point if you can no longer work there. But the time for a change is actually unfavorable. Try to get five successful GF years. Precisely because you were previously in the more staff-like central function and this is your big operational test. You don't "throw" them without need. And a lack of joy does not count as a need. As a consolation: Your frequently changing GF acquaintances

are walking on very thin ice, which will break with the next shock. And they are certainly not all GFs for the first time.

There is no good answer to your question 2. The truth would comevery bad – always a worrying sign And the commute between home and work? You knew everything beforehand. But now I'm suspicious: Is what is actually a central argument seemingly harmlessly hidden in the last sentence? Something like this is convincing in applications for clerks, but not for managing directors. Hold on for three more years. With a different attitude, you can enjoy your great position again. I understand your feelings, but I advise against the conclusions you draw from them.

2.3.3.3 "Even a GF has his problems"/reader reaction

Ask

I have been reading your articles in the VDI nachrichten for almost 20 years now. I think the vast majority is correct. You can also justifiably be proud of having steered a large part of the readers onto the right career path. However, I see the content of the article "Even a GF has his problems" critically. The decision-making process at a GF level is much more complicated. A reduction to "the owner or Chairperson is decisive and everyone else has to conform to it" is too simplistic.

1. In the meantime, also because of the views you propagate, we are experiencing too many adapted top and middle managers in our economy who are ultimately only executive and politically active units. According to the motto: "Where is the strongest wind blowing from, then I point my flag ... and primarily I am concerned with determining the right wind direction" – far too little work is being done on the actual factual question. Your contribution is another nail in the coffin that fits into this picture.

2. I am convinced that with such an attitude, companies will gradually lose their competitiveness. It must be the task of successful owners and their representatives to deal with conflicting opinions from responsible managers and employees, as long as they are justified. In the end, it is up to the owner or CEO to assess whether these opinions are really helpful or whether they come from others, e.g. B. personal interests result. In the medium to long term, it will also affect this "wind

direction-seeking" manager. If the company is sold or if he gets new managers, he has meanwhile lost the connection and thus the competence to his actual area of responsibility. I meet such fates more and more.

3. Managers who are responsible for several hundred employees and a considerable budget in the millions report and reported to me. In fact, I crave their opinions and assessments when it comes to important corporate decisions. If I can combine this opinion with my own evaluation and even with the assessment of the owners, then I have already fulfilled my task in an important part. To do this, I work out similarities and contradictions, address the contradictions and resolve them in a large number of discussions. This phase is over after a defined period of time. The remaining contradictions are often still there and cannot be solved in the short term, but are transparent due to the previous process. The final decision is understandable for everyone.

4. Admittedly, if you don't get the long-term trust of the owners and/or superiors, you run the risk of failing before your own beliefs even
take effect. I can tell from my own experience2.3

to report. In the medium term, however, this experience will help to dare a new, all the more successful start.

5. Conclusion: An active and productive acceptance of the assigned responsibility and position, which is in contrast to superiors and/or owners, can certainly lead to (great) professional success, even if the path can be a bit rocky (and risky).

Answer

I extracted this aspect from the (even) longer submission, it gives us enough material for a weekly post.

With all due discretion: The sender of this reader reaction to the earlier article of the same title has been working as Director XY on the second management level of a large company for a short time and, according to his CV, must have experienced something that corresponds to my warnings in the original article (see also 6. His question, with special reference to the words "can", "more difficult" and "more risky"). I would be more reassured if he could already look back on three to five years of successful (as defined by supervisors and owners) service in the new position.

Dear sender, don't you also think that it is a bit daring to present your current working style - which I do not criticize at all - as a recipe for success when the new working time is practically still measured in weeks? I do not name your area of expertise, your education and your age, so you cannot be identified by third parties. I have a slight suspicion that you are also processing special experiences with previous employers, especially the last one. So, that was my reaction provoked by your "coffin nail", now to the point:
We're not that far apart at all:

6.

7. On 1 (the numbering of your paragraphs is mine, it simplifies the answer): There is a legal basis according to which the owners can do almost "everything" with their company (decide the business policy, divide the

company, sell it, shut it down , restructure, change the product range, relocate everything abroad, etc.). Measured against this, the employed management is practically "not allowed to do anything". As always in this series, the facts dominate, not theoretical discussions of how it should be.

8. And: The owner (or his representative) hires the subordinate management. If he feels like it, he'll fire it again (or not renew a GF contract); in this question, which is existential for a subordinate GF, he is also almost absolutely sovereign.
9. No, I'm afraid it's the situation first of all
10. "simple" as I put it. I even subscribe to your exaggeration:
"The owneror chairman is crucial and everyone else has to judge by that." It's not a question of whether that's nice, but it is. And it is the intention of the creators of the "rules of the system".

The number of managers who later found out with great pain that this is the case must be legion. I then have many of them as partners in outplacement, in new placement or in career advice. And from their fate it can be deduced: It really is that "simple". Those were the basics.

To 2: You say: "We are experiencing ... in our economy too many adapted top and middle managers ...". Correct, that is unfortunately the case – if one assumes that "the companies" are a kind of "third force" with equal rights, alongside the owners and employees, who both play a precisely defined role and have defined rights. "The Company" however does not have these rights – it has no enforceable interests and claims of its own. If the owners (shareholders) want to sell a top

corporation to someone who will certainly do more harm to "the company" than good, then they can and will do so. Whether this is also in the interest of this company is not even a relevant question.
"On the actual factualquestion is worked far too little"
– I agree with that in principle, but the devil is in the details: What is the "actual factual question"? These are again the "interests of the company", which do not exist in an enforceable form.

You see, even a house that belongs to you, for example, could definitely have "actual objective interests". In this context, it could undoubtedly make sense to re-cover the roof to maintain its value. The owner would have to make money for this. But he doesn't want that, he tears down the house and sells the property to a supermarket chain.

11.

12. My example may lag a bit, but the principle is comparable. I have both a (small) business and a house. Both have no rights to assert with regard to optimal well-being. Who would want to formulate that? So the legal system has left the definition of the interests of companies and houses in the hands of the owners - neither the employed managers nor the employed caretakers (although both of them would certainly know much better what would be in the interest of the company or the house).

a. That would remain my "nail in the coffin", which represents my contribution to a conceivable optimum (although if the owner could no longer act without restrictions in the company, there would hardly be any buyers, founders or investors, but let's leave that out for a moment). That's right, my enlightening presentation is, within a certain framework, quite capable of cementing existing circumstances. And of course you can regret that. But: a) With my reporting ("that's the way it is, prepare yourself for it"), I might support the conditions desired in and by the system, by law and jurisdiction. So "coffin nail" whose? A revolution in circumstances, a conceivable change that has by no means proven that it would be any better afterwards?

b. The legislature could (theoretically) have been close to implementing a change in your interest (disempower owners, empower new groups or at least bring owners to their senses), but after reading my contribution they refrain from doing so. Probability?

c. The owners may have just come to their senses, read my reply and left things as they were. Unfortunately, I cannot reach the owners and CEOs who are currently the only authoritative ones. So I can't do any harm in that regard either.

d. Perhaps many middle managers think like you. And maybe some weredetermined to stand up to their CEOs and owners "in the interest of the company" (for which they have no mandate). And maybe I stopped some from doing it. Then I'm proud of it. Because I don't tend to have people run up against machine guns with wooden clubs, for example.

To 3: It is very conceivable that the real conditions, as I describe them, run counter to the interests of the company (and thus actually also those of the owners as well as those of the managers and employees). But: see to 2, these interests in a defined way do not officially exist.

"It must be the task of successful owners... especially

with opposing opinions..." Yes, it should. And: All the owners I know only want the best – for themselves, their company, etc. Very many also listen to a dissenting opinion presented in an appropriate form. In my opinion, presenting this at least once is one of the clear duties of the employed manager. But if he does not assert himself, he can be expected to implement the completely opposite specification/instruction of his senior superiors with commitment and full commitment. This also includes, if necessary, inspiring your own employees for something that they are not at all convinced of.

13. I share your shock at the professional competence of some
14. company managers - and I find broad approval. Anywhere in a free society
e.g. B. in politics, the system flushes the incompetent to the top. Especially in an unfree society. The hired middle manager who sees something like this draws his "sword", resigns and leaves. But be careful: in the technical assessment There is a special kind of arrogance in the way top managers and shareholders are treated by subordinates – someone is not automatically right just because they are in a lower rank.

To 5: Exactly, exactly, one "runs the risk". But I have to doubt whether the experience of a failure in this regard will help everyone "to dare a new, all the more successful start". Well, experience is the sum of self-made mistakes. But: "From failure to success" seems to me to be a very daring strategy. I see managers who have failed so badly that they have never recovered.

Regarding 6: You too will be in your current position, to which you are absolutely rightare proud of, ultimately less because of, but rather in spite of, the contrast to superiors in previous positions. I'm happy to believe that such contrasts and overcoming them have done you good and that you have personally matured as a result. But the following still applies: When it comes to applications from managers, I advise against giving reasons for leaving the old employer such as "I could not and did not want to follow the ideas of my boss about business policy" if in doubt. The possible new boss basically feels closer to the old one. Exceptions are conceivable, but rare. Don't count on it.

15.

Internal change during the probationary period

As a career starter, I am a project engineer during my probationary period at a large chemical company (Bachelor Eng. Mechanical Engineering). I am currently employed in the area of plant planning and construction. I enjoy the work. I'm a kind of middleman between the companies and the planning department, which also enables me to have contact with the practice.

Now it is planned to transfer me to another location (within Germany) because there is an absolute shortage of staff there. I'm supposed to work there in project cost controlling. The joy about the new job is limited, since the practical relevance that I currently have and which is very important to me would be greatly reduced.

Now I noticed an internal job posting from another division. There they are looking for a technical clerk for a specific type of machine. The practical relevance would be even greater than today. The position would also suit my training profile.

I see several possibilities:

1. I am applying the "normal" way (I assume: as an external applicant at my own company; H. Mell). Do I then mention the current time (several months) that I have been working as a project engineer in the company? How is my application treated in the company? The executives will certainly talk to each other.

2. I speak to my current boss and tell him what I intend to do.

3. I contact the head of department for the advertised position and ask about my chances, stating what I am doing today.
4. I do not apply and have myself transferred to the new location as planned. I'll take my new job in cost controlling with me as experience and I'll apply at a later date for a position similar to the one currently advertised.

Answer

Bosses usually know what they're doing when they're doing it. Your current superiors also know very well that the transfer at this point in time is quite a "slap in the office" for you. Your first few months are practically "dead" for your CV, there are no plans to go back, and the transfer after such a short time will still raise questions in five years' time if you then apply externally. Your bosses have also noticed that you don't want to work in cost controlling or at the other location. Yet they made that decision. This could be for one of these reasons:

a. The whole story is primarily against you. At the end of the probationary period, your bosses will have recognized that you will not "bring well" in today's job. For social reasons and because one does not like to dismiss such people in times of a shortage of engineers, one looked internally, found the cost controlling department that was "blessed" with vacancies and put them there
– the further away, the better.
In this case, your current boss was the "motor of the

transfer idea" and wants to get rid of you, no matter how. He doesn't care where you stay.

b. You do a good job, inspire hope, your performance and your personality please your boss. But with your few months of service, as a beginner in the "1st Apprenticeship year" is of course not yet an indispensable top performer.

Now comes a desperate oneRequest from an external department that simply cannot find any applicants at their location, your boss helps out. If this department belongs to the same area as your boss, then the common higherThe superiors of both department heads put pressure on yours – he didn't want to give you up, but he had to.

If the two heads of department do not have a common boss, yours would hardly voluntarily make a promising man. And certainly not a vacancy! In this case, the evidence would support a.

It is imperative that you find out whether a or b applies. If necessary, ask your current boss very carefully. And of course all colleagues have long known what's going on.

Forget the internal advertisement. If a is correct, no one will take you internally (except for cost controlling, which is desperate – perhaps also because of its location).

Your idea of behaving like a "normal" (external) applicant and even concealing your current job is ridiculous. You would have to indicate where you are today. So either a applies, in which case this third department will not take you, or b applies, in which case your appointment will not be approved for that department head – because "higher company interests" are at stake. Also forget 2., except to find out whether a or b is true. Act according to variant 4 and see it as an opportunity. Anything else is unrealistic

2.3.3.4   problems withservice provider

Ask

I've been employed by an engineering service provider for almost two years,
whose employees – including myself – are hired out to a large corporation. When I signed the contract back then, I was not familiar with the service industry.

The project I am currently working on is very interesting and I have learned a lot. At the end of the day, however, I work for the clerk in the group, but I have no way of assuming technical responsibility sooner or later,
e.g. B. to take over a project management. I can see that I'm getting better and better at my job, but I don't have the prospects. Just supplying someone and not being able to make decisions yourself, I don't want that for a long time. I'm thinking about changing employers, but I'm undecided on where and what exactly I want to do.

It makes sense to apply to the company I'm working for. I've built up a network there and know the processes, even if not all of them. You have immediate responsibility in this house at clerk level In general, advancement in this company should be very difficult. On the one hand I get to know a lot of people in this big company and benefit from their knowledge, on the other hand I don't like the corporate culture of the company. If you express your opinion freely, it doesn't necessarily get you anywhere. I don't feel comfortable in the company either.

Should I try and still apply to the group? Does it look

better from the inside, inside the company, than what I see from the outside?

My previous professional experience is not yet the world. But when I change, I start all over again to build up new knowledge and a new network. However, if I stay with the service provider for a longer period of time, I cannot claim to have completed a task or a project when I apply later. The clerk reaps the laurels.

I would like to further my education, e.g. B. through postgraduate studies in the field of technology + business. Should I start now?

Answer

Now always nice and slowly with the young horses!

You are still very young, very inexperienced and – even in your own opinion – you are in an extremely unsatisfactory overall professional situation. And without any perspective.

Considering your situation, the "right" job at the company you are loaned to would already be a huge step forward by several steps. Then this company is one of the top addresses worldwide for certain high-quality products, which people lick their fingers for in China as well as in Hamburg or New York. My God, "the store" is just world class, nothing more. It must be a dream for you to work there. I'm talking three to five years, not necessarily life. And you think the corporate culture doesn't appeal to you, that promotion there should be difficult
- and you're not even in it yet.

Oh yes, and "if you express your opinion freely, it doesn't necessarily get you anywhere." That, dear sender, is a globally valid standard for employees, nothing more. Your joke was good, honestly.

For you, a job with this group would be a great "promotion" – also in its later effect on your CV(!). Simply seen within this overall constellation. And three years later you "may" think about whether the corporate culture is able to meet your requirements.

.

PS: Of course they only cook with water there, there are problems, incompetent bosses and lazy employees. You just: You won't find it much better in the country, the professional world is no better than the people who shape it and who live in it. And if you don't make the leap, someone who looks at your CV later will say: "Why didn't the company take on this employee after they had known him for a number of years? Well, I know: weighed and found wanting."

Conclusion: The store there is world-class, but the world is imperfect (which youwould you know, e.g. B. read this series from the beginning of the course).

Staying with your current employer for more than two years will do you no good. So: a) Immediately initiate efforts to be taken over by the group. b) If you fail, you should switch, e.g. B. to a large supplier.

Clarify your career path first. You don't even have a classic job at a company where you can and are allowed to shape something. If you have such a position and the probationary period is over, you can think about part-time further training. That's not your central problem.

2.3.3.5   Reapplying after your own rejection?

Ask

Let's assume that engineer A applies to each of the companies today
B, C and D. The interviews are going well, all three companies are interested and offer applicant A employment. A chooses company C. After five years, engineer A wants to change employers to move up the career ladder. Company B still seems attractive to him, so A applies there again.

How does company B react to this application from an engineer who had already turned down a job offer from this company a few years earlier? With the same interest as back then? With reluctance (because this applicant "could do it again and again", as one of your quotes goes)?

I am aware that the labor market situation also has an influence on the answer - but I am sure that you still have good pointers on the subject.

Answer

So let's assume that A applies for a job after working for C for five years
now with company B. First of all, this does not raise any particular gene up. The man has been with the current employer for a sufficiently long period of time – if he can think of a reasonable justification for the change project, everything is fine so far.

Now, five years ago, the candidate not only sent an application to B, he also caused a lot of work there. For an interview, maybe even for preparing a contract offer. And he declined, preferred another offer and - one might think - disappointed, offended or even made B angry. The people there could remember this applicant, still resent his rejection at the time – and suspect that he is only provoking a lot of effort now, maybe just testing his market value and then rejecting it again. The following arguments:

1. That applicant A is a clever man. He knows that one never leaves "scorched earth" behind when dealing with potential employers, but expects from the outset that one "always meets twice" in life. So he wrote a rejection letter with this content at the time:
"... I was very pleased about your contract offer. I would like to express my sincere thanks for the trust you are placing in me.
During our contacts, your company turned out to be a very interesting potential employer for me, and one I would have liked to work for.
Unfortunately, after very careful consideration, I have now decided on another offer for special reasons. It is clear to me that this decision can also be wrong, only time will tell. If you allow me, I would like to reserve the right to apply to you again at a later date.
Thank you again for the information you gave me and for the interesting discussion.
Best regards...."
Or something like that. It's not like people at B memorize something like that and immediately remember it when A's name comes up again after several years. But A feels better about it if he later wants something from B again.
And he wouldn't feel good at all if he had written back

then: "You can keep your second-rate offer. Fortunately, there are still companies that can correctly assess the value of an applicant. Good luck for the future."

2. Five years is a long time in a modern company. There is probably "not a stone left unturned" there – the structures are different, the people have changed or have different responsibilities. And even if not: After such a long time, no one remembers an applicant who "only" didn't accept an offer.

3. Applicants are no longer associated with their names shortly after they have become acquainted – too many of them simply come and go for that. If you remember anything, then the names of well-known employers from which they come. But today A comes from an employer who didn't even appear in his application at the time.

4. Even if a company should go to the trouble of recording all applicant contacts with all the details in a file, which is hardly to be expected, the following still applies: new game, new luck. Years later, the position is different, the line manager has different standards (or is a different person), a changed labor market situation forces you to think differently. The company reads the application "neutrally" and is generally interested.

Also, you will no longer care about the sameApply for a position like five years ago, you wanted to "climb the next step on the career ladder" (which, by the way, doesn't work that way; you either "take" the next one Step" up a ladder or, better yet, you "climb" the next "step".the same - but you don't climb steps).

Conclusion: You can apply there again without any worries. I would not mention the old case in the written application. Whether or not you do it in the interview depends on the course of the interview.

But: There is not the slightest certainty that you will now be made an offer again. As you know: new game, new luck – and new competitors.

5.

" Change employer every 4 years?

Ask

They recommend to the career ambitiousengineer to change employers every four to five years.

Answer

I don't do that - and I didn't do it!

To be on the safe side, here are the recommendations I have written down many times:

1. The "minimum length of stay" per employer should be around five years on average. If things are going well, it is better to stay for at least seven to eight years – this is how you build up a "cushion of service time" for any "rapid" changes that may suddenly become necessary later in your career.

   "At least" means: rather more. And there was never any talk of a recommendation to change in any case after five years.

2. An exception applies to career starters after graduation. They even tolerate two years of service in this first job. The same applies here: longer is better, with a "cushion of service time" you make provisions for various possible disasters.

3. Since everything that is basically good and useful to urgently advisable can also be harmful above a certain amount (like salt in the soup), there are upper limits that are also fluid and do not have to be taken slavishly narrow:

   After ten years of service per employer, you should start to think about whether a change might not be advisable.

4. This recommendation to change is reinforced by a similar, unchanged activity/position in those ten or more years. It is mitigated by many internal changes (which are reflected in the CV) and above all by real internal progress (promotions). After more than ten years, recognizable changes in the CV should therefore appear: either due to internal changes in tasks/promotions or due to a change of employer. In general, people tend to change too much rather than too little in the country. There are CVs with ten employers in twenty years.

In times of good economic activity, employers easily overlook boundaries of this kind, as well as when the applicant specializes in a rare, urgently sought-after field: If a position absolutely has to be filled, the shirt is closer to the employer than the pants (otherwise it would not come to these careers of extreme changers). But in the next crisis or when certain age limits are exceeded, the same employer suddenly pulls the ripcord and rejects such candidates. And there they are...

Therefore, as a kind of "life insurance" (that's factually wrong, but memorable), it's recommended to stay on the safe side. But don't say I would call for a change "every four to five years".

And with that being said: staying with one employer for 25 years is perfectly fine – as long as you can be sure that you will never

want or need to change more. Can you be sure? Unfortunately you cannot. By the way (so that you are warned): The critical phase in which something suddenly happens against all expectations is between about 48 and 52 years.

2.3.3.6   Atthe notice period failed

Ask

I'm in my late 40s and head a department in an international group.

I recently applied externally and had an interview. The position offered, the location, the size of the company and the industry were very much in line with my expectations. I later received word that I was third in the candidate selection. The reason for my weaker classification was my long notice period of six months to the end of the month.

This decision gave me a lot to think about. After all, neither in the ad nor in the interview was I given a target starting date. Don't get me wrong, I didn't expect that the notice period could be to my disadvantage. When I was hired by my current employer at the time, this period was non-negotiable.

Is this deadline unreasonably high at my hierarchy level or did I respond to the wrong ad? Isn't such a deadline also an appreciation of my function? Isn't it the case that after more than five years of service, the legislature provides appropriate notice periods to protect the employee?
How will this be dealt with in the future?

Answer

The following aspects play a role:

1. The actually existing/applicable period of notice, whether it is individually written in the contract or whether it is influenced by the collective agreement

and/or the law, is a problem for the applicant. He must know them and be able to name them correctly and bindingly in the application or in the interview. The disadvantages that may result from this also affect him alone.

Recipients of applications (future employers) make their decision regarding employment dependent on the following criteria on the part of the applicant, among others: Professional qualifications, personal charisma, "format" appropriate to the position, feeling of sympathy from the future manager, special knowledge, age, gender, certificates, career, salary - and also "availability".

And of course they playcompetitors play a role. Of course, the one-eyed man is king among the blind – but even the best of twenty candidates ultimately cannot fit well enough and is rejected. You can (!) fail at each of the points mentioned. Or the photo. Or an incorrect use of a foreign word that appears "uneducated" (in extreme cases). Or a period of notice that is subjectively perceived as too long.

2. There are different ones on the employer sideRequirement situations (which the applicant usually does not know) and which lead to different priorities in the selection. The whole selection process, which has been running in an orderly manner up to now, can suddenly tip over because an appropriately active employee of the searching company is unexpectedly absent (dismissal, illness, death) and a calm search for a successor to the head of department results in the hectic striving for one as quickly as possible available candidates.

3. As a precaution, it should be said: There is nothing within this process that does not exist. Fortunately, these are isolated cases - but yours could be one of them.

4. Back to the period of notice: Normally, an applicant is sought who is in an employment relationship that has not been terminated, has a solid period of notice that corresponds to his current position (which makes the relationship that has not been terminated really believable) – and who can start at very short notice.

   Do you think that contradicts itself? So what?Where does it say that companies of all things are only allowed to think logically?

5. The speed of change in the entire economic process is constantly increasing. In a well-organized large company, hardly anyone is still sitting in their current chair after two years, and almost nobody is planning concrete personnel for a longer period of time.

   "We have to react extremely quickly, the markets demand it, theyCompetitors do it too. What was core competence yesterday is thrown out today – and vice versa (it goes back in)."

   And in this environment, a department head position is being filled. For whatever reason. The day before yesterday a decision was made, yesterday you advertised, today you're talking to an applicant. The position is important (na-

   of course, otherwise they would have been deleted), the expectations of the new owner are high: the higher management wants the results of the new structure and/or the new staffing. Or everything should remain as it was, but the department manager is gone and the shop there is not working efficiently for so long. Only the employees always think it would work without a boss, the management sees it completely differently.

Whatever the case – the new head of department has to come. Preferably yesterday, worst tomorrow; everything awaits him.

Please don't say that if that's the case, then at least the "casting" decision-making process could be significantly shortened. But somehow that doesn't work. Do you find that strange? So what? (See above.)

So: The new head of department has to sit there quickly andbring results. But of course he shouldn't be unemployed either. Now you think something like this:

"We still need two months for the selection process. Then the candidate signs his contract. Then he resigns. Then his notice period expires. Six months to the end of the month, with a bit of bad luck, that's almost seven. Now it's November, so this one comes on August 1st. n.J. at. Then it's the main vacation time, and nothing happens here. So he begins his induction period around 15.09. For this he needs at least three months. Then it's Christmas. So we're not going to see any results from the new one for the whole of next year. Maybe his ideas aren't even worth anything. Then we lost this whole year. But the board wants results, and they want them now! So it doesn't work like that– isn't there an applicant who doesn't have such a stupid notice period?" You know the rest.

PS: An analysis of the circumstances at this searching company could show that without exception all department heads there also have six months to the end of the month, some even to the end of the quarter. But that's usually dismissed with a shrug: "So what?"

6. Employment contracts are drafted and pre-formulated by employers, including notice periods.

   With a relatively long period of time, the company protects itself against the sudden departure of employees in key positions. At the same time, one has to recognize that this also protects the employee against a sudden loss of income.

   But it's like the salt in the soup: too much of it makes historyinedible. For the employee. And it works like this: If you give department heads nine months to the quarter, they won't find a new job "outside" at all if the current employer doesn't generously agree to a reduction - which you can't expect beforehand .

   This is "original" for the company until someone calculates that every dismissal will cost a lot of money – and until you realize that you won't find anyone on the job market who will sign such a contract offer. But with the employees you have under contract in this way, it is up to the current employer alone to determine whether they ever leave (because they will only get a new job if their early departure is approved).

7. My appeal to employers: Employees, especially managers, shouldstay with the company because they want to. Only then will they be motivated, committed, happy and willing to work overtime. Anyone who only stands by the flag" because excessive notice periods prevent their long-planned departure is "dead capital", nothing more.

8. This also applies to holders of key positions. Leading them correctly also means looking after them in such a way that you know what moves them, what ambitions

and wishes they still have, where their goals lie. Then you can react in good time and counteract migration tendencies. " And when a manager finally resigns and has to stay for another nine months – what do you still get from him during this time? He thinks ahead, his future lies in the new company that awaits him urgently. What should he still decide here if he no longer has to bear the consequences, what should he plan if he no longer "experiences" the realization? It is not without reason that some corporations basically release managers at certain levels if they have resigned.

9. suggestions for employees,how to deal with the problem:

a. Be careful when signing the contract. Some companies act as if they wouldn't budge a millimeter - but after the umpteenth application rejection for this reason, they do move. And, dear applicants, you don't have any problems with rejecting offers because of the wrong location, because the salary is too low or because there are no opportunities for advancement. Getting stuck one day because of too long a notice period is also not desirable (see the specific case of the sender).

b. In the letter of application you should express the hope that a shortening is possible (hope dies last), this does not really oblige you.

You can't talk to your current employer beforehand "so completely non-bindingly" about a "conceivable shortening of the period in the event of termination", that's out of the question. All you can do is cancel and then ask for a cut. Since you may not get Do you need a starting date in the new employment contract at a point in time after your regular notice period has expired (possibly with the addition: "Mr before the latest entry

date mentioned").
That's all you can do.

10. The applicant is not particularly enthusiastic about the "respect" that you enjoy (in his eyes) with your long deadline: It disturbs his circles, probably applies to all managers at your level in your company regardless of your person and weighs the late possible entry date does not occur.

11. I'll try recommendations once. For example, the following can be regarded as customary in the market and relatively unproblematic (including minor deviations): clerk:

4 weeks to the end of the month/4 or 6 weeks to the end of the quarter AT employees, team/group leaders:

3 months to the end of the month/3 months to the end of the quarter Head of Department:

3 months to the end of the month/3 months to the end of the quarter/6 months to the end of the month

The following applies in each case: If you apply, the shorter deadlines are usually moretiger. However, if you are threatened with termination, the longer period promises more financial security.

And just so you don't think that this was an exhaustive treatment of the topic: Applications keep coming up that say "6 months to the half-year" or "6 months to the end of the year". Anyone who has signed such an employment contract is practically unemployable.

Whatever is possible: You have a long period of notice, you first give notice and then apply. But this is highly risky and not recommended. The ideal to strive for is and remains the application from a position that has not been terminated.

2.3.3.7 "In one pieceor in slices?"

At my current employer, staff changes are rather frequent for a variety of reasons. Against this background, I had interim references issued to me at regular intervals. This refers to this
the most recent testimony to the previous ones. In the case of an application, this would mean that the addressee would have to read five to six pages of references in order to grasp the entire content. To what extent is this a problem in your opinion? Would this certificate structure also be retained for the final certificate in the event of a withdrawal?

With this method, the earlier documents become part of the later ones. Actually, you would then have to enclose all of them in an application, but your reference to the flood of data is justified.

Suggested solution: Attach the last two interim references from the current employment relationship to your application, that's enough. However, when mentioning the "enclosures", write very clearly: "enclosed are the last two interim references from my current employer; older documents from this company are available on request."

In the case of a final certificate, all interim certificates and the rest of the service period are usually summarized in just one document. Occasionally one sees a specific interim reference mentioned in it, more would be unpleasant. In your case, you should only ask for one complete document.

2.3.3.8   Successful internally, not externally

Ask

I recently achieved my next career goal and I'm looking forward to it
mynew area of responsibility.

In the past application phase, I could observe extremely different reactions to my applications, which I cannot classify. For all three internal applications I was invited to an interview with my long-term employer, a major supplier, and I decided on the first position that was offered to me.

My applications to external employers were much less successful. I applied ten times and was only called once for an interview. I received a rejection, but I would have turned it down myself because the job offer on the Internet differed from the area of responsibility that was presented verbally.
My assumptions as to why I was so unsuccessful externally:

1. Compared to my competitors, less professional experience as an engineer (you have ten years, that's basically enough "for everything"; H. Mell).
2. I've been with my current employer for too longemployed (you've only been there ten years, that's absolutely unproblematic; H. Mell).
3. The length of my employment in the last department was too short (just under a year; but that doesn't matter at all from the point of view of "frequency of changes / length of service", it is covered by the ten years with this very company; H. Mell).
4. The youngest (internal)Change from production to

(technical) project managementcommunication with customers is unusual or critical.

5. An (external) change of company type, industry, product range could be considered difficult.

6. The vast majority of external applications came from human resources consultancies. Are such applicants tended to be disadvantaged by the searching company because a successful placement involves considerable costs?

7. My unusual name (first and last name).
For me, the next application phase will certainly only come in a few years. Nevertheless, I would like to know the reasons for the bad performance of my external applications and would like to ask for your help. Documents are attached.

Answer

I have already been able to deal with questions no. 1 to 3 with short comments,
The rest remains for us. And to satisfy the curiosity of the other readers ("what's his name then?"), I'll start at the end:

Regarding 7.: There is nothing unusual about your name (as far as I can tell), you are clearly of Turkish origin. "Turk" is the colloquial classification that you will find out from practically all applicants. You were born in Turkey, next to the city or region you give an additional abbreviation that sounds mysterious, but it says "Turkey" after it.

In the matter is thatStrictly from a citizenship point of view, it is completely different: your citizenship is now "German" – apparently for quite a long time, at any rate you have already gone to school in Germany, completed

your training and your university degree here (with presentable results after a 2nd educational path). Officially, that probably means "German with a Turkish migration background", but nobody says that, people say "Turkish" – just like you
"Ostfriese" or "Saxon" would say, even if he had lived in Bavaria for many years.

In such a case, that means absolutely nothing negative! Nice, there are always people who reject others across the board, also for reasons related to their country of origin – that can also happen to Europeans in Europe or Germans in Germany. But given your special background with school, studies and ten years of practice in Germany, the high level of acceptance that you enjoy from your current employer should be more typical. The refusal of your external applications in this massive form cannot be due to the name you entered as an assumption (you actually mean status).
To 6.: I don't quite understand that. I know

a. Advertisements from companies that are looking for consultants and to which applicants are applying. There are no problems with this.
b. Ads from consultants in which the company actually searching is either named (sometimes) or not (usually). Here the consultant has the task of looking for suitable applicants. The company knows in advance that a consultant's fee is due and in what amount. Here, too, there are no problems for the applicant, and no disadvantages either (since it is the only way).

Now I have to be speculative: You obviously entrusted your documents to consultants. As I understand you, these consultants do not have a specific procurement order at all, but read published job advertisements from companies and then place e.g. B. Your documents- and expect a placement fee or commission from the searching company. Yes, why are you doing this? You can also read the published vacancies and write there yourself. So if companies that are looking go public with their needs and then get two groups of similarly qualified applicants, one of whom costs a placement fee and the other doesn't, then I too fear that the group, which costs nothing, has a clear advantage.

On 5.: Let's just take a look at one of your attached cases: First you write "Dear Ms. Müller"; Do not do that! In the address, that may be fine, but it's not wise there either. In the direct form of address, one always writes "Frau" – that's how long it takes. That also applies to "Mr".

But then we are right in the topic of your specific question:

The envisaged job is a "Project Manager in Project Management" (I didn't write the headline), it's about "leading customer projects", it's about "establishing a project structure" and "planning, overseeing monitoring and control of the project process" at a well-known supplier. We are looking for "familiarity with the tools and methods of project management", fluent English and other languages – as well as "experience in leading interdisciplinary teams".

In your CV you state that the current position is "Project Engineer", the job before that was "Process Engineer". Before that, there was also a project management function, but that was about the "wrong" production planning. The problem with this: your entire development seems to the reader as if you had been demoted: first as a project manager (in the wrong department), then twice as an "engineer" without a manager. This is not a good basis for a promotion application.

Then the applicant also wants practical experience in the chassis area, your experience comes from "higher regions" (of a car). After all, you only want to reveal your "motivation to change in a personal meeting" - and define your specific target remuneration as a kind of "reasonable" wish. This is not ideal.

When reading your CV, another assumption comes to mind: You have presented everything clearly, correctly and clearly by way of example, and you are certainly using the usual internal designations for the presentation of the individual activities. Every reader understands them internally. This is also the reason for the high level of internal acceptance.

But: The companies are organized differently and use different (varying pompous) designations for certain tasks and activities. The external reader – e.g. B. I – has great difficulty in answering the simple but fundamental question: What is this applicant actually doing? This begs the question: What can he do? Because you can only prove what you have done. Everything else is speculative. You also have to think of the reading speakers from the human resources department. They are business graduates or business economists, maybe even ("even" in the sense of "even further away from technology") graduate psychologists. And they don't understand everything, but they quickly see: In your – important – last two positions, the central terms of the advertisement ("project manager" and "project management") do not appear at all.

On 4.: You write above: "The recent change from production to (technical) project management with customer contact is unusual..." It is. But where is "project management" in your CV today, and where is it?

"Customer contact" (in the description of the last two positions)? I can't find any of that.

The most recent interim reference states: "He completed his tasks very properly, quickly and conscientiously." That is – quite decent, but does not yet describe convincing potential for a future career.

Conclusion: You are known internally, hardly anyone reads your application in detail - and if they do, you understand everything immediately. When it came to presenting yourself "outside", you failed because of the facts (formerly leaders, not anymore) and because of your presentation skills. There should be no doubts or unanswered questions when it comes to external applications, especially when making the leap to management level. Internally, your qualifications were openly on the table, externally would be - with identical documents
– also a "Max Müller,born in Munich" failed.

PS: Don't let the "just because I have this name" story become an overriding obsession

c.

2.3.3.9   If the board problemsdon't want to hear

Ask

I'm in a managerial position in a larger company - and inan age when you no longer change employers.

After a change in the board of directors, the organization was also changed. Sales divisions, to which sales were assigned directly, were placed directly under the board of directors.

I have known for a long time – as have my colleagues – that two of the sales managers are unable to carry out their tasks. This damages the sales units, which can be clearly seen in the sales figures and the result. The responsible salespeople are largely responsible for this. They are afraid of necessary price increases, show little activity in terms of new acquisitions and are by no means pushing new articles.

When asked about the problemthe Board of Management merely responded by saying that colleagues should be left to work in peace. This is difficult to accept, since "necessary personnel measures in the lower echelons" are already being discussed. These levels can do little to change the situation. How should/can we position ourselves here?

Answer

The story cries out for an answer to the question: who are you?
where do you stand in this constellation? I draw my conclusions from the following evidence:

1. You have to be pretty far from the sale being addressed

- otherwise you would know to never (in any relevant language) write "Aquise". You have to assume this knowledge as a minimum standard for a seller (by the way, the word means acquisition).

2. Your compassion for the "lower echelons" is most easily understood when you belong there yourself. There is also a very tried-and-tested company rule: Don't worry about problems that don't concern you at all (unless you take part in the company suggestion system or CIP).

3. Your question printed at the end of your submission suddenly jumps from the neutral description of the problem to the "we" of those affected.

Conclusion I (initial situation): You are a middle manager in a newly structured sales division, but you don't sell yourself. The division thrives on sales, and the board has appointed someone who you think is incompetent. Due to poor sales figures, the area is threatened with the dreaded cost-cutting measures. The board of directors doesn't want to know anything about your point of view, they still think savings are the solution.

Now for the "evidence"you cite to blame:

a. Ultimately, only supervisors have the right to classify employees as incompetent. Colleagues at the same level or even subordinate ranks have neither the right to do so nor - according to the general opinion
- the necessary "perspective" for it.

b. Especially for people who don't sell themselves, the solution to sales or profit problems is apparently so obvious: you just have to sell more, charge higher prices or advertise new products that are considered future-oriented, then everyone would be helped.

However, it is extremely difficult, often impossible, to

achieve higher prices in highly competitive markets, and there is even a risk of losing customers entirely. That's what your scolded sales people are afraid of (of enforcing price increases, not of the price increases themselves). Then: Unless you have carefully and intensively motivated every sales person, he shies away from selling new products within a larger program: You have to laboriously familiarize yourself with the new technology, the customer does not want it spontaneously, it takes a lot of work to convince him of it – and that with every customer from the beginning.

Sellers like to take the easier route if they have alternatives. Your superiors need to know this, see it in detail and take action against it. But: You cannot force superiors (board members!) to do this from "below".

c. Their "evidence" of the vendors' incompetence is flimsy and not "admissible in court". These people may simply have been mismanaged and insufficiently motivated.

Conclusion II: You don't think so much of the sales people, you think the board of directors as incompetent. That could well be the case, but I advise against pursuing this idea. You just can't survive something like that.

Having already been 'sensitized' to the matter by the board and saying you should stay out of it, it's already on 'amber alert' so beware.

For the money it pays you, the Executive Board can expect you to be committed and almost enthusiastic about implementing its(!) ideas, regardless of their quality. So try to act accordingly. Help the sellers as much as you can, talk to them. Above all, don't put up any protracted resistance to the Board of Management.

This is life-threatening. And you are not responsible for the well-being of the company, the owners have put that in the hands of the Management Board. If this was the wrong hands, the owners were unlucky, that's all. "The company" has no right to the right strategic orientation, optimal factual or personal decisions. Whoever owns it may trample on it with impunity...

2.3.3.10 Notes from practice

Answers that were important to me, even if there was no suitable question at the time

About free development the personality

I know I'm repeating myself occasionally, but there's no other way: the employee is employed. Anyone who takes offense at any detail or gets upset about the details of the professional system should let this core sentence melt in their mouth (it's not mine, it runs through all official definitions, textbooks, etc.). So if you want to become an employee or have already become one, you have to accept this concept of dependency as indispensable. Everything else is window dressing.

But there are also people for whom the free development of their personality is very important. You can understand that - but everyone will see that dependence on the one hand and the desire for free development (of whatever) on the other hand unfortunately lead to conflicts. Concrete:

During my dailyTerm of service as a dependent employee can logically not be that far away from my free development, to say the least.

Even more specifically: "I want to secure my existence as an employee and I'm striving for maximum free development of my personality" - that just can't work. The attempt is doomed to failure, examples can be found in sufficient numbers on the job market.

As far as the regular readers sufficiently well-known. But this introduction had to be done, otherwise you wouldn't do justice to the topic.

Now the new thing: It's not all that bad in many areas of professional life (let's leave out the tragic and/or dramatic exceptional cases that we all know). There are 25 valuable years between the age of 25 (examination) and 50 (beginning of a significant reduction in the "market value" on the job market), in which, with a little good will and a lot of skill, a satisfactory balance can be struck between dependency and free development - tion is possible I was an employee for 28 years, so I have enough of my own and still a lot of stored external experiences from CVs, job interviews, career advice, etc. So it's a bit like the crash barriers on the left and right of the freeway: Once I've got on the next section of road (of my own free will, I could have left it), then I only have the choice between two or three lanes - if the traffic allows me to do so. But the crash barriers set narrow limits to the right and left, so suddenly swerving off-road is not possible. Only on the next descent can I make my own decisions again. Is that reasonable, is anyone still upset about it, is that why driving on the motorway is discouraged? Yes, no, no.

Nice, some days you can already feel the dependency of the employee. There are always and everywhere such days, even in private relationships. But then there is still some freedom that you can use. And even if working life was not primarily created for having fun, there are still sufficient opportunities to enjoy the thing from case to case, to develop and not to perceive the "guard rails" as a real handicap.

I see these basic requirementsI have these recommendations in this context:
You have to be very good at your job – that's a minimum requirement. What you are doing there may only require about 80% of your technical skills, and even 95% at peak times. But whatever comes, stay calm still have reserves. This makes you "highly valued" and generally considered to behard to expend.

So you have to be sovereign when it comes to the tasks assigned to you. This means being able to cope with a situation or task at any time, even to be superior. (foreign word Duden definition for "sovereign"). By the way, anyone can anywhere

be "like that" - even if it's "crate stacking". If you don't have that feeling today, you're not in the best job.

The better you are at your place, the less dependent you feel. Don't worry about whether this demand is statistically enforceable for everyone and whether it is possible for everyone to fulfill it - it's about you, work out your personal basis here.

1. Then you need healthy self-confidence (beyond the arrogance limit), a healthy willingness to take risks and no "fear of your own courage". For example, I get inquiries from applicants who have been sent an offer of employment. They then ask something like: "It says that the salary is reviewed annually. Does that mean it can also be changed downwards?" These are questions from losers.

2. A petty, narrow-minded persistence in the details is incompatible with the required sovereignty.

There you are at oneYou got stuck on a tram ticket on a business trip and you weren't paid for two hours of overtime. So what? You survive that – and you actually have demanding professional goals, so what do those peas you're counting mean? This also applies to the technical/factual area of daily work. Mimosa-like sensitivity and constant personal concern only do harm.

3.

It is said that regulations are quite important when managing complex organizations. You need to know them too, but often solutions can only be found if you make the best of them. Anyone who, to be on the safe side, only drives 65 km/h when the maximum speed is70 km/h will pull a queue behind them. And when there are queues of cars, the slowest one drives ahead

– this is not an honorary title. Symbolically, you should rather drive 80 if it says 70 on the signs (no, no, not really on the road, just pictorially).

4. You need to understand what is going on around you. Why does this (e.g. my) boss react this way in that situation, what are they angry about and what are they happy about? Why is the management now issuing such general instructions and why do the colleagues not like it when...? You cannot master a system that you do not understand.

You must know the rules by which this game runs. It's even like that in football - if you don't know why this or that is happening now, you'll hardly enjoy it as a spectator, and certainly not as a "player".There is a reason for everything that happens in the professional field – if possible, you need to know it. A small example: Your boss is a reasonable man. If you give a good reason why you missed a deadline, he usually responds with understanding, or at least listens to your arguments. But if his boss is also present, he is unrecognizable and may scold you at the slightest mishap. Why? Because it makes a difference whether he is "fair" to you or whether he appears to his boss as someone who might be "too soft" in leadership, who doesn't get through with his people - and because he might be exactly that The accusation only had to be heard three days ago. In the long run, there can only be answers to the question

"Why is/do things work like this in the company in such cases?", not a shrug of the shoulders. You can't play golf or poker or even bridge without knowing the written and unwritten rules. And especially the top-class professionals (as well as your superiors) of every discipline do nothing in their "sport" without reason.

5. Now the high school of it all: You needinformation, you must know something! Something? That's far too little, "everything" would be impossible to achieve, but things are heading in that direction. I'm sitting across from graduate engineers who express the assumption that their boss doesn't like them and has something against them. Then the questioner is a university graduate - and he doesn't know what the boss is. Doesn't he know! That doesn't necessarily have to be the solution, but if you don't know that, you don't know enough.

   Knowledge is power, too much of it (of knowledge) ishardly conceivable. In order to really understand people like bosses, bosses, colleagues, etc., I have to be interested in them. And at least listen carefully when they say something. It is then necessary to ask one or the other skilful additional question from time to time (eavesdropping is frowned upon!).

   Don't ask me how to do this, it depends on your bosses, your colleagues and your own personality. The main thing is that you see the need to know as much as possible about your professional environment. Since bosses are often good actors and like to chat about themselves, there are many opportunities to get information.

   Example: you havea 1.x high school diploma and an adequate university degree. The official rule is: the better, the more valuable. So you might think: He's my boss, so probably even better than me. So when the topic of training qualities or grades comes up on a business trip or over a beer in the evening, I clearly point out – in a roundabout way, but nonetheless – that my grades are very good. However, there are bosses who have much worse results in their papers.

It wouldn't be so good for you then. But there are even bosses who have sons who just failed the Abitur. Then your repeated reference to how you excelled in high school would have been a bad mistake.

So you have to know "something like that". And if he doesn't tell you voluntarily, ask him when you get a chance. Not: "What grades did you get?", but something like:

"You have a lot of experience in recruiting. We recently discussed it in a circle of friends: What role do you actually attribute to Abitur and exam grades?" From his answers one can draw conclusions (all people with bad grades tend to think that "something like that" means nothing). .

Such information is not only about the boss, it is also about plans, likes and dislikes of the board of directors, about long-term corporate concepts, etc. In the company you know people who in turn know people who ...

However you want to see it, not knowing after five years of work whether your boss is a TH or FH graduate must be seen as criminally careless. Because you can only treat someone properly if you can classify and assign them.

6. So ideally you are

- very good in your field,
- self-confident, confident and – within limits – willing to take risks,
- generous in detail and not mimosa-like sensitive; not a bean counter, but an employee with an eye for the connections, for the essentials,
- someone who understands his environment, knows the rules,
- provided with sufficient information about your environment - so that you can avoid pitfalls and take advantage of opportunities in a targeted manner.

They always are thoughstill an employee, but come quite close to a free development of your personality.

Or: It's only fun to play the piano if you've mastered the instrument to some extent, everything else is jingling.

7. The question of the possible development possibilities now remains:

a. Look past the "kitchen" or "poetry album" philosophy of this saying and judge only the content:

If the hard word 'you have to' torments you in your heart, then use the proud word 'I WANT' to replace it, strong and quiet.

You are not annoyed about a deadline that has been set for you, you want(!) to get it done by then. If you open yourself up to it, it works (free spaces are also a matter of perception and definition).

b. In every job there is freedom that you open up and that you expandcan. The salami tactic ("slice by slice") works best. And as the saying goes in every larger organization: "If you don't have a say here, it's your own fault" (this is not linguistically clean, but memorable).

c. Who, as a boss, would unnecessarily restrict the freedom of a technically very good, very committed employee who understands his or her superiors, knows the rules and is interested in everything? Of course, the required points 1-4 also include that you show your superiors the necessary respect, that you do not give the impression of sawing their chair and other things of this kind.

The more afraidthe boss has, this "great" employee could quit, the better for the latter - and for his freedom.

d. I was young once too.And analytically strong, rhetorically agile, self-confident - a downright disgusting combination from the point of view of my senior boss. And I've been right too many times. I liked to discuss and always had only one goal: mine was to win. Until his experienced secretary told me it wasn't going well - and "he also wants to win sometime". That was my key experience. So I let him (win) a lot. It was an investment, it paid off very well. In general, the best way to avoid getting angry at the boss is very "simple": become the boss yourself. That is fun. And then you don't just get angry at your boss, but also at your employees. Or half of both.

The job you have is only "half the battle"

There are some facts and insights that you can ignore, but you really can't deny them. And yet the attempt is always made with pleasure:

- The employee - and especially the hired manager - needsemployment by an employer. Without them, he is somewhere between "out of function" and "depending on transfer payments".
- He can lose the job he currently has. Anytime, without warningand also through no fault of your own. He can never be sure that an existing employment relationship

will last "forever".

- The involuntary loss of the respective job is a life-threatening oneCatastrophe. There is only one sensible solution: a new job in a comparable or better position with a new employer.
- Anyone who is in a non-terminated, "unthreatening" employment relationship is also
  in the realization of professional (e.g.Ascent) plans rely on a to find a new job in a rather better position with a new employer. This case of necessity can also occur at any time.
- The rule to be derived from this is: You always need a) one freeending job and b)the certainty of finding a job that is just as good or better if necessary (!) at any time (preferably several, people want to have a choice). And that too as quickly as possible.
  To make it short: a) it's in the minds of the employees, b) it's not. It is frightening to see that long-standing clerks pay just as little attention to this as high-ranking managers. The following applies to everyone:

- The job you are doing right now is only halfso "great" if you don't have theknowing that you can find a suitable replacement at any time. For this you need two starting points:

1. Such jobs have to exist often enough (industry, activity, type and size of company, remuneration, etc.). Holding the only position of a certain kind in the country shouldn't make you proud - it's rather stupid.
2. Your special qualifications in professional and personal terms must correspond to the standard requirements of existing, comparable jobs.

Fortunately, this information is now "on the street". Job advertisements contain a lot of what you need to know - every three to six months you should look at the job boards and see if you can find alternatives. And every few years, one or two concrete applications can do no harm. Perhaps this campaign will even give you momentum in your career planning.

So the "high school" of career planning consists of only accepting jobs for which there is a sufficient number of substitutes in an emergency. Therefore, the following also applies: "Don't despise the standard for me" (loosely adapted from "Die Meistersinger von Nürnberg" by Richard Wagner).

2.3.4 Look for alternatives, make decisions, take riskscarry

In the twenty-five to thirty years between starting your career and the end of your mobility on the job market, you keep coming across "road crossings" and "junctions" where there are no signposts. What now?

2.3.4.1   Change after more than 20 years?

Ask

For more than 20 years I have been a manager in sales for a German
industrial group active.

Some time ago there was a change of ownership and due to other unfavorable circumstances of an internal nature, the company is not in a very good economic condition today. Loss-making business areas have already been closed, employees over the age of 57 are being sent into "early retirement", other (particularly younger) employees with potential have left the company due to a lack of prospects.

In this situation, I am considering the idea of a change, for which I would of course have to apply externally.

Do you recommend a change under the circumstances presented? How promising is an application now, considering my age (early 50), the length of service and the future condition of the job market? What about the employability of older executives?

Answer

Your introductory sentencethat's not true! It may be a small thing, but fight back
the beginning" (after Ovid, "Remedy for love"). I pick this up becausethe candidates also deal with facts in such a "confident" way in applications. And you work in sales, so mistrust is always appropriate when it comes to details (life experience).

You have been working for a group of companies that

has been subject to the vicissitudes of business life for "more than 20 years", that is correct, your CV clearly shows it. But at the beginning you were a career starter and the first few years that followed – of course – not a manager. You've been the latter for less than 20 years. Applications, which I always have "in the back of my mind" here, are always a work sample, so be warned and be careful.

First of all, to reassure readers who often classify me as "very harsh judgement" (in my professional world that is much better than "too soft, too forgiving, a do-gooder" it would be): You, dear sender, have an Education at its finest: TU engineer, doctorate, additional training in business administration, so don't need any special leniency either.

And then you fabricate something like the third paragraph: For me, the first part of the sentence screams something out into the world – we just have to find out what that is. I suspect your subconscious, shaped by those more than 20 years without an external change, shows us here how "unthinkable" a separation from this only employer landscape that you know still seems to you.

In case someone can't understand my thoughts spontaneously: First of all, one would say "in this situation" as an introduction, not "at". But that's a trifle. But then "I consider the idea of changing". First of all, that's not nice: "Thoughts of change" are no good, it should then be called "Thoughts of a change". But just "I ponder the thought" is somehow enormous. Had one of our great old philosophers ever thought of it? A man of action thinks and ponders actions, that is quite enough.

A cool and matter-of-fact thinking engineer would have formulated here, for example: "In this situation I am considering a change" or "... I am considering a change". No, with you one believes one can literally feel the emotional outburst,
mer triggered.

However, the following applies: Employees have employment contracts with mutual termination options. It is to be expected at any time that one side or the other will make use of it. It is therefore a completely normal process when an employee (including a manager) changes several times during their working life. Today, people like me even recommend changing after about ten to fifteen years of service with an employer, even if there is no urgent reason. This is also done so that if you do have to go one day later, you'll be in practice and won't be overwhelmed. The latter can happen at any time, as you can read from me again and again. Then, however, the search for a new employer should not be an almost unthinkable monstrosity, but a reasonably familiar routine. I can help you in certain areas, but I cannot solve your central problem. To do this, you have to make one of those typical decisions where you don't know what the outcome of the possible courses of action will be (at the moment, from your point of view there are only two, namely "stay" or "change"; but when things really get going , there are also the problems of whether external offer A is better than B or whether you shouldn't choose C. Believe me: that's when it gets really difficult).
Let's approach the relevant problem areas:

Your career so far: From the perspective of an outsider,

it peaked a few years ago. Before that you were managing director a sales company with xxx million sales and responsibility for a large number of employees in a large number of countries. Since then you have been in a different function, no longer MD, your responsibility for sales is now around a third, your scope of management is less than a tenth

"Size". There may be explanations for the insider, but all three indicators (rank, turnover, employees) are pointing downwards, and it's not that easy to tease out a promotion. It is not about whether you are "to blame" for that change, whether it is related to your performance or not.

On the other hand, the question is simply: why did you put up with the cut that took place a few years ago? They were younger then and had a good reason to step outside! If that point in time coincided with the aforementioned change of ownership, then you would have had two very good reasons.

a. Your chances on the job market, especially considering your age: I think I can see from certain details in your submission that this question is particularly pressing on you. That, in turn, is absolutely unjustified. Because you can get the answer to this part of the question without much effort and without any particular risk: just write about ten applications and see if you are interesting.

Since you let the managing director and the very high sales and employee responsibility be taken away from you without a fight (that's how it looks), it is best to apply to (partial) sales managements that correspond to your current area of responsibility. Industry and customers should come as close as possible to today's environment.

The principle: Applicants aged around and above all over 50 market what they can prove, i.e. what they have done up to now. In contrast, those in their late thirties market their presumed potential for what they could possibly be able to do. The assumption is that the 50-year-old has already gotten everything out of himself that was in it; he can do what he is doing today (or what he did last time), he offers this qualification. That in turn is his advantage over the younger climber, who has never worked in exactly the responsibility that is now under discussion.

And you need a comprehensible reason for the change you are now striving for. With the reference already in the application letter to

"Economic uncertainties" and "Uncertainties with regard to the continued existence of the company in its current form" do you have such – good – reasons. If they are missing, you give room to the assumption that your bosses are dissatisfied with your performance.

What should you do now? Try out your chances on the job market, you only need to make the final decision when you have job offers that are ready to be signed. Just to be on the safe side: You apply "secretly" behind the back of your previous employer and only give notice when you have signed a new employment contract. The job market gives executives around 50 good opportunities, especially in medium-sized companies.

b. Risks of staying with todayEmployer:
- the situation can get even worse;
- the GAU is the termination by the employer if you are three years older (and still far from retiring);

- no one can give you security, not even your boss; he should have similar worries as you; if anyone knows anything at all, it is the owners, but they will not make any binding statements.
c. Risks of switching (or attempting to):
- the fact that you may not be able to find a new job is not one of the problems; then you just have to stay, you have no choice and you haven't really done anything wrong by staying;
- You have been attuned to a certain company environment for twenty years, your instinctive thoughts and actions are geared towards this; You will be amazed at how "different" other companies can be in all areas; the risk of making serious mistakes, especially at the beginning, is great;
- You lack the routine to select suitable positions from advertisements and job descriptions, to recognize the character of a boss in the job interview; They don't know what questions to ask, how to distinguish good offers from bad ones, etc.; Statistically speaking, you are in great danger of having to or wanting to apply again after about a year or two (but then you would be in a much worse position than you are today);
- You can go from bad to worse with no chance of knowing beforehand – problems can be greater with a new employer than with the old one (companies have been sold three days after a new manager has joined).
Conclusion: Your main problem, "How popular am I in my special situation on the job market?" is easy to solve - just try it out. As long as you don't sign a contract, nothing happens ultimate importance. If no one wants you (which I don't believe), you don't have to make any

decisions. Then the following applies: Rely on sticking with it. But then you would have finally discarded your only weapon in the struggle for existence, that invisible sword at your side that says "Resignation".of

2.3.4.2 My boss doesn't want me as successor

I'm "around 40", Dipl.-Ing. (FH), originally come from the Ser-
vice and start-up of branch X, which, on superficial inspection, could definitely be considered something special (at least from the point of view of my current environment).

For about four years I have been responsible for a technical area (maintenance, among other things) in a production plant of a large group in the chemical industry. I have significant personal responsibilities. I really enjoy the task and (almost) all boundary conditions are good.

In two to three years I would like to take over the position of my manager as a technical manager and deputy plant manager will take over when my boss retires.

I work very closely with the responsible HR manager. I found out from him that my manager should nominate a possible successor. As a result, I recently approached my boss and asked about possible career development. After about five years in my current position, he recommended that I look for the next career step within our group. He did not point out a concrete possibility in our work, he did not speak of his successor.

As expected, he then asked me about my ideas and concepts. I immediately brought up his successor as the next step.

Unfortunately, his answer was not very specific. If

asked, he could give three names, one of which would be mine. However, the Management Board of our sub-group also plays a key role in deciding who to fill the position. He would have little control over that. I am not satisfied with this open result.

That HR manager casually sent me the information that I would have to bring myself more into the conversation "at another (higher?) position" in order to get ahead My idea is to get an appointment with the next higher supervisor (plant manager) in the next few months so that I can be discussed as a successor. Is this a viable way, can I burn myself doing it? I have a very good relationship with my manager and I don't want to risk that.

A foreign plant in my industry from the area is looking for a new technical manager. A commissioned personnel consulting company asked for my documents. A conversation is pending.

I think that a short-term change would be a bit too early for me. What's your opinion?

Answer

I have to explain a special feature of your industry here for the other readers:

In mechanical engineering and related areas, the technical manager is one level below the GF and is the head of development/construction and production, among other things. He also has maintenance etc. In chemistry and similar areas, the technical manager is in principle responsible for the production facilities, their design and smooth operation. He is not responsible for ongoing production, and certainly not for product development.

Why is this important? Because technical managers from chemistry who apply for technical management in mechanical engineering often do not understand that they are comparing apples with oranges and don't have the slightest chance. And vice versa.

Your boss, that's clear, doesn't want you as his successor, his behavior istypical of that. First he doesn't even talk about the well-known case of his successor, then he makes you one of several candidates, finally he brings the executive board into play – whatever is decided, he doesn't want it to have been.

BasicallyThe following applies: keep an employed manager (opposite example: owner) out of the search for their successor or at least out of the decision about their successor. There are several very good reasons for this. However, if your HR manager is right, your boss is actually involved in the search for a crucial successor.

But: Whether with or without direct influence on the filling of your own position: Your boss could never guarantee that you will get the job, because his bosses are directly responsible for this. But in any case, his power is enough to prevent you. Then:

.

People want to see proven good things about others, but they immediately believe bad things.
Whether your supervisor is ultimately responsible or remains responsible for the question of succession or not: If he explains "upstairs" that you can't do that, you are "dead" to these considerations.

By the way: I don't believe the very good relationship you claim you have with your boss!

According to popular belief, 'very good' would imply more understanding from your boss of your desire to succeed him - and your placement higher up on his list of candidates. However, he seems to be thinking about you:

"Quite a good man, but nothing more..." Conclusion: In recent years you have not been able to convince him of your potential to follow in his footsteps. And of course he has long since communicated this reserved attitude towards you internally.

As far as the appointment with the plant manager is concerned: the project could also do you harm. If this next-higher boss informs your direct superior about your corresponding initiative (50% probability), the latter will be annoyed.

But the HR manager didn't even mean this single appointment! You shouldn't talk to this one man, you should be "talking about" with the higher management level, they should know you, appreciate you, talk about you and "automatically" take you into account when talking about interesting positions becomes. This is a project of years of intense effort, there is nothing to be gained with a single appointment. It applies (it should have applied) to attract attention from "higher places" with achievements, suggestions, initiatives - past your boss, without arousing his displeasure. This is possible, but requires a high level of energy, tactical skill and instinct. Or let's put it this way: if you can't do that, you can't easily become the successor to the boss.

I remember an example:Once upon a time there was a little boy whose school got a new principal. And the interested parents asked over the meal what the new headmaster would be like. According to the little one, he was all right. And added calmly: "Know me, greet me." That was - transferred to that environment - what is meant here. How the fellow achieved this has never been explained.

A career can hardly be made with good specialist qualifications alone. What goes beyond that is crucial to success. I'm afraid that from today's perspective, your chances of succeeding your boss are rather slim. In this context, it is a relief for you that you work in a group in which many employees have much longer service periods than your few years and that you as Side entrants came from a completely different branch with certainly different structures. In this environment you weren't "dyed in the wool" at first.

With the "foreign work" from your industry, there is a possibility, but that's all it is at first. And the personnel consultant collects potential candidates, but does not decide on the filling of the position.

You are "around 40", age is good for almost any position. You have well over ten years of professional experience, which is sufficient for any middle management position. For eight years you have been entrusted with managerial tasks and for almost four years you have been responsible for a large number of people. Your length of service with your current employer is very short, your boss doesn't want you as his successor, you yourself want to move up the ranks, but would have considered a point in time in two years to be ideal. This is the starting position.

The request, however, comes now. Internally there will probably not be a chance in two years; we do not know what the situation will be in the labor market. If you wait another two years for your current position but are not promoted internally, you are a little more frustrated every day. I would try it externally from now on. This request from the consultant is a first step on the way, maybe the decisive one for you. There is never complete certainty, neither when choosing the time, the new job, the new employer or the new boss. Responding courageously when an opportunity presents itself along the way is definitely one of the secrets of success. Or you follow the intentions of your boss and come to the conclusion that you are rather unsuitable for such a position.

2.3.4.3   Bicycle versus managerial status

I have a migration background, my parents are from Turkey. I went to secondary school and continued to develop: apprenticeship, high school diploma, graduate engineer. The thesis received an award.

I switched to my second job about four years ago. I really enjoyed working there, my colleagues were great. Everything was very harmonious and very good. I really enjoyed going to work, it took about 15 minutes by bike. If I had something to do in the morning, I could easily do it or leave earlier in the afternoon. I had a relationship with my supervisor that was great, great, great. For me he was more than a boss, I could talk to him without hesitation. I miss him now. However, in this position there was little change. I also wanted to expand my international orientation, but didn't find an opportunity to do so.

I found an interesting job advertisement on the intranet of my large employer and applied successfully (more income, classification as a manager, more project responsibility, also international work). I was really looking forward to the work and was and am highly motivated for it. There are new challenges, I'm getting to know new processes and I also have opportunities to develop further here. In the previous area, I would have had to wait another three years to get to the current salary level. The new colleagues also seem to be fine; the new supervisor is a good, nice person, as far as I can judge so far.

What is wrong? At my old job, I lived "around the

corner" and rode my bike - no traffic jams, no car journeys. The new location is 65 km away. I've been driving this route for five days now (you'll say that's nothing - actually I would say so). I had prepared myself mentally for the trip beforehand and knew the route from occasional business trips and seminars. Now I've realized with a start that I'm not cut out for those car commutes, including the traffic jams. I won't be moving either (family has settled into the previous place of residence, I'm taking care of my elderly parents).

I spoke openly to my former superior that he would take me back immediately (but not as a manager and for a lower salary). He indicated opportunities for development – I would be upgraded in about three years, but would then have to wait longer for the next upgrade. What can I do? How can I find out what is better for me?

Answer

Anyone who deals with applicants on a daily basis also thinks that this is quite possible,
so much in advance. Let's just hope that our Chinese friends - or whoever else we have to compete against in the world market - have the same problems. I mean: to compensate, because of equal opportunities and such.
To the point: If the donkey is too comfortable, he goes on the ice. This is a German proverb, describes your situation in the "old" position and contains, I say this to be on the safe side, no condescending elements towards you. But that's how it is – when people are doing too well, they leave paradise (Adam practiced something similar, he probably got a little bored too). But:

Basically, your decision was the same as before, despite good circumstances Job to leave and for the purpose of personal development
break new ground,absolutely right. Something like this will eventually become easy
"due".

By the way: Under no circumstances go back to the old position! They were bored there then - and would be again in a few days. Look forward, not back!

Nobody loves long daily commutes, and only the most opinionated people love traffic jams. But both are the price you pay for a good job in this country. 65 km is a bit far, you shouldn't do it until you retire. But three to four years is basically reasonable at your young age. You got something for that. You will find that you pay a price for achieving goals more often. There are no all-around ideal circumstances for ascension, certainly not. Show that you have what it takes to be a leader and just persevere! Running away from the first problem is not a solution

2.3.4.4   stay or go

Ask

I'm in my mid/late 40s and have been at my job for more than fifteen years-
geber, an American company.

As you can see from the attached documents, I have held various positions in the course of this employment relationship. In addition to the actual work content, my focus has always been on expanding my tasks, ideally accompanied by a promotion. I really appreciate opportunities like this in American companies.

I know your concerns about ten-plus years of service. Since some of my functions had very different content, I would be interested in your opinion on the extent to which you maintain your fundamental concerns about possible operational blindness. Would the individual sections possibly be counted as individual stations, which would then again be fully within the framework, or does your recommendation relate more to the aspect of "belonging to an individual company" than to the individual activities?

Answer

The recommendation derived from the thinking of typical job applicants is: After having been with the employer for around ten years, start thinking about whether a change might not be common considerations might be advisable. The reason for this is the reluctance that can often be seen towards applicants with very long service periods. This, in turn, is not only based on instinct, but also on experience: You can very often see that in such CVs after e.g. B. fourteen or twenty-one years of service followed by a very short period of employment, so a new change was due.

a. Man is a "creature of habit": habits dig deep into our consciousness; At some point we no longer perceive the special features of our environment as such; we have long since stopped behaving contrary to the code that prevails at our long-standing employer. And we soon lack the ability to distinguish what is on the

"House rituals" of our long-standing employer is standard on the market, which must be considered a special feature and which may even represent an "exotic" exception.

There is a suspicion that a new employee with such a long formative service at the previous company is no longer able to adjust to the new environment or even refuses. This aspect also includes the working methods.

b. On the other hand, if you changed your first job after maybe three years, your second after eight years and now want to change your third job after maybe four years, you have experience of how "different" new employers can be – and have already repeated such changes passed successfully. Above all: He knows that he has to adapt and is sensitive to the problems that will come his way.

A small (realistic) example: After eighteen years of service at company A, department manager Müller comes to B. Heimmediately offers "his people" the first name, because that was usual with A and he doesn't know anything else. B doesn't appreciate that at all - the first thick spot on Müller's waistcoat is there, his bosses are eyeing suspiciously "what else is he probably doing". And: At the next change, Müller will be smarter and more careful (hopefully); he knows where "traps" can be lurking.

c.

d. The one mentionedReservations against long periods of service of significantly more than ten years basically refer to the affiliation with a single employer, that is the central "bracket".

e. It is intensified when these many years have been spent with largely the same activity, always in the same organizational unit at the same hierarchical level. It is clearly(!) weakened if several of these criteria have changed several times. Promotions are particularly helpful There is no fixed formula for weighting here. The applicant is at the mercy of or subjected to the very different feelings of different decision-makers. Among them are people who have been doing their job for twenty years and those who are new to the company. The respective situation on the labor market (many or few competitors) also reinforces or mitigates such concerns.

But: Anyone who has not had much more than ten years of service with an employer is better prepared in the event of a sudden termination by the employer. On the other hand, if you know for sure that you never want to leave there and that you never have to leave there, you don't have to pay attention to this aspect. But then he would also have the talent for clairvoyance.

.After second degreeorientation problems

Ask

I am Dipl.-Ing. (Uni), early 30s, four years of work. At first I was
accounting engineer, today - after a change of employer - I work in the software development of a well-known company.

When I was with my first employer, I started a part-time business administration degree with a focus on marketing management, which will soon be completed. This decision was triggered by short-time work at the time. I wanted to use this to lay the foundation for later leadership/management tasks. Due to the specialization in my second degree, I see my future at the interface between market and technology, ie in technical sales or product management.

I enjoy my current development work, I've settled in well over the past two years and I'm well able to cope with the tasks given to me. A new development project will be started next year. I was given the signal (without obligation) that I could lead a small team during this time: the project duration is roughly two to three years.

At our location, there is hardly any opportunity to get a position in sales/product management. Moving to the company headquarters is out of the question for me. A professional reorientation towards
"Application of the second degree" would therefore be associated with a change of employer, which I would definitely consider.

My question: What makes more sense, the management task or the professional reorientation?

I'm concerned that by accepting the leadership role, I'm setting the course in the wrong direction. In the case of a subsequent reorientation, there would already be a gap of two to three years between the completion of the second degree and an application in sales/product management. During this time, I miss the opportunity to gain relevant work experience in this new field.

On the other hand, changing employers shouldn't happen too quickly, and having fulfilled your first managerial task will probably not harm my CV or my personal development.

Answer

No, it probably won't. But I will your personal development
harm if I don't restrain myself strongly. I'll list the problem areas:

1. I would say that business administration graduates are vastly superior to engineers in terms of general qualifications. Evidence: You have your one poor little degree in your pocket, go and have a career. Without any feelings of inferiority, without the slightest desire to first complete a supplementary engineering degree in order to – I quote you – "lay the foundation for later leadership/management tasks".
What kind of guys must they be!
Seriously: A solid engineering degree (TU/FH) is enough – like any other individual degree – to make a career up to the highest hierarchical levels. In the case of the engineer up to the technical director or board member. Of course, on the way there you have to be

willing to think outside the box, to be interested in circumstances outside of pure technology, but in principle you can also acquire all the necessary knowledge while growing into ever larger areas of responsibility - which will inevitably be a gradual process acquire. As thousands have successfully practiced before.

2. A supplementary course of study never does any harm – seen in principle – and even adorns its wearer immensely. Above all, the knowledge that one acquires can (and 5% of it will) be extremely helpful at some point for and in practicing the "old" profession.

– It can only be that the – considerable – effort exceeds the benefit in individual cases.

And it may be that it then tempts the person in question to consider and plan things that are not good for them. And here we are in the middle of our case The story goes like this: A - for example - Dipl.-Ing. E-technology will one day be a job. Let's say that everything he has acquired in the course of basic and detailed knowledge makes up 100 "points". Then he easily accepts that he can use perhaps 5% of it in his future field of activity. He may never need the remaining 95 "knowledge points", maybe he can use fractions of them somewhere when completing an important activity. His broad knowledge will never harm him, and he not only crammed knowledge during his studies, but also acquired and trained skills. But everyone lives with this 5% quota (if you are skeptical, take 10).

And no e-engineer who is now developing software for mobile phones, but who also knows something about the generation of electrical energy and the function of emotors from his studies, now demands that his cellphones also answer him in questions of electromotive rotation and demand for energy production. No, he lives using that 5%. But let our electrical engineer do an additional course in business administration with specialization X: Then there is nothing with 5% use of knowledge from this additional training, but a new job must be found in which you (estimated) use about 75% of the additional knowledge can. And right away.

– Therefore, I firmly believe in the following connections: From the additionally acquired knowledge, no additional study will fundamentally harm. In fact, it will always be useful if you calmly store the newly acquired knowledge, occasionally refresh it in details and keep it ready for the day when you need parts of it (5%) in your original main job.

Example: An electrical engineer will eventually become a development manager. And then grapples with development budgets (business administration), target costing (business administration), market and target group-oriented product development (marketing) and the annual financial statements of a newly purchased small subsidiary (business administration), where he is also appointed to the management board. Then he needs this additional knowledge, whether it was acquired during his studies or self-taught.

Additional studies are good for this. They only become dangerous if a new job is sought immediately(!) after graduation, for which the new knowledge would be absolutely necessary. I think it's possible that in many cases it does more harm than good.

The rule is: Additional studies serve above all to be able to solve the tasks arising in the "main job", which in turn are based on the specialist knowledge from the main study, even better, more convincingly and more effectively for one's own career.

This aspect is underlined when the main study is at university level and the additional study is at FH level.

3. You, dear sender, started your additional studies during your first employment and then switched to today's company. You knew beforehand that there were no jobs of the kind you were looking for at the location you were looking for and that you didn't want to move – which is almost always a mistake when you have high job demands. You also knew that you would have to change employers immediately after completing your additional studies in order to achieve your professional goals. S.a. 4.

4. However, you cannot and must not change employers now. It would then be the third in a good four years - that's not responsible. For orientation: You should have stayed with the first employer for at least two years and with the second around five years. Then you would be on the safe side. Also in the event that something "happens" at the third employer. In addition, given your two short periods of service (so far), you also have two job titles that sound very different, if you take the titles you formulated yourself in your CV. Under no circumstances should you now start a third area (sales/marketing), as you would lose the common thread completely.

5. My recommendation: Everything is fine - as long as you stay where you are, seize the opportunity that is offered

to you with both hands and continue professionally what you "enjoy". You only need to give the additional study the – subordinate – rank that it deserves.

And it is by no means certain that good developersalso become good sales people or product managers. The areas are not particularly close on the human talent scale, to say the least.

6. The "interface function" you brought into play deserves a special chapter.

I admit that it basically sounds good: Here, the focus of day-to-day business is not the profane everyday direction A or B or C, here you don't sit on a standard chair – but somehow more between several chairs (because on several at the same time, yes does not work). I have to try to explain:

– There is nothing, absolutely nothing, that speaks against the completely normal standard positions without any special interface component. Examples: development engineer, production engineer, sales engineer. Their advantage is twofold:

– There are a lot of them on the job market. Anyone who has such a job and no personal handicaps always finds new opportunities.

– These positions are part of an existing career path that leads straight to the top. From here you can declare any final (MD) or intermediate position (development/production/sales manager) as a career goal and generally also reach.

Your disadvantage: Standard functions often only sound averagely "exciting" or "fascinating" to the beginner. At the same time, the top of the career ladder sounds very ordinary: "Managing Director" is a "normal everyday job", every larger company has at least one. Nevertheless, this is the culmination of a career.

– The advantages and disadvantages of the interface functions are exactly the opposite, the latter are:

– There are only a few of them on the market. It is often difficult, when forced to change, to find sufficiently new positions of the kind one has lost or is about to give up. Many of these positions stand alone as they are not part of a predetermined career path. Often there is no predetermined path to the top, whoever wants to rise from there has to fight, explain, take detours and accept losses. As a consolation: temptations always look appealing – otherwise they wouldn't be. But for many (as the saying goes) "the big end comes after".

2.3.4.5 Have I the "stuff for more"?

Ask

I'm in my early 40s and was a development engineer at one for many years
medium-sized company with a very large development department. In the last two years I have worked successfully as a group leader. Then there was an extensive restructuring, the department was dissolved, the employees were distributed to other departments.
Although, in the eyes of my previous manager, I had always done an excellent job and enjoyed special trust, as did many colleagues was a valued mentor, I was only intended as a clerk in the new structure. In the various departments, other employees were deployed as department or group leaders.

When I signed an employment contract with a new company and resigned, there was little attempt to change my mind. Now I am working in the new company in a clerical position. Functions as a group or department head only come within reach after a few years, if at all.

I'm thinking about whether I might never be anything other than a clerk. Is there a realistic way to find out.

Answer

Who likes to be the bearer of bad news? But may I just say what i enjoy?
– So, I do think there's a way to phrase your final
– .

question-answer. Two notesFirst of all: What I am now listing here is circumstantial evidence, not proof. It is not possible to make a definitive, reliable prognosis about the development of a person. And: None of these indications are suitable on their own to justify a well-founded statement - but in combination they are serious:

1. Due to special circumstances in Germany, which was still divided at the time, you spent valuable years of your youth as a kind of bus driver and skilled worker. When you later finished your FH studies, you were of course quite old. As a result, you missed the academic youth years in which one learns easily, absorbs environmental conditions without any problems and allows one's personality to be shaped and shaped by this new environment with lasting effect.
I am not saying that the situation you were in at the time was always disadvantageous or that you could be a bad person because of it. But a career starter at 32 is

"different", less up to standard (to which all circumstances are tailored) than someone with e.g. B. 25 years. And being "different," "not conforming to the standard," is always more dangerous than beneficial. You then also develop "differently", often not corresponding to the usual expectations of your bosses. A basis for a very special development could have been laid here.

From your attached curriculum vitae, I am looked at by someone who appears to be without a smile, and is therefore very serious and also very young man on. He is dressed in an open "lumberjack shirt". This is not, never, not at all the application appearance of a man who dreams of management positions.

You just don't do something like that, anyone with a talent for a career would have an instinct for it.

2. Of course, I'm concentrating on the testimony of your nominated, long-term employer.

That describes you as a very accomplished, very capable and successful development engineer - without any limitations. All statements are of the finest in this regard. It says "... always and in every respect to our extraordinary satisfaction". This can be equated with "very good". The resignation at one's own request is certified, which is very much regretted. Finally, the "always very good performance" is expressly mentioned again.

So you are an excellent development engineer, no question about it. But I'm actually looking for the slightest hint of management/leadership qualities - and I can't find anything. Although your group leader status is listed last in the list of activities, leadership is then no longer mentioned.

So your old boss didn't (on purpose?) say anything about it - and you didn't notice it.

3.

In all likelihood, your whole description suggests that they saw you internally as a very capable developer and not as a talented leader.

4. You were a group leader, were demoted by the transfer, were clerks again and left. That's right, that's how people generally react to it. But there was only one good reason for changing companies: you should have fought for a group manager job in the new company with all the energy you are capable of. Or you could have given yourself the whole change. Somehow you know that too. At one point in your letter it says: "I also worked in a similar environment (as today) in the old company. The only difference is that I ... am considered a beginner in the new company." That's great progress!

Now you have also done something in your CV that is worse than the demotion at the old employer (which is not at all visible in the certificate): According to the CV and according to the certificate, you were a group leader at company A. Then you leave there voluntarily - and go to B as a clerk (!) at the age of 40. How else should one evaluate that than the admission that your qualifications as a group leader are not particularly far away and not with your urge to go there either? Those who have not advanced at this age only make it in exceptional cases.

Conclusion: You are a great professional; As your very good technical college entrance qualification already suggested, you can deal with all technical problems very well. But the talent and the will to lead are only weakly developed, you probably lack the instinct for power.

And while I leaf through your documents again and again, I find another clue. Not serious in the matter, but critical in the eyes of the expert, it shows that you don't really "live" in this professional world with its various intricacies. You write, among other things:

"I applied with the enclosed CV and after just under a week I got a second interview and the job. And that, although I didn't have a job reference at the time." The latter, dear sender, is always like that, completely normal, nothing special - and not worth mentioning!

You were in an ongoing employment relationship when you applied. You don't have a certificate, that's the way it is, it's accepted without any problems. Sometimes you have an interim certificate, but mostly not. And you don't get your final certificate until the last working day at the earliest - but then you've already had the whole application process behind you.

So I believe there is an answer to the question you asked. As a consolation: There are no absolute statements in this profession. Despite my misgivings, you may stumble upon the opportunity of a lifetime tomorrow. Just how likely is that?

2.3.4.6   Stay, switch with severance pay, rising up?

Ask

I'm in my mid-40s and work as a project manager in in-house engineering
of production facilities in a large chemical company. I don't have any leadership outside of the respective project team.

I have been working for this company for more than fifteen years and I am actually quite satisfied. Unfortunately, I've been put off by my management for a long time when it comes to promotion. I would primarily be interested in a group leader position without disciplinary management responsibility. I know well that as a technical college engineer in the chemical industry, I like the higher ranks
e.g. B. that of a department head practicallyremain closed.
My last hopes of increasing my career have recently been dashed because the group wants to significantly downsize its staff. The The process has already begun, there will be layoffs and outsourcing from individual areas.

High severance bonuses are also offered if you leave the company voluntarily.

I am currently considering leaving the group and striving for a position with personnel management in another company of a similar, possibly smaller size, with the practical effect of then "taking along" the severance pay.

a. Does it make sense to quit in this situation and get the opportunity to manage staff elsewhere?

There is a verbal promise to start as a project manager at another company without managing employees, but that is not my primary goal.

b. Is it better to keep your feet still and wait out the "firestorm" of layoffs? There are clear signs that I will not be affected.
c. Does it even make sense to switch at my age? If there are problems in a new position, I'm 50 and then I have to go back to the job market.
d. If I change, I would of course like to take the severance pay with me. Would that be viewed negatively by the old or new employer?
e. How do you rate the risks and chances of going or staying? As a solid father, should I stay or is it "last chance to get started"?

Answer

The peculiarity outlined in the last sentence of your second paragraph does not have to apply to every single chemical company, but the industry does have this image that logically needs to be underpinned. It is based on the fact that – easy to understand – the chemical industry is shaped by chemists and is also dominated in many areas. The classic chemist now has a university degree and – a special feature of this field – almost always a doctorate.

For this reason, the many chemists in the company who have a doctorate are traditionally placed as partners in the technical departments with (doctoral) TH/TU/university engineers.

That no longer has to be the case everywhere, but as

our sender explains, it is still the case in this group (sales in the eleven-digit euro range).

With the compensation offers we have the poodle core (freely based on Faust, Goethe). And in connection with the appearance of the poodle, which shortly afterwards turns out to be Mephisto, Faust says beforehand: "And if I'm not mistaken, then a whirlpool of fire/ will follow along on its paths."

We'll come to the details later. Let's get to the core:

- Let's summarize what we've got so far in terms of larger topics Above write:"Unfortunately, my managementment in terms of advancement." Precisely because your company is so big, we have to take it very seriously: After more than fifteen years, your superiors still don't want you to become "just" a group leader. Your bosses really cannot excuse the lack of opportunities for such a promotion. Face the truth: Your superiors ultimately do not consider you suitable. Then:

"Put it off" means it was talked about. This in turn means that your bosses know perfectly well that you have ambitions in this direction. Then these superiors also know (guaranteed!): "If we don't give the man what he wants so badly, there's a risk that he'll leave." But they decided: he should go, but he won't become a group leader here.

In large companies in particular, the following applies: it was not a grumpy, incompetent boss who threw off your promotion, but "the system" made a negative decision. In the case of large employers in particular, the superiors are individuals who think and act individually, but to a large extent represent "the industry in this branch and company size".

So be careful: These people could be right, then you could also fail in another similarly structured house. I think that's a real danger. My view is supported by the following consideration:

The man who is made of the cloth from which group leaders or even higher-ranking executives are made does very good work somewhere for five years and distinguishes himself. Let's be generous, let him work like this for seven years. Then, if everything goes well, his bosses promoted him of their own accord. If they: have risked it, not this great performer To have been "rewarded" accordingly, the claim is made politely but unmistakably. Then he gives his bosses a maximum of one year – and then he's gone.

The conclusions to be drawn for you are not: I am unsuitable as a "group leader and more", but to put it more eloquently: "I probably do not meet the ideal standards of the management of such a large corporation; which in turn could be seen everywhere. So I'm changing the type of company, aiming specifically as a group leader in medium-sized companies, then I also have the 'bonus' of coming from a larger, more renowned company, which will impress my new employer." Or you can leave this project alone. You have to decide.

- The Compensation: Hold a glass of mustard to a group of peopleback and encourage them to spoon it up. Nobody will "bite". Now offer 100 EUR, someone will find themselves doing something because of this "premium" that they would otherwise not do. There you have the principle of severance pay: You are thereby tempted to act in the interest of the other side, which has disadvantages for you and which you would not seriously consider without this bonus.

The risk is that, tempted by the "easy" money, you will get carried away into something whose downsides you "whitewash" yourself. The thing is comparable to those dollar signs that block Uncle Scrooge's view of everything around him when he smells money somewhere. In addition, severance offers are usually limited in time, so you have to find a new job under time pressure. That's not good for the matter anyway.

Then it may be (ask beforehand) that you will receive a reference from which the intention of the employer to get rid of you (while keeping others) becomes evident for the rest of your working life. Depending on the further course of your career, this can cause serious damage to you.

But can't you take the opportunity and take the severance pay with you if you're about to change anyway and already have a draft of the new employment contract on the table? Read the previous paragraph with the testimony again - and think of the probability of the whole constellation. No, the company wants to move employees who would otherwise stay. And even if the circumstances were so favorable (a new offer happens to come along), there's still a chance you'll sign where you wouldn't have signed otherwise. Money is one of the great temptations. be yourself at least aware of the dangers. The result "Money in the account, career ruined" is of no help to you either.

Never forget whose interests dominate here: ThatCompany wants to get rid of employees and lures with money. It's less about making you happy.

Note: I might appear to be torpedoing company plans to downsize by warning employees not to accept severance offers. There is no reason for such misgivings: money that someone waves is such a strong temptation that there are always people who will "spoon out a glass of mustard" for it.

Basically, you had long since made your peace with your current situation – only the severance pay thing is giving you "ideas".

I advise you, taking into account all aspects:

- Enter the goal of personnel management on the way to an external applicationto want to obtain (if something else comes up internally, grab it). Striving for personnel management because a severance offer triggered the idea is nonsense anyway. They would have to achieve a double goal (take severance pay, gain a management position) under the time pressure of a limited severance pay campaign, which leads to chaos.

- According to the tried-and-tested principle "every application should be a (!) progressachieved", you could now switch to the same level (without management) with little risk and take the darn severance pay with you. This is where progress would lie - you could also convince yourself that you have no chance of further development in today's boss environment, but that could be the case in the new one. This move to a position that you have mastered from your current job and where the risk of failure would be low could be defended. You would have the severance payment to cushion the ever-remaining risk.

- Just for the sake of good order: notice is only given after the signatureunder a new employment contract, and think of the question mentioned as to what will appear in the reference (who gave notice to whom?).

- The old (today's) employer wants to get rid of employees, so he pays for itfinally even. So he'll be happy when you leave. Your boss might be sad, but has to reckon with such layoffs.

  You do not have to and should not tell the new employer anything about the severance payment. If he finds out, the timing of the change and the severance pay was just coincidence. Since you are on the same hierarchical level

  change and not as a manager, the demands on the "story" that you have to tell are not extremely high.

- If youIf you're still unsure, do what you can without would have made a severance offer.

  Don't forget: money is being used to trick you into doing something that is probablyis not good for you (otherwise you wouldn't have to pay a "company leaving bonus"). The story with "I wanted to leave anyway, so I can pay the severance pay..." is extremely unlikely: If the employees had left anyway, no bonus should have been offered.

2.3.4.7   Flexible, mobileand forever for rent?

Ask

As a Dipl.-Ing. mechanical engineering for many years in the field of
active energies, for several years as a team leader. I will soon
40. My wife devotes herself entirely to the upbringing of our children.

For years you have been propagating in careers advice that an engineer would do well not to be tied to one location. I've followed this rule to this day and I have to say that I've improved substantially since my last move, which is now a few years ago. This would not have been possible with a local change, especially since my industry is – still – quite narrow.

At the moment we live in a semi-detached house for rent and feel at home in the rural environment. We are now planning to move to a small town. On the one hand we would like to see secondary schools for our children locally, on the other hand we would like to finally design the house and garden according to our own ideas. Therefore, we would like to build or buy a house in the new location. This would bind us regionally in the long term. You don't build in order to move out again immediately. In such a case, realistically speaking, you would lose the additional construction or purchase costs i. hv 15-20% full, the value of landscaped grounds etc. about half.

Now, in many guidebooks on old-age provision and asset accumulation, the motto "rent-free in retirement" is issued. Can this goal also apply to career-conscious engineers? Or do I have to rent for the next 27 years in order to remain flexible?

Answer

It's basically part of the old central problem of "profession versus private life",
which you describe clearly. According to the question, let's concentrate on the house problem There is no one-size-fits-all solution that can be implemented anywhere and anytime! In the end, the only thing that remains is to find a compromise in each individual case after weighing up all aspects. The following can be used to help:

1. This series focuses on professional aspects. The following clearly applies here: Anyone who has career ambitions and wants to fully exploit their potential must be prepared at all times to accept a position based anywhere in Germany. This applies to both external transfers and internal transfers.
Principle: You don't turn down the chairmanship of VW because the office would then be in Wolfsburg (that's just one example, I don't want to offend the home-loving residents of this city).

2. Even an employee who is willing to make a career for the benefit of his housedoing without, cannot avoid the principle according to 1.: One day he loses his job – with or without fault – and cannot find anything in the immediate vicinity. Then he is faced with a choice again: unemployed in the old house or ready to move.

3. A change of place of work, which only a few people are spared during a career, can be "processed spatially" as

follows:

- They commute very long distances (e.g. more than 50-80 km) daily. That costs time, nerves, car running costs and displeases some bosses. In the long run, this is an "endless horror" and unsatisfactory.
- You take a small apartment at the new place of work, the family keeps the old place of residence, you commute at the weekend. This gives you a lot of time on four weekdays in the evening that you can use professionally, but at the weekend it brings with it a great deal of stress due to the driving and can(!) alienate you from your family. In addition, some bosses also dislike that. In particular, medium-sized companies "in the provinces" often like to see (or insist) that the (senior) employee lives at the place of work. This pendulum solution also has something of the "endless terror".

On 3.1 and 3.2: Almost all employers have had bad experiences with these variants: After a while, the resulting stress is often felt by the employee and/or his family as unbearable - a better solution is needed! This is practically never due to the family moving to the place of work, but leads to activities by the employee concerned to look for a new job at the familiar ("old") place of residence. Then the current job loses-

give the new employee back - without any chance of being able to do anything about it.

- The "cleanest" solution is to sell or rent the property in connection with a move.

This can certainly be associated with financial losses, no question. But: You always change jobs (usually also the employer and then the location as well) because the new commitment is associated with advantages – including financial ones. Then you have to count against each other. And: If I'm a clerk and want to be a department manager one day, then I must have been a department manager at some point on the way to my individual goal, no question. If I now have to accept disadvantages in one area when moving from group to department head, that can be perfectly fine overall! At: the end, a balance is drawn

4. For some reason we are a people who give great room to fear of the possible, even the improbable. After we once wanted to conquer the world – megalomaniacs – we now export "German Angst". We shouldn't overdo it. A life without risk is not possible, but you don't have to miss a football game just because a fully fueled passenger plane could fall on the stadium.

5. So if we have to and can (!) live with a limited risk, then the following applies to your house construction plans:

- If you have been with your employer for at least 1-2 years, if your career planning does not speak against being able to stay there for at least another five years, even better ten years, if you have all the information you have about the company and bosses , shows no particular risk, then build or buy your house. It works 80 times out of 100. Trust that you're one of those 80.

- Nevertheless, plan that you will probably not build "for eternity". Do not design your individual dream object in every detail - according to your taste, which is unparalleled, with materials or a room layout that has never been seen before. Build a standard house in an area with similar objects

  – look for easy resale (or rental opportunities). Do not

ask an architect about this, but (preferably her) a broker – who knows what the local market wants. By the way, brokers say that the location is everything for a house, the rest is not so important.

- Nobody likes to move out of a house they just moved into. Ten years later things are different: families are changing, houses are rigid. And so they only fit one moment in family history. Newly arriving children or old parents who have been taken in lead to space problems, and offspring who move out early leads to uneconomical vacancies. What would seem unbearable to you shortly after construction (moving out/selling) will one day be conceivable again, even for partners.

- Finally, I recommend once again Mell's priority list, which is very close to my heart: Write down everything that is important to you, arrange it according to priorities - and force yourself to occupy each place on this list with only one aspect. On number 1, write "I want a house" or "I want to be a group leader" - but only one of them, the other goes on number 2 or lower. You can also write "world peace" or "a life without nuclear power plants" there, the main thing is to observe the core principle: clear decisions at every occupation. You can change the list shortly, but don't water down the principle. By the way, you learn how to make decisions and practice a classic managerial virtue. A company owner cannot say: I want to get a high profit on my private account and invest a lot of money in the company. He, too, can only occupy No. 1 once. But he, too, may change his priorities next year.

2.3.4.8   searched for an alternative

I've been working as a development engineer at my first job for nine years.
employer in a technically very demanding industry. The product is technically attractive, the pay is right and the working atmosphere in my department is everything you could wish for. Internal changes without promotion have broadened my horizons and my network in the company.

Nevertheless, I now have a certain feeling of a lack of professional prospects. Also, given the advice in this series, I shudder at the thought of staying in my position until retirement and am concerned about how to actively shape my career in a meaningful way.

I don't just want to be able to look to the future with no worries when I'm fifty, I want to be accompanied by the feeling that I've made something out of my professional life.

I consider myself to be professionally committed and also privately hold positions on the boards of clubs and the like, although in no case as a chairman or leader. I am not striving for personal responsibility and I am particularly skeptical about such a step in view of my life experience to date. To take this risk without necessity seems foolish to me, although I gather from your series again and again that there is no alternative in the long term to a career path without any sort of upward mobility.

In my specific situation, I see three possibilities:

I. Staying in my current position, developing my

professional qualifications and hoping not to be laid off for the next 30 years. There are numerous and valued older colleagues who have found their niche somewhere; fluctuation is also low.

II. Expand my CV and experience and change employers. The unavoidable change of location with all the consequences and the risk that every change of company entails have been sufficiently discussed in this series. The question is what the chances are if the change does not involve any noticeable advancement, i.e. I end up doing the same job somewhere else for the same salary and will sooner or later face the same problem.

III. Recognize that I am not in the right place in the world (you would write, "in the system") of the private sector and do something completely different. A change to public service, to a supervisory authority, to the consulting industry, or something more exotic, such as a job as a development worker, would be conceivable.

Variant III is certainly the most attractive. However, I suspect that you are particularly skeptical about this and I look forward to your analysis and your advice.

Answer

In the first three paragraphs of your question, we are dealing with interesting starting points:

a. I can promise you that your "certain feeling of a lack of professional prospects" will remain and grow – unless you actively do something about it.

b. For an employee in the private sector, there is no guaranteed worry-free view of the future. That is part of the principle of the system. Carefree works, carefree doesn't.

   Imagine that a few years ago you were a specialist in a specific,now in daily public discussionexisting power plant technology. Which originally could have been a very sensible idea. Then at the political level it says "exit this technology", then again it says "extend the service life" (this could have extended many specialists to retirement), then suddenly "exit immediately" – until the next change of heart. You can also have it one size smaller: from the always possible bankruptcy to quarrels with bosses.

   No, this one of your wishes is almost impossible to fulfill. That doesn't mean that corresponding existential worries are guaranteed, but it does mean that you are called upon to be vigilant and cautious tactics throughout your professional life.

c. One day they want to be sure "... that they have made something out of my professional life". This is a very human endeavor, it's ancient, and can be narrowed down by two fairly well-known quotes:

   "The trace of my days on earth cannot perish in aeons"

says Goethe's Faust II. What is expressed is the human desire to create something lasting, to "have made something out of life". In this demanding form (it's about a kind of dam) only a few succeed, but the principle becomes clear.

"He lived, took a wife and died" (from "The Old Man" by Ch. F. Gellert) describes the life of a man about whom there is nothing of importance to say at the end.

In between we orientate ourselves. Somehow. Now, not everyone can leave a legacy. That's why I react to considerations of this kind ("made something out of my professional life...") with the recommendation: Get out of yourself what you can do, develop your individual abilities. Here is a small example: think how unpopular a skat player is who never exhausts his hand and who, out of sheer caution, always falls short of what he could have done.

You worded the last sentence of your fourth paragraph in a misleading way. It should read "with any rise". Incidentally, I never said there was no alternative. Practice also shows that there are at least two alternatives to classic promotion with personnel responsibility:

– You simply remain a clerk until you retire. If you look around, you will see: the departments of many companies are full of such employees ter, who also make a valuable contribution to the success of the whole, who above all have special technical know-how and a wide range of experience; Hardly any company can do without both.

– You start an internal specialist career – if your employer offers it. There you can rise to the specialist level, take on technical responsibility and achieve salary dimensions comparable to management careers.

The limitations: These specialist career paths are primarily intended to bind the relevant employees to the respective company and to expand in-house specialist qualifications. The instrument has been around for a very long time, it also has very convincing advantages for the company and also some for the employees. whether it is e.g. For example, I cannot say in general terms that it is still possible for you, with your nine years of professional experience, to jump into a specialist career as an external applicant in another company. This path is particularly well suited for specialists who have been active in the respective company from the start. A big problem can arise if you are in the higher stages of your specialist career and want or have to change. Your professional orientation is then highly specialized, the number of suitable new employers is extremely small - and if they don't have a specialist career on top of that, they can't do anything with the "extremely highly paid clerk without managerial experience". All of this needs to be carefully considered.

But: A professional life with classic advancement is not without an alternative. Cross out I. This doesn't eliminate your problem, on the contrary, it only makes it bigger. And if you had to switch at 45, you would hardly have a chance.

In order to make your case more transparent for the other readers, you are Dipl.-Ing. (univ.), mid-30s, single (that's why the development worker would go), your 1.x in the Abitur corresponds exactly to the 1.x in the exam. I accept your dislike of, or your presumed lack of, talent for leadership. However, I would deny your suitability for forty years of work at the same level in an unchanged environment.

You know my (very general) 5-year rule: promotion every 5 years (if you are interested in a career), at least 5 years per employer, be careful if you have been in the same job for more than 5 years, beware of overestimating the experience growth curve, which initially rises steeply but only slightly after 5 years Except for serial authors who consult on HR, of course). It seems that a career change after this period would do people good.

In your case too, your almost ten years are divided between two different activities – now you are getting restless. And you're far too alert not to get nervous at the thought of thirty more years. Oh, just try to find out how high the proportion of 1.x exams is among the "numerous and valued colleagues" who "found their niche somewhere". Despite your – correct – arguments, I don't like No. II all that bad. So far you only know this one company. It could be very special. A change would force you into new professionally relevant activities, give you new insights and ultimately give you a completely different working environment. The latter will challenge you in other fields, bring you closer to other career examples and other leadership personalities. Perhaps this will make strings ring in you that you didn't even know existed - with all sorts of consequences.

Also: Until you have really digested this experiment, another five years have passed. You are changing during

this time, I wish you a wife, three children and a mortgage for a house (professional life is tailored to this standard type, who is also better able to find the answers to central questions about the meaning of life).
(
The chances are at II. So in conceivable perspectives of any kind - in comparison to the guaranteed "yawning boredom" today. My hope is that someone there will give you a great, exhausting project – and will challenge you professionally and personally(!) to the bone.
So you wouldn't do anything wrong with II. and - presumably - open new doors into the big professional world.
Now to III.: "I would like to do something completely different" is a dream often dreamed of by dissatisfied people. If I were a soul therapist, I would occasionally advise it. But now I'm a career advisor in a system riddled with minefields – and I tend to advise against it. Partly as a matter of principle, partly because some people who seek advice give me the arguments "free to the door".
For example you: What are the alternatives you mentioned
"public service/supervisory authority", "consulting industry" or "development worker" to do with your current job as a development engineer, which you have chosen yourself in a free country? What connects these activities together - apart from the very, very flimsy aspect,
to be "different"? How do you or the recipient of a corresponding application intend to gain sufficient certainty that the new start is the professional direction you have finally found and that you would not be asking

the same questions again in ten years? And as "Wanderer Between Worlds" end?

Did I already say in this series that being allowed to deal with 1,x candidates can also be a cross? And if someone then refuses to let their untapped performance potential be exhausted by the demanding, demanding and appropriate task provided for in the system (because they say: Cheers me up, but I don't want to lead), then they also bring hard-nosed ones Career advisor still in a rage.

Conclusion: You are not sufficiently challenged by your current job as a development engineer. head of department e.g. B. complain less often that they are under-challenged.

And: Of course it could be that you would be a great development worker, but how should I know? But if you couldn't or didn't want to do this until you retire: what would happen after that in your case?

– Maybe you should have done your doctorate back then on the basis of your good exams, maybe that would have opened up a different dimension for you professionally. Try it now with No. II, which will definitely bring you new challenges and possibly new perspectives. I care a little bit about "I" and a little less about "the company" to which you are committed and about "the shareholders" to whom you are particularly committed. You accepted the office – reluctantly, but then you did. Now you have to try to fill it and list less of the things you hate. Unless you have alternatives, which I don't see specifically.

The employee, in this sense also the managing director, is employed as a dependent employee. They are a kind of vicarious agent for the shareholders – it's never really a piece of cake. They are employed there primarily to "enjoy" the shareholders, not should be, noneDesire to train myself - despite multiple complaints also with the GF. A two-year induction period was originally planned; this plan was dropped and the job holder persuaded to continue working, I was fired during the probationary period.

After a year of unemployment, I took a job as a developer (without personal responsibility). I was fired again after the probationary period because, as I later learned, my supervisor was afraid of losing his job (he was much younger and completely inexperienced as a supervisor).

After another six months of unemployment, I tried my hand as a project engineer - again without success. My experience wasn't good enough for that (my guess), and the owner was a domineering dictator, and we occasionally clashed personally.

I pondered the reasons for my problems for a long time and recognized one thing in common: I'm too nice. In each of the last three appointments, I would have had to let higher-ranking, incompetent people "jump over the blade". But during the probationary period?

What now? I would like to work as head of design and development again, I think I'm in the right place. But I'm afraid I'm too big
"burned" that my application immediately ends up in the trash. What are theat all for alternatives?

2.3.5 Special cases - the career is a "broad field"

The longer the career path, the more specific the problems one encounters.

2.3.5.1 How do I get back down?

Ask

Many readers will dismiss my case as a luxury problem. my most important
Data: Age well over 50, Dr.-Ing., in a small family-owned company for more than ten years. First development manager there, then managing director, finally sole managing director.

The first years with my current employer were a great time. As a development manager, I led a team of nice, conscientious, capable employees. Success came quickly, we were able to grow and get a significantly better result. Then the shareholders asked me to join the management team. I decided on the request and unequivocally contradicted it, there would have been other solutions. Nevertheless, I was pressured so massively that I finally agreed.

This was a mistake! My desire to include some sort of exit clause in the contract that would have allowed me to return to my old position after a few years fell on deaf ears.

I hate doing things I can't do. I hate having to deal with every chore that inevitably comes up in such a small business. But what I hate most is that I don't have enough time to take care of the things that are important to me and that I'm good at. A neglected product development is a ticking time bomb.

So I want to go back to my old job, but how do I go about it? Since I'm rather frugal, money isn't that important to me, nor is my company car and status. But how do I convey my wish to the shareholders? I want to descend a rung or two but not jump.

Answer

2. The factual-"technical" side of the matter:
- For difficult internal company problems that a manager encounters, there is first of all the solution via the external labor market. It doesn't help us here for two reasons (in the combination of both aspects, the story is hopeless):
- For classicChange of any kind you are now too old.
- Nobody likes external applicants who are currently in a significantly higher position than the desired one. Anyone who was once the sole manager already has problems if he "only" wants to become a department manager afterwards - the ex-"sole ruler" is no longer of any use at department head level.
- Whether the shareholders went along with it or not, it wouldn't work if you went back internally accordingly. You would lose face, you would risk becoming a sad figure both internally and externally – and nobody would believe that you did it voluntarily. Such a step is so rare that no one can do anything with it. The usual way of dealing with a sole manager who can no longer do it (in the eyes of the shareholders) or who no longer wants to (which is difficult to convey to the environment): the man leaves, he leaves the company – sometimes involuntarily , partly at my own request. What becomes of him "outside" no longer interests

anyone internally.

– If anything is a "ticking time bomb", then it is a department head who has previously been the sole MD of this company. Any sensible successor in the MD function would have to try to get rid of this "strange saint" who is now "playing" the department head as quickly as possible. He would never look up to the sole manager with respect, but would probably say to his wife in the evening: "The manager shouldn't puff himself up, after all I was what he is now." And nothing on earth protects you from a successor in the GF who, of all things, has development as a hobby and takes care of every detail there.

3. The professional philosophy("moral") side of the matter:

– You are certainly not a standard personality, as one usually finds on such a chair:

– There is your description of the team in the development department:

"Nice, conscientious and capable" were the people. Who starts with "nice" when listing the characteristics of a team that is enormously important for the existence of the company? You instinctively put what you consider most important at the top. Kind?

– In the penultimate paragraph of your presentation, you really rage: "I hate" is written three times, it's about things that "are important to me". Without you in development, the company is in danger of going under. What kind of solo GF is that they have there? How can he neglect development when it is so indispensable? And why hasn't he installed a new department head there long ago who is making things as good as he used to be? Or did he keep this job free for selfish reasons and against his duties so that he could slip back into it himself if necessary?

however, to do what you enjoy most or hate least.

- Now we will climb up a little higher and look for "protective help" there for our problem:

- While everyone was talking about it, Frederick the Great is just right for us. He also hated all sorts of things he was supposed to be and do, but then adapted to his position and finally formulated: "I am the first servant of the state." Putting it a little bit smaller, something like that would also be good for a sole managing director decorate.

- The cimier (according to the dictionary of foreign words, a knight's helmet adornment) of the Prince of Wales contains a banner with the text – actually written in German –: "I serve." That would also be good food for thought. Humility, modesty despite healthy self-confidence.

4. The options you now have:

- A relatively easy, absolutely clean chance to return to the old

  I don't see a "small" job (once GF, always GF).

- A serious attempt to do this could first annoy your shareholders and ultimately fail - you would then be worse off than before.

- You can quit and leave; But I don't see any chance of finding the small job I'm looking for "out there".

- You can think everything through, carefully analyze your overall situation, and make your peace with where you are today. It's a matter of attitude. If there is something to do, just do it, don't waste time putting it into different hate categories. And think of the alternatives you have. Like so many others, I think there are worse things than having to come to terms with a managerial position. Some would give their left arm for it...

For potential copycats Our sender was unsuccessful in rejecting the top job, which was unloved then as now. That was unfortunate in several respects. I don't know how he argued at the time, but I suspect ("I hate") that he mainly used "I don't want to".

Now a high-ranking boss (a shareholder) who wants something himself(!) is hardly impressed by the argument that the subordinate does not like it. Resistance from below is there to be overcome! So you have to offer more than defiance (don't want to), which you can also break or overcome with good persuasion. It's more effective then

5. :

6. It's okay to put forward serious (apparent) factual arguments that you can't get rid of under pressure, something like this: "Thank you very much, the offer is a great honor for me. However, in the interest of the matter (shareholder interests, concerns of the company) I have to politely decline - because I cannot do justice to the position. You think I'm capable of it, that's an honor, but I know myself better. I've often asked myself in the past whether I'd like to be CEO one day. And then I analyzed the position and its requirements on the one hand and my strengths and weaknesses on the other and came to the conclusion: I shouldn't aspire to such a position because it wouldn't be responsible, I'm not the right man for it, I can not that, I would be overwhelmed. Would I accept the offer

7. Anyone who then promoted him would be acting irresponsibly.

2.3.5.2   I am too nice

I, too, belong to the large circle of your fans who have been devouring "career advice" for many years and at least try to apply as many tips as possible in professional life. I have to admit, however, that I only managed to do so incompletely; After looking through my CV, you will surely agree with me.

Why? Well, I wasn't interested in a career at all, I just wanted a job where I could best use my skills. Then I've had bad luck a few times lately. Or? Do you see any fundamentals or similarities in my last three (failed) attempts to gain a foothold in professional life again?

After seventeen years of working for the subsidiary of a very large international group as test manager and technical manager of a product area, my job was rationalized away. As one of many, I could have muddled on at a larger company location, but I decided to make a change.

This second job was my dream job. Unfortunately, the company had to be streamlined due to economic difficulties, four of eight executives were dismissed, and I was there (social selection). I found my next job as a future design manager at another medium-sized company.

During my probationary period, however, I didn't get a single order; recently there was 100% short-time work. In addition, the man whose successor I had

Answer

Two explanationsin advance:

a. I'm actually not too nice. That's a good thing for the author of such a series, because unfortunately I often have to put my finger in wounds and then dig into them a bit. So be prepared, whatever.
b. How we are, what we can do is reflected in a – especially a longer – curriculum vitae. When things pile up, suspicion quickly becomes certainty. If the symptoms increase there, there is also a "disease" behind it.

Let's start with the analysis of the basis on which you started your professional life:

Abitur with 3.4. You can do that, but it's dangerous. One or two tenth notes later you get "shot", so it doesn't get much worse than that. Such a result should inspire humility. One should realize that one's own trees will not grow into the sky. One shouldn't trying to build a big house on a weak foundation. You now chose the leap from this weak basis into the thin air of the elite: Studying a particularly demanding subject at the TU. Six years(!) later you had found out what I've often spread here (even if some people don't like to hear it, for whatever reason): With a 3.x Abitur you should better avoid the university. Otherwise there is a risk of what you then experienced: studying without a degree.

Change to the University of Applied Sciences. lies with the documentsa diploma, but no sheet with references to grades. Well, life experience teaches that this procedure would not be typical, e.g. B. for straight-A candidates.

At the age of 29 you had your FH exams, about the quality of which we know nothing. And - you would have to have the disposition of a butcher dog, if that weren't the case - the defeat of not achieving your TU degree after so many years has certainly done damage to your self-confidence, something like that is not so easily dismissed.

The description in the 3rd paragraph sounds convincing at every regulars' table. But I am suspicious by profession and have the certificates at hand. The document on the big corporation's letterhead (you know, "cut in marble") confirms the seventeen years. As a test engineer. Nothing leader, neither from the experiment, nor from a product area. No change whatsoever during the extremely long period of activity there.

The "school grade" of the document, which is short for the long period of service, is good, not very good.

When big companies rationalize away the job of a long-time, proven, and capable employee, and thus innocently squeeze them out, they are often generous with severance pay, but almost always generous with wording of references. The note is embellished accordingly (paper costs nothing). About half a note to a note. The expert deducts them again while reading. But where am I in this case? 2.5 or 3 - not acceptable after seventeen years in such a company.
Your cheating with the "leader" is unacceptable.

And one more thing: If it says, "Mr. X continues to

murder", then he has already murdered before. According to your description, you, dear sender, could have "muddled on" at the other job offered to you. So you've been mumbling before. That's how the company may have seen it, but you made that suspicion yourself. The testimonial from this group and your first employer certifies that you are leaving at your own request – now you should stick with it in writing and verbally (you were the only one who wanted to leave, there was never any reasoning away).

After those seventeen years as an executive engineer, according to your documents, you then took over the management of technology and construction at a small medium-sized company. The employment relationship lasted for two years, the testimonials are "good", the resignation was involuntary due to "strategic corporate restructuring measures". You are described as an "entrepreneurial manager".
How about some "engineering" precision? At your third job

- write "design manager" in your CV
- write in the letter to me "design manager in future",
- writes the certificate (which is just a certificate of employment without an evaluation
is) "deputyDesign manager of a division".

The following applies to applications: the "certificate" is right if you deviate from it,has lied. It's all rather unimportant as a matter of fact, but it doesn't reflect well on you. In addition, this certificate is not good, it confirms the dismissal, speaks of "economic reasons", but regrets nothing.

There is a detailed certificate from the penultimate employer (developer). This confirms dismissal by the employer, regrets it(!), but gives no justification whatsoever. This is not good.

In the letter to me, you call the last position that you have already completed "Project Engineer", in your CV "Project Manager", there is no certificate.

By the way, as a small employee you don't "clash" with an owner (or managing director/board member). That sounds like fighting on an equal footing - which isn't there, not at all. Formally, you would have to say: "Unfortunately, I gave my highest boss the opportunity to be extremely dissatisfied with me. Then, as was to be expected, he fired me." But don't bother.

I don't know if I can help you anymore. In addition, you are now 51 years old. This is still possible to some extent in the management area, but in executive (administrative) positions it is a high hurdle. But in any case, this is a good lesson I can use to show other readers what to do and what not to do.

So, dear sender, I think a central core of your problems lies here: you lack humility. This applies to assessing your own qualities, assessing the options you have, appreciating opportunities and dealing with information. As well as for dealing with bosses First of all, I try to list mistakes and unfortunate decisions, based on misjudgment of one's own possibilities, etc.:

1. Your handling of information in your records is absolutely not to beaccept. Any serious application to reputable companies must fail because of this alone. You should never(!) make "more" of yourself (cover

letter and/or CV) than the reference shows.

2. Going through your training (study) was already a very bad professional start. The fact that you try to study at a technical university with such a lousy high school diploma and realize after six years(!) that it's not possible should have shown you - and shows every application reader again and again - that there are limits. On that basis, "not being interested in a career at all" was actually reasonable.

3. You then had a suitable job as a ... engineer with your first employer for many years. Why do you have to inflate that against the wording of the reference to the "leader", why do you explain that you considered the alternative job offered, in which you were "one of many" at the other location, to be beneath your dignity? If you had just "muddled on" in this company, after having done your first job for such an awfully long time, you would be in a much better position than you are today.

4. Position No. 2 as head of construction was your dream. By the way, you got it based on an application with the CV that you used as a
"Head" with employer no. 1 reported - the different certificate without
"Head" only existed after you left. Who wants to rule out that your bosses there later noticed this discrepancy!
and therefore put you on the redundancy list? And: You have a "dreamlike" certificate of your dream position, e.g. B. A very good one (especially if you include the "discount" for the "innocent" dismissal).
And above all: Even if everything were perfect here, it is still only one of five positions, only two of a total of twenty-two years of service. This is not a convincing

record.

5. You saw yourself as the "leader" in the first position, you were in the second. The – brave – attempts to only work in executive/non-leadership after that were high-risk adventures. One has had extremely bad experiences with the use of former executives - even those who only "felt" - in low-ranking positions. Read your own corresponding accounts: It abounds with incompetent or unwilling superiors, malicious owners, etc.

3   So far, my statement is clear and well-founded. Now you expect advice for the future, if possible with a guarantee of success. The latter can never exist.

4   As a piece of advice: look within yourself and see if I might not be right in my analysis. Then accept that you will no longer get a serious managerial position with this "preload" on your CV. Revise your CV and oral presentation. You have never been a manager. The only point where something like that comes up is position no. 2. Pull that down on the CV to "design engineer, responsible for a product group" and write below in the CV: "(internally mainly because of the effect on customers as a head of department, but that was of no importance in the day-to-day business of the small company)", refrain from any criticism of superiors in writing and verbally (interview!) – and accept that you cause of

5   "self-made mistake" are where you are.

6   Then apply broadly to the implementation level, market your/a specialist qualification, also think of companies in unattractive locations and temporary workers.

7   be

2.3.5.3   Warning shot in the middle of working life

Ask

I'm just over 50, in the middle management of an industrial company
mens - and satisfied with my previous career path. I was able to implement demanding, exciting and complex projects and enjoyed the appreciation of my employees and superiors.

Probably due to years of extreme stress, I suffered a mild heart attack.

I now perceive insecurities of my superiors regarding my future career. Their ambivalent attitude is that, on the one hand, they would like me to get back to work as a well-known top performer, but on the other hand, there seems to be a (justified) fear that at some point I will collapse completely. I imagine that from a management perspective, a younger fresh replacement (if one is found) and my departure would be the best solution for the company.
What alternative solution strategiesI have?

From a health point of view, the immediate pension would of course be the variant with the highest life expectancy. Unfortunately also the most unrealistic. I am missing Assets, an occupational disability pension because of a slight heart attack does not exist either.

I. Look for a stress-free biotope in the company. That doesn't exist in my company; I can't go back to the operative business as a simple engineering clerk either, I've been "out of business" there for too long.

II. Changing jobs to a less stressful company: impossible at my age with the health problems.

III. The healthIgnore the warning shot and continue 100% as before. That would be my boss's preference. But this variant is the most risky in terms of health.

IV. I could try to muddle through somehow, introduce stress-reducing measures, but still keep the old job. It's an egg dance, a compromise solution "deliberate loss of performance vs. health benefit".

Answer

V.

Let's deal with one detail quickly before it gets lost in the main topic: people tend to put what is most important to them first in lists. It happens very instinctively.

However, a middle manager is not primarily there to gain the appreciation of their employees (your first paragraph). This is useful from time to time, but she is deployed and paid for by her superiors, whose vicarious agents she is in her area of responsibility. Don't make any mistakes in the distribution of priorities! Not even in thinking. Situations are conceivable in which managers must and can do without the appreciation of their employees (keyword:

"Reduction of staff in the department"). But there is no conceivable situation in which they can survive without the appreciation of their superiors.

First some basic statements (although we don't know anything about the medical prognosis or the urgent recommendation of the doctors; I'm also a medical layman, but everyone else involved is too):

1. what happened to youis generally considered a "warning shot". It shows that your potential is finite.

Everyone assumes that something like this can happen again, although you have no guarantee that it will only be a "minor" heart attack.

Conclusion: In your own interest, you cannot continue as before. The previous professional life is over, there must be a change for you. This change can only go in the direction of "career light":

Less stress, less commitment, less the key performer, less the (almost) indispensable doer, but willingness to go back. Your previous professional life has to die so that you can go on living. Think more of yourself, be – besides everything else – also selfish.

Accept this point - and face the consequences.

2. It's always helpful to be ruthless about your own market value - assuming that everyone knew the whole truth. A very brief consideration shows: As a man over 50 who has just survived his first heart attack, you have no chance as an applicant. No matter how competent and – formerly – powerful they may have been; now they are seen as an incalculable risk. No, your (almost only) chance lies within the company, in the environment that knows you, appreciates you and knows about your merits. But: Even that does not protect you forever and against all impairments.

   What is required of you is sensitivity, putting yourself in the shoes of your superiors and the willingness to keep a low profile so that you don't become a constant nuisance in the eyes of the company.

3. Your superiors will initially show you human sympathy and show an understanding of you and your situation derived from this. After all, they are also men, also over 50 (or will soon be) and also executives. When it's their

turn one day, they want to be treated fairly decently. But: Your bosses are also dependent employees who have to be responsible for the sensible management of the resources entrusted to them in terms of profit optimization. And a classic type of company is not a social office. Many companies are also social, but never primarily. So their bosses have to find a compromise between maximum efficiency of their subordinates, the supervisor's duty of care for each individual employee, the impact of their measures on the public inside and outside the company, etc. This is what they are looking for, this still existing uncertainty appears to you as ambivalence. In addition: For cases like yours, there is no predefined scheme, here you have to approach a halfway satisfactory individual solution.

It is particularly problematic that there is no clear medical prognosis for you. Nobody knows exactly what burdens you can bear, if and when the next heart attack will come and what will happen afterwards. Counterexample:

a complicated (mechanical) broken leg. There are mostly forecasts with x weeks in hospital and y months of rehab until complete recovery.

So your bosses don't have it easy either; they would have as the most important basislike planning security – which cannot exist here. In any case, they expect help: from you; You are the problem, the solution should come from you. And there are three more aspects that you have to see - and that will also influence the perspective of your bosses in the long run:

a. There is no evidence that your heart attack was due to any special operationalor even overload. Malibu beach retirees get it too, some people seem more susceptible than others.

b. In principle, the performance of an employee in the past is compensated with the salary of yesterday and the day before yesterday. Practically all that counts for his future in the company is the value he will have in this one.

c. Let me remind you that there is no justice in our professional system – there is no justice in the product markets either. The system is not unfair either, it simply cannot do anything with the demand for justice.

4. So you should come up with a solution that you can live with (you can't get out of this situation without paying a price), that you believe could be acceptable to your bosses and that it could "work" objectively. Don't give priority to your employees again, you no longer have the strength to protect them from unwanted changes.
This proposal needs to reduce your commitment, relieve your stress, serve the company (by keeping your skills and experience alive and valuable). Loss of power, influence, hierarchy and money included. Make it clear that you want to continue working and get involved, that you are allowed to do this within the proposed framework, that you do not want to unilaterally burden the company with the risk you are currently facing, and that you know that the matter is also extremely difficult for the company and your bosses. Give up a larger part of your previous position. Stop worrying about whether they would like to get rid of you. Remember point 1, which says: Be selfish too. But make it quick We are not that terribly far apart when it comes to concrete

solution strategies. I - IV are out of the question for both of us. I plead for a tightened V., but without the core idea of "retaining the old area of activity". This will not work. Suggest splitting the department or giving it to another leader, or reverting to leadership of group X yourself, or remaining department leader but giving group Y to a colleague or reporting directly to your boss. You will have to accept a financial sacrifice for the additional costs presumably associated with this. Surviving is more important than making as much money as possible.

2.3.5.4 Correct, but "dead" or a scammer with a job?

Ask

In my professional life there is an incident that I am responsible for, his
telling the truth would cost me my job and ruin any job opportunity. I managed to prepare the documents in such a way that this is not recognizable. Now I have a boss who trusts me and therefore shames me. I would like to tell him the truth.

Answer

If your boss is owner and so sovereign, a confession maybe
make sense, it remains dangerous. However, he isEmployee, he has to answer "above". He can't just carry on with the knowledge, he needs to get his back up and "take your case" to his bosses - which might mean your end there. Otherwise he jeopardizes his career. I give you about a 30-40% "chance of survival" with a boss, but not really with a salaried employee – or he has to resign in order not to become disloyal. Don't do this to him. I don't have a better solution. Accept your moral burden as part of a deserved punishment.

2.3.5.5 Where are the young men in the women's quota?

Ask

In my opinion, the topic is highly explosive, especially for young engineers with career aspirations: the preferential treatment of women in managerial positions required by the state. The sword of Damocles of a women's quota not only for supervisory board positions threatens to fall on us at any time; especially when the economy isn't picking up.

The following section was copied fromhttp://m.faz.net/aktuell/wirt-	schaft/people-economy/women's-quota-louder-lost-men-11771952. html; Article drawn with Bettina Weiguny.
The quote from Dr. Zetsche sums it up:
"What makes alpha girls and women advocates happy slows down a generation of young men: those between the early 30s and 45s. Suddenly everything has to happen at lightning speed. Faster than at all possible, as Daimler boss Dieter Zetsche criticizes. His dilemma: 'Where should I sort all the men? Force everyone to retire so there are enough vacancies?'

No, the old gentlemen don't have to worry about their jobs. The newcomers have to pay for the men-only mentality that has been practiced for decades. 'When in doubt, go for the woman' is the top priority in human resources policy, it may also officially mean: 'When in doubt, only by qualification.'" (End of quote).

My experience is that in recent years, women have been increasingly favored and men discriminated against. It is not performance that counts, but gender; at Daimler AG, where I worked for 20 years and also at

universities, e.g. B. when appointing professors in STEM subjects (there are – at least at my university – internal quotas for women).
signed Prof. Dr.-Ing. ...

Answer

First of all, every quota is inevitably associated with injustice, there is no other way. It's safe to assume that the EU folks who started this knew that. So the injustice towards men that can now be observed is intentional or is consciously accepted. It is unthinkable that this effect surprised people at EU or national level. Anyone who wants more women somewhere "up there" and does not drastically increase the number of corresponding positions by decree wants fewer men - a truism.

It's like having a big hole in the middle of the lawn in your own garden, but no soil reserves at hand. So you take away earth somewhere else, dig a new hole there - and fill in the old one with it. You didn't win much overall, you just exchanged one hole for another. Children experience this in sandbox games, only supposed justice fanatics and do-gooders feel better about it.

It would be a bit polemical, but not wrong in the matter at all

Calling a "promotion quota for women" a "reduction quota for men". Because you can't have one without the other. What was primarily wanted is not decisive – what "comes out at the end" is ultimately what matters.

Also, an injustice that has existed up to now will not be compensated for by any reversal of the circumstances. The previously existing without a doubt Dominance of men in the management area of certain institutions and companies - by no means everywhere, from our government down there are numerous organizations firmly in women's hands - was based exclusively on tradition, usual behavior, "automatic" continuation of the organization in a "proven way" (permanence) , conservative thinking and an aversion to change that is often pronounced in people. But before women were promoted, there was no valid law that would have preferred men, and certainly no quota for men.

Compared to the "mixed situation" that has led to the dominance of men in those positions, the preference for women now decreed from above is, within a certain framework, quite a big "club".

I think it's totally inappropriate. In a free, fully democratic society, there is no need to artificially encourage a group that accounts for pretty much exactly 50% of the electorate - such a group can fend for itself if it wants to. With our chancellor it also worked "without", we almost got a female federal president.

With a group as large as that of women, the following applies: quality, combined with the will to power, prevails even without a populist quota – as long as both of the above conditions are met.

Why do I think the quota (like any other of this kind) is absolutely wrong? Because it can be an instrument that saws the branch on which we are all sitting: We do not live from our raw materials or other undeserved resources that have come into our power, we live exclusively from the abilities of our people – that applies to every individual place in those institutions that support the state, if only because they feed and clothe the people of the state. And in each of those places goes the best candidate money can buy. If you are subject to a quota, this can no longer be guaranteed in theory, certainly not in practice. Every woman who gets promoted just because of the quota – and there will

be one – is just as bad as a quota woman in the Chancellery or a quota man at the head of a corporation would be. The best – admittedly only imperfectly to be determined – must be placed in the relevant places, not those who meet a quota. I consider this principle to be indispensable.

If those best in a case are women, then put women there. About 80% as far as I'm concerned. But if better men should offer themselves, then kindly take them.

I see no point in the question of whether women could generally be better managers or, for example, university professors. Whoever can do it best should become it.

I am for women, if necessary even in double at the head of state. I've worked with absolutely convincing managing directors and with outstanding clerks. I know overwhelmed company heirs on the one hand and men who work happily under female bosses on the other. Of course, I also know women who are very committed to emphasizing: "Whatever you want, but never again under a woman." All this is also possible with men.

And I am in favor of promoting possible talents that have not yet been discovered or have not made a breakthrough: promote mathematics classes for girls, promote women's studies in subjects that lead to management (no, pedagogy is more like it not), encourages companies that offer working conditions that meet the needs of mothers and those that offer management courses for women (if that makes sense).

And if a CEO has to appoint a person to the board: If he wants the best, and this is a woman and his male board colleagues should grumble, then he has to assert himself.

But stop interfering with the structures of one of the most successful industrial countries in the world with primitive instruments such as quotas - neither for women nor for people of a certain descent, race, homeland and origin, belief, religious or political belief. This enumeration corresponds almost exactly to that in Art. 3, Paragraph 3 of the Basic Law. It says who is not allowed to be "disadvantaged or preferred". But every quota does that, there is no shaking it.

I'm still missing two aspects that I wouldn't want to forego addressing:

1. The previous male dominance in management and in other senior positions is not only due to male defensiveness, but also to widespread female disinterest. We are primarily talking to and from engineers here. There are now many female graduates of this subject, as well as corresponding clerks in companies in almost all operational areas. But if, for example, we advertise a "Design Manager (m/f)" or a "Parts Production Manager (m/f)" or a technical team, group or project leader, then there are either no female applicants at all or there are only a proportion of them is in the meager single-digit percentage range. Where, if you please, is there an injustice that must be eliminated by quota?

The women also have to want it, there is no other way. Of course, you also have to give them the opportunity through women-friendly working conditions en, I have already commented on this above. But a "club" is the wrong measure.

Before the quota was introduced, did anyone even ask women whether they now wanted to flock to the career paths that were open to them? Does such a banality even interest you?

2. So what does this mean for the young men? It is inevitable that there will certainly be massive new injustices in the attempt to eliminate alleged previous injustices.

If a corporation decides (or has already decided) to introduce a women's quota in management, then in twenty years' time the consequences will only be manageable: the quota has been achieved, may even have already been surpassed, may even be the result of the corresponding practice outdated, has fallen into oblivion or – may God grant them their wits – been abolished again. But: Every student already knows what to expect, every career starter knows it, every climber with practical experience knows it too.

Once the quota has been met, every new appointment to a management position is again a largely open race. Since one day there will be enough women in the company where the quota wants them to be, there is an opportunity for each individual appointment to actually select "the best" (who can be a man or a woman). If it is a man in construction and a woman in marketing at the same time, then the quota is right again. Or the other way around.

Certainly, the wind will blow harder for the young men, and the number of promotion positions will be fewer. But you can adapt to that. Those men will fall by the wayside, for whom one does not know today what their qualification actually consists of - some of them will be replaced by those women, for whom one does not know what actually...

But the real male top executives don't let that get them down. The competition is tougher – so what? The "per capita qualification" of male managers should actually increase, but some average climbers may fall by the wayside. This does little harm to the economy.

But that relates to the situation in twenty years. However, what is true

"today", i.e. when the quota was introduced? That will be a "blow in the office" for the young hopefuls who started under different conditions, one has to assume that. Life plans are destroyed, hope Gen disappointed, profound frustration justified. And those affected were blameless and have no chance.

External applications? In the case of corporations of the same type and size that also have the quota, it's pretty hopeless. Striving more towards the non-quota middle class would be a way out that not everyone wants to take and not everyone can take because of wrong talent. And medium-sized companies don't have more jobs to offer than before, just because corporations promote according to quotas.

If it's any consolation: Every far-reaching change "burns up" large parts of an entire generation. This has often been the case – from the French Revolution to the fall of communism in the former GDR; sometimes it hit the people of nobility, most recently the system-compliant leadership elite. By which I don't want to say more than is stated here, I didn't intend to make any more extensive comparisons. But as the saying goes: where there is planing, there are shavings. In my opinion, which is irrelevant in this case, the quota goes beyond Section 3 of the Basic Law. It says in paragraph 2: "The state promotes the actual assertion of women and men and works towards the elimination of existing disadvantages." I consider the quota to be an instinctless coercive measure that goes far beyond this goal.

"Promotion" is required, not the exercise of coercion, as was the case with the supervisory board quota.

What remains for us: to see in twenty years what has come out of it. And always fighting for the best principle. Regardless of gender, descent, race etc. etc.

2.3.5.6 Take over dad's company directly?

Ask

I am currently studying mechanical engineering at the university in ..., but I will
need about two more semesters for the bachelor's degree due to initial problems with math and because of a special student commitment.

My father is the managing director and shareholder of a medium-sized automotive supplier, the company is doing very well at the moment. The company was not affected by the economic crisis and already has orders from well-known automobile manufacturers and important large suppliers for the next few years.
According to my father's ideas, I should take over the company immediately after my studies so that he can withdraw and retire after he has trained me. Since he doesn't like to close the company just like that wants me to make a relatively quick decision on this matter so that there is still time to find an alternative if necessary.

Personally, I am very undecided as to whether it is a good idea to move up into management directly after graduation without much professional experience. On the other hand, it would be a unique opportunity for me and my career. I know that I definitely want to be in management one day and have already learned a lot during the holidays in my father's company.

But right after graduation? What if I fail? I have often read from you that it is difficult to find a new position as a failed CEO.

Answer

The temptation has come up to you - and at least you have noticed that it is one. Temptations are characterized by the fact that they include an offer that appears extremely attractive, for which either an equally high price has to be paid or for which a particularly great risk has to be accepted.

I don't know what your father's arguments are for making this push now (his age, health, other interests), so let's focus on your side of the matter:

1. The management of a manufacturing industrial company in the tough business environment of the automotive industry is not a job for a young professional and someone in their early twenties, even after the induction by the previous owner.
The probability is extremely high that you would be overwhelmed and ultimately drive the company against the wall.
There are three additional aspects to consider:

a. The customers, who represent the largest and most important asset of such a company, look for the certainty that their requirements will always and reliably be met when the managerial position is filled. After all, supplying your production lines with the appropriate parts and assemblies would depend on you personally. They would not place this trust in you in the years to come. As a rule of thumb: not before the new boss is at least(!) 30 years old. That alone would take well over five years.
As the boss at the head of a medium-sized company of this type, you are just as challenged as a production and development technician as a businessman in accounting and tax issues and as a buyer in negotiations with

suppliers. Of course you would have employees in all these areas, but the final decision would always remain yours. And it's easy to imagine how banks would react to you if you needed a loan. The requirements for your qualifications would be high, the status of heir alone is not enough.

b. Rules have been developed for the advancement of young people in "foreign" companies: They work for a few years at the executive level, then increasingly take on responsibility and personnel management. Around the age of 38, one finds among them the first department managers or even managing directors. Increasing personal maturity, knowledge and experience as well as increasing performance are roughly balanced. This path of advancement should also be the general guideline in the family-owned company, whereby the path to the top may well be about a step steeper and faster than it would be outside (there is less resistance if everyone is aware that the future boss is growing up here; he can against the background of his special position risk a little more than foreign managers,

2. Should you for any reasonafter a failure one day want or have to appear as an applicant on the job market (both are conceivable), then the following applies:

a. It is almost like "life insurance" if you have worked successfully externally for a number of years and received very good reviews as an employee before joining the family-owned company. Then you returned to your old professional home in that emergency, but without this basis you would be entering completely new territory.

b. Your entire "career" in the family-owned company, your

advancement there, the references you are given - none of it would have any value "outside". It is well known that "blood is thicker than water", so that quite incompetent heirs have "proceeded" in companies of this kind. And: Anyone who decides later on your possible external application had to work it out themselves, there was no "pre-warmed executive chair" after graduation. You can accuse him of envy, but that doesn't change the intensity of his rejection.

c.

3. It would be good for your personality development as well as for your professional qualifications to have worked and learned in a different company. Your own company will also benefit from this. It is useful,
to gain such experience in the right industry, the employer should be larger than the company to be managed later.

4. The takeover of an existing, well-established company owned by one's own family is basically a "road of no return". If everything goes well, you have had a unique chance in life and successfully realized it. If things go wrong, the later solution is not simply a change to comparable positions as an employee. Then it's better if you have a little fortune left over and build up something new in the self-employed area or you withdraw into private life, depending on the duration of the "experiment" and the size of the final catastrophe. In one case you "played and won", in the other "played and lost".

5. As an exception, i.e. in special circumstances, the period of professional activity with a lot of learning and

experience before being promoted to management is also conceivable in the family-owned company. But: You don't recognize your limits when everyone knows that this is the owner's son and future boss; you only learn what is already known in the company, you don't bring any new impulses with you later, the company "cooks in its own juice" in the long term (which always applies if only your own employees are promoted and new managers never come from outside) . And if one day things went wrong, the concerns from 2a and 2b will have full effect.

6. Without knowing the situation in your family business, here is the general recommendation:

a. You start in a larger, well-known automotive company, stay there for at least three, better five years, try to work in as many and varied areas of activity as possible and strive to rise as high as possible and with a very good assessment (certificate as "life insurance ") to leave. Only then will you join your father's company, provided that it still exists.

b. Your father bridges these years by either staying there longer than intended or by hiring an interim manager who will run the company for the next few years, who will keep the successor open to you and who will be available for your induction. Or he sells and leaves you the corresponding fortune. With this behind you, your future employment will either be much more fun or you can build your own independent existence.

As a final general warning: For ambitious young people, having their own father often seems to be a fundamental problem. It won't get any easier if this father also becomes the boss. And: Never trust an owner who says he will retire.

Ultimately, he will not do it - so in any case, clear agreements must be made in writing.

Ask   2.3.5.7   How do promotions work?

Of course, since I never received a professional promotion as a student, I have no experience of how promotions are decided and carried out. Are there common processes or patterns in professional practice according to which employees are promoted?

Does the head of department stand in front of the astonished clerk one day and solemnly announce that he is now the group leader? Or, for example, in large corporations, is each individual advancement promoted by an internal job advertisement?

Answer

Students are not promoted, and as a rule, young professionals are not either. First the exam, then the start in practice, then at least three, probably five years of work - during this whole time practically nothing happens in terms of the question. Except that you will become more and more familiar with the system, gain experience, observe all possible personnel decisions around you, have heated discussions with your colleagues – and constantly expand your knowledge about it. And just before you get promoted for the first time - stop asking that question. You then only wait for positive news about your first ascent, but no longer ask how something like that works. I guarantee you, count on it.

On the other hand: Is this explanation satisfactory for the sender of a question that appears to be justified?

Probably not. So some additional information:

There areThere is no uniform system in the German economy according to which employees are promoted. Some corporations have one. There you have to B. first be accepted into a "sponsorship group" before you even get a chance. This special offspring is often systematically trained "on the side". There are often meaningful personnel appraisals with detailed criticism discussions in which one learns something about one's basic chances.

Sometimes companies plan the long-term succession of a manager and consistently develop an employee for this purpose. In the course of sudden structural changes or e.g. when a superior dies, for example, a spontaneous solution often has to be found. However, three iron rules always apply:

1. No company promotes an employee simply because they deserve it, are qualified or even "it's up". There must always be an internal need, e.g. B. a vacant group leader position. That means: Coincidence plays a major role. And: The companies primarily use promotions to solve their problems ("fill the gaps") and less so those of their employees ("I am so longingly waiting for it").

2. A mandatory basic requirement is what the supervisor thinks is first-class, committed, above-average performance in the current job (i.e. before promotion). And that for a few years.

3. If you want to become a group leader, you have to spend a long timeThink, act and act like one for a long time. In his current job, he has to show "potential" for promotion to the next level. Sometimes there are

separate test systems (assessment centers) for this aspect. Attention: "Promote me first, then I'll do better", that doesn't work.

And then, just as an aside, there are also "promotion prevention constellations": It may be that a department has five highly qualified top clerks, each of whom could become a group leader, but no one will. "They are so equal and at the same time jealous – if I promote one, the other four will quit. I don't risk that, so someone comes from outside," says the head of department.

This applicant "from outside" is often more important than your own employees. We also know the weaknesses of the latter, but not of the external candidates. The same applies: If you are "mature" for a promotion but nothing is happening internally, you must make an effort externally – in your own best interests.

So it is a wide field that lies before you here. But after a few years of work, you will "internalize" everything that is written here. And maybe a little more.

2.3.5.8   demoted

Ask

I completed my FH degree at the age of 27 on the second educational path
closed and developed through a few professional positions from project manager to department manager. In this capacity I have more than five years with my current employer. I knew my boss at the time from a previous job.

This boss retired after a few years of good cooperation. The manager, with whom I had little to do, changed the organization. He created the position of Senior Division Manager with extensive responsibility for multiple departments. This position was filled externally by a candidate who was known to the managing director and to me from working together. This department manager made it a condition that he was given direct technical and personnel management of my department. I was relieved of managerial responsibility and the managing director asked me to stay.

The new department head explained to me that he could not rely on me and that he expected me to look for a managerial position in another company. And he doesn't expect that we would become "close friends". That's about three years ago now. i'm still there

How do I explain this in an interviewChange plausible? Like the long time I've been holding out? Can I (curriculum vitae attached) change the company again?

Due to our house I am local. During the last crisis, I

couldn't find a management position within a 100 km radius. In the meantime, I might be willing to take a room at a new job.

Answer

It starts very simply:

1. A person with a degree who wants to work in a demanding manner over the long term should be ready to move.
2. A person with a degree who wants to build up a successful management career and keep it permanently (!) must be willing to move, real estate must not stand in the way of this.
3. In the case of possible conflicts between professional and private aspects, it hardly ever pays off to put professional matters aside in favor of private ones:
   "Early man was a hunter-gatherer." Reading this "occupational" definition in that way, does it trigger any particular reactions, such as amazement? It doesn't. At most, a theoretically conceivable alternative definition would amaze: "The early man conquered a cave, which he defended tooth and claw and never gave up.
   Moved the herds of mammothsleft that area, he accepted the painstaking task of chasing rabbits and birds and being barely able to feed the family." Do you read something like that as a definition of this type of person? No, rather not.
   Amazing insight: We define people through their "professional" activities (hunters and gatherers), not through their private lives. We still classify today: "Mr. Müller is a forester." Not something like: "Mr. Müller

owns an apartment."

4. What your new division head told you at the time was a clear invitation to leave. This request was factually correct

– nobody likes to have a degraded ex-head of department under them as an employee. The basic rule here is: those who are demoted should change externally, as quickly as possible.

5. As your curriculum vitae shows, you endured this demotion for almost three years. That was way too long. Now you have two dilemmas to choose from:

a. You explain that you have been dealing intensively for three yearsapplied for a managerial position, but nobody would have taken you. That would be bad.

b. You say it took you almost three years to realize that you didn't like the demotion and you're only now applying. That would be bad too.

6. I can't think of a really convincing reason for accepting this "negative promotion" either – the time that has elapsed is simply too long. One will conclude from this that wanting to lead the "flame" and being able to do so does not burn hot enough in you. Even the manager responsible for the removal will have had something in mind about not letting you have this responsibility any longer (the fact that he asked you to stay means nothing). And even your new boss, who somehow knew you before he joined, didn't want you as a subordinate and preferred to manage your former employees himself. All of this condenses into an opinion that makes the success of an application for a management position made today less likely.

7. My advice: you should leave the company. The new job

should preferably be sought at the level of your current job (the three years in which you have already worked without managerial responsibility are good for this). And then you have to convince the new employer with your performance and hope for internal opportunities. In today's company, where everyone knows your destiny, you no longer have any prospects.

2.3.5.9 Manager, 50, unemployed, seeks...

Ask

As an F! fan (it means "Formula 1", as I found out with difficulty; H. Mell) and one of your fans, you are the "Niki Lauda" of career advice for me. i.e. They show competence, experience and clarity in assessing the letters or the questions, problems or situations described in them, which is very rare to find.

From the "bottom up" I got my start as an engineer via the 2nd educational path.nieur (process engineering, FH) in plant construction. It was an arduous journey to be the first from a working-class family to suddenly go to university. For ten years, I worked as a project engineer and project manager for various companies, planning and realizing plants with a focus on environmental technology for customers. Until the market collapsed in 2000 and was no longer attractive to me.

That's why I switched to facility management at a German company of an American group (2000-2005). I had a tough school to go through, but I learned a lot, for which I am very grateful.

I would have liked to have done my third job until the end of my working life. I was manager of technical services in the subsidiary of an international group, responsible for the supply and disposal of a site.

Well, unfortunately, my superior changed to another company because the highest boss had a management behavior "like the ax in the forest". I managed to "dive under" for almost a year after that just to avoid getting caught in the line of fire. But in the end, things turned out as my superior had predicted: I had to sign a termination agreement after four years of employment.

It took me a long time to get over this loss. Because I had filled this job – and this one had filled me. I had been (or we as a family were) happy.

Through my personal contacts I managed to get a new (fourth) position with a seamless connection:

As a specialist and leader, I was supposed to build up the business area of technical building management. The commercial success, for which I could not be responsible after a few months, was unsatisfactory. This and the way in which I implemented my diverse tasks and how the GF perceived it led to my dismissal in due time after almost a year of service.

A conceivable alternative solution at a large corporation fell through, so that I am now looking for a job for the first time.

Despite intensive application activity(50 pieces), research, contacts and discussions, the success has not been satisfactory so far. So at the moment I'm only there with a specific offer of a six-month job at half the previous salary.

My outplacement consultant has shown a tendency not to accept this position, but to use the time to find an adequate position with all his might. My wife shares this opinion.

I, on the other hand, would like to go back to work because it is good for me and I long for it. In addition, there will hopefully be vacancies over time that I could also accept from this temporary position. What do you advise me?

Answer

According to the description in
Outline credentials as "Management position in maintenance/maintenance/asset availability" with more than 10 subordinate employees.

This certificate says: "... he mastered his field of work with confidence", "he did his job... justice", "... he always completed the tasks assigned to him to our complete satisfaction". And then it says – in a different wording – "We fired him". Without pretended concrete reasons, without any regrets or an attempt to relieve this employee.

As a side note and mentioned with great reluctance: The last sentence says "We wish him for his private and professional future...". According to an unconfirmed(!) rumor that is circulating in our profession, the conspicuous, because factually incorrect preference of the private over the professional side has an indicative character (problems in the private/personal area). But this is unproven, the enumeration order can also be random. Only: If it were written in a certificate with "resignation at one's own request", "always to our complete satisfaction" and "to our extraordinary regret", one would shrug one's shoulders. Here, however, one is looking for an explanation for the sudden involuntary departure which the employer does not even regret.

So it's 2005 - and things aren't looking so good for you. The opportunity for you: In the applications at that time, this certificate does not play a role, you get the next job without having to or being able to present this document.

, The development in the third company is actually an extremely fatal repetition of the development in the previous employer. But here your memory is fooling you: the problem doesn't even exist! At least not according to the all-important "files". You will be given a certificate of a comfortable length confirming that you are leaving at your own request. one does not regret this, but thanks for the always very good and productive cooperation. And you are granted the rating "always to our complete satisfaction", which corresponds to the "school mark" being very good. And your CV shows a new job the day after you leave, so it doesn't arouse any suspicions.

Contrary to what you describe, this is the positive highlight of your entire career without any problem(!). Unless you "invent" one.

So you have to sell this phase as the "files" say: successful, great, super, everything is fine. You left voluntarily – not even conspicuously early – because your boss had left and there was a risk of restructuring with incalculable risks. But of course that was long before any kind of trouble came your way or could have come your way. "As the law commanded." (Freely based on Schiller's translation of the commemorative distich for the fallen soldiers at Thermopylae).

If you let any difficulties shine through in the oral or written part of the application process with regard to this employment relationship, this is "suicidal" because it is unnecessary.

It's 2009 now - and things are looking a lot better again.

Most recently (No. 4) you were responsible for maintenance and modification work as well as for the costs of the systems in the area of supply and disposal for a building service provider. Despite the short period of service, the corresponding reference is pleasantly long, which has a positive effect.

The main statements are consistently "good", the overall rating "always to our full satisfaction" is on this level. At the end is the

"Naked" dismissal for operational reasons, at least with express thanks for the "productive cooperation", leaving is "very regretted" (this is logically questionable, but one recognizes the good will to say something nice).

Here the not so bad overall assessment is "eaten up" by the short period of service with dismissal from the employer, the impression from the assessment does not match the extremely negative facts.

a. You write to this on your emailNewspaper, which, according to the broadcast log, was published on May 19th. J., "A-town, March 19," and then enclose your case description, which you also date March 19. After putting a lot of effort into "unraveling" this puzzle, I simply believe that you are confusing March with May twice in the same process. It was all about me here, but if you do the same thing in day-to-day business or when applying for jobs, that's very questionable!

b. The "real facts" of your case are: 50 years, first worked in specialty X, then switched to Y. Since then had three jobs, all of which had been "resigned" at the employer's request, today unemployed. This combination is fatal to hopeless!

c. The "sellable facts" are better: 50 years remain, as does the change of subject. For the first involuntary departure since then you would have to
– only for the interview, don't go into it in the written application – find a factual explanation, which of course must not have anything to do with you personally. It wasn't you who were actively dismissed, the position was eliminated during restructuring – and you were superfluous through no fault of your own.
There was never any trouble with the second employer! Make use of what the certificate certifies: all very well, left at your own request. You were fine, you are on the tender for the
3. Employers who suggested to you that things could be even better there. Your mistake, you should have stayed with #2. Unfortunately, the job there is now occupied by someone else.
The third catastrophe is officially the only one. This company, which has a completely different structure, started from assumptions that unfortunately turned out to be unrealistic. Your mistake, you should have recognized that (or realized that you couldn't tell from the outside).
Then accept the fixed-term contract. Because everything is better than nothing. Unemployed is nothing. end of discussion. And: Continuation of the application process alongside the new temporary job with all my might.
You must then make sure that you argue in exactly the same way in the interview: at the first company you were the innocent victim of a structural corporate decision in faraway America, at the second

everything(!) was great, at the third you didn't realize that the expectations were unfulfillable, your mistake . And you accepted the fixed-term contract because you had hopes of permanent employment. Now that you're there, you see it's unlikely to come to anything. So have to You are looking externally again. And of course you have to be ready to move anywhere in Germany!

d.

2.3.5.10 There is no easy way back
2.3.5.11

I have been the head of purchasing in a company for over fifteen years. I was now offered the opportunity to change to international key account management internally in order to take care of sales for large customers. But then there is no internal way back to purchasing.

Would it be viewed negatively if, after a certain period of time, I found that key account management is not the area in which I find satisfaction and I would like to switch back to external procurement?

There are internalAreas that appear to have similar requirements, where a change seems logical, but in which completely different personality types are required (example: production/maintenance, purchasing/sales, development/sales).

1. When you switch from one area to the other after three to five years, there is a certain logic to it. After fifteen years, she hasn't. You've either been a second-rate buyer for fifteen years whose true talent is in sales, or it's just a crazy idea.

2. Anyone who makes you an offer to switchwants to solve one of his problems, not yours.

3. Today you have managerial responsibility, but not as a key account manager. You only do something like that if you show: I don't want to and can't lead at all.

4. Do not do it. If you are "in the mood for something new", then it is better to apply externally for a position as purchasing manager with more purchasing volume, more employees and a higher salary.

5. If you still want to become a key accounter and later want to go back to external purchasing, you have a chance (no guarantee!) if
   - no more than about one to two years have passed,
   - You state that you responded to an urgent request from your management at the time to help the company in sales in a problem situation (the crazy idea was not yours),
   - You apply for a purchasing position that is exactly the same as what you are today (so you cannot make any progress compared to today).

2.3.5.12   Risks at 50

Ask

I'm concerned with the extent to which people over 50 still support the American
"Hire and fire mentality" is appropriate.

As Vice President (how do you actually translate that into German: head of department?) I've arrived at a level where there are relatively few further career steps to choose from. I would describe my job as fairly secure and my performance as good to very good. My employer is very strongly focused on shareholder value. As a consequence, this leads to a policy of "hire and fire". Layoffs are the order of the day, especially in times of economic challenges.

I'll be 50 in a few years. Even if I don't feel that "old", I remember your recommendation that by the time you're 50 you've reached the position that you can hold on to until you retire if you have to.

Should I be very actively looking for a new challenge externally in the near future so that I can get into a new position while I'm still under 50? Or should I put up with my current employer so that if I am laid off in a few (hopefully only five to ten) years, I can bridge the time until I retire with a severance payment?

Answer

You underscore what I said earlier if you don't know how to describe your current position in the local job market, which would be yours if the worst came to the worst. This is exactly one of the problems when someone sees a single employer as "my world" - and he no longer knows any of the other worlds.

I can't definitively answer your question about the translation of the term VP either, in the end you would have to take care of it. Simply writing "VP" in an application would be very critical, because you then surrender yourself to what the respective applicant thinks: Presenting your qualifications in such a way that the reader of the application can do something with them is an "obligation" on your part .

Even those who are not familiar with American conditions know about the President of the USA. He has a single second man, the vice president. Our observer might imagine the VP of your company to be something like this. If this is not correct, you should write something like this (on your CV):

"Management of the area ... in theRegion ...with sales of ..., (internal rank Vice President - a designation applied group-wide to managers of the
...th and ...th management level is assigned)."

You would have to check this and, if necessary, reformulate it in a way that suits your company. Caution: It is not in your interests if the reader suspects more than is actually true; suspected overqualification is just as harmful as the opposite.

Regarding your key question: I don't think that in your particular situation you should be advised to switch across the board:

a. When changing, you should only change the type of company if you didn't get along well with the previous one. This is absolutely not the case with you. So you should aim for a company like yours today - and you would be exposed to the same dangers there, only you would have a much shorter service life. So they would get worse.

b. Any move can go wrong, and that's always to be expected. If you were then affected by it, it would hit you at the age of 50 or more. Consider this: besides everything else, you might simply not like it with your new employer, e.g. B. in terms of area of responsibility or competencies. This is not a threat at all with the current employer.

Conclusion: According to the "principle of the lesser evil" this would mean staying with you.

A general rule also fits your question, which can be well illustrated with this example:

Professional life is combat: with occasional battles, frequent skirmishes and frequent small one-on-one skirmishes. First you fight to become something and then later (say, from the age of 50) to secure what you have achieved. But: There are always "soldiers" who survive a complete "world war" without ever firing or even hearing a live shot. You just don't know in advance whether you'll belong to this group or that group.

2.3.5.13   Alone against many

Ask

I work for a manageable, economically very(!) successful
medium-sized companies (high return on sales). However, there is a massive corruption problem: A technical manager sells production waste from valuable metals to a special scrap metal dealer on his own account.

Several thousand euros per month flow into the pocket of the relevant manager. A larger group of employees from this department who are aware of this practice are financially involved with smaller amounts. Another group of employees knows about this practice but does not accept any money. Through more or less clear blackmailing of the manager concerned, these employees enjoy all the freedom, productivity is poor as a result.

In addition, that executive has special products made in the company that she sells privately. Management is clueless, although one might be suspicious of that executive's circumstances - hobbies, vacations, cars. I learned about this practice without the knowledge of the perpetrator. So now the question: what to do?

I don't want to just stand still and do nothing, that goes against my work ethic and my sense of justice. I could rat out the manager anonymously or openly – both have their own pitfalls. I don't want to leave, I like it here. I also find it illogical that I should leave when someone else is cheating.

To make it short: The man has to go (although I am

aware that his entire existence is at stake as a result). How would you solve this problem?

A remark in advance: The existence of a criminal does not exist because of the
cover his act at stake, but because ofindeed! It is not the policeman who "catches" him who has to worry that the poor person will be severely punished, but the perpetrator himself should have had such thoughts beforehand. But that's only marginally.

Now we're doing something unexpected, we're looking at the story from the point of view of the management, which - by whatever means - just officially found out about the scams. There are two prerequisites for this: an initial check has substantiated the allegations – and the company is still doing well, "loudly" well.

Five minutes ago, the managing directors were still extremely successful, high-earning (high returns = high GF bonuses) entrepreneurial top managers. Now they are suddenly just "poor pigs" who have a large pile of - e.g. T. hardly solvable - see problems in front of you:

History falls back on them: how did this happen, why didn't anyone from GF notice, why aren't there any systems and controls in place to prevent it? A simple "recyclables accounting" would have It suffices: the weight of the purchased material per unit of time compared to the weight of the parts produced and the officially sold amount of waste.

So: The managing directors get their share of the scandal, trouble or whatever you want to call it. Think

of the attention the case will draw from the public (that's almost gang crime). And the anger of the company owners at the
"incompetent" managing directors - who could also damage their careers because of this matter.

1. So, from the GF's point of view, something has to happen - but what? Possibilities for this:

- The executive concerned must be dismissed immediately without notice, and a report must also be made to the public prosecutor's office.
- That larger group of fellow profiteers (who pocketed the money) should also be dismissed immediately and probably reported as well, otherwise you lose credibility.
- The other group, who knew everything, benefited from it (without accepting money) and who did not report it, should either also be released (perhaps on time), or at least warnings are due here.

That leaves the not entirely unimportant question: And who does the day-to-day work in the house when we have fired or demoralized everyone who deserved it?

Who will then secure our particularly attractive return on sales for the next few months?

I guarantee you: the managing directors will not be really happy once the full extent of the catastrophe is revealed to them. And with all the anger at the scammers, they will hardly find the time or desire to be particularly grateful to the person who uncovered the scandal.

2. Since membership in the various groups mentioned affects practically half the workforce (even if it is because they know it), the management also knows that

the person who uncovered it (ie you) is almost everyone's

"the real culprit"will be viewed. No one will want to work with this man any more, they would have to reckon with being bullied out of the company. Officially, the GF should actually commend him, but that would only fuel the general anger and contempt of the many perpetrators and their friends. In fulfillment of their duty of care towards you, the GF would even have to worry about your physical integrity. One more problem. And if an anonymous complaint had been received, there would only be one topic for everyone in the house: Who was that? A tiny indication is enough and the anger of the people and probably the unwillingness of the management boiled up.

Now let's turn to the classic view of the problem, namely to your options (you know yourself and the people involved, I don't know either of these parties; you have to find your own way):

a. There is a powder keg in your professional environment that can explode at any time and cause a great deal of mischief. You can no longer ignore what is theoretically conceivable.

b. They're up to their necks in the mud. You're going to have to pay a hefty price to get out of there. It won't work without him. You got in there through no fault of your own? Life's answer to such objections is: So what?

c. They are now accomplices, which is also morally reprehensible. You also have a duty of loyalty to your employer. If you're considering doing nothing: If the story one day blows up

– and it will – then everyone will blame everyone. And the management (perhaps also the organs of the judiciary) will meticulously investigate the question who knew about it? If even just one person knows that you "already knew then", you shouldn't be able to sleep peacefully for that reason alone.

d. If you are up to your neck in the mud and want to be rescued, it is unwise to reject individual rescue proposals on principle. Despite your apparent reluctance, I'll bring up the option "leave the company as soon as possible". That may be the smallest price you would have to pay. Also, if everyone involved leaves or gets fired, you won't have much of an uplifting environment.

e. You could speak to the executive concerned, tell them that the story is more widely known than they know, and ask them to either leave the company immediately, or at least to "stop" it immediately. So maybe you could at least reach an end. But you are still covering up the fraud from the past – if the perpetrator is found out later, he will involve you.
So that's not a viable solution either.
And: In every better thriller, the group of perpetrators involved would try to eliminate you for good, no matter what.

3.

f. You could speak to one of the managers privately (perhaps you can visit him at his home without an appointment) and tell him what you know (only since yesterday, of course). Assure him that you know that the matter is huge and could endanger the entire company (if everyone involved is fired). You just wanted to do your duty and let him know. They left it entirely up to him what he would do, if at all. Nobody in the house knew about this conversation, it would stay: that way under all circumstances. You would be able to understand every conceivable reaction of the GF (meaning one according to the following point I). Outlook: There are two other variants that I would like to share with you:

I. It might be the best solution for a very pragmatic GF - to do nothing at all (but which requires information from you after f). The hole is plugged by a process optimization measure that appears to have been introduced by accident ("recyclable material accounting" or similar). In addition, there are general-sounding warnings against fraud to the entire workforce. Money earned has always been good and will continue to be good. The stolen assets are irretrievably lost. If the perpetrators are all jailed or even fired, future returns are at risk. Simply ruling out future recurrences and allowing operations to continue could be the lesser evil. In the medium term, of course, you have to fire the main culprit, for whatever reason ("God forgives, Django never").
"heroes". But in the way that best suits the needs of the company.

II. I experienced this from relatively close by: In a large company it came out that a production manager had simple transport carts built "on the side" at operating costs and sold them privately with great success. After careful consideration of the best way to get hold of the embezzled money, a decision was made: the production manager would start his own business with the production of carts, the company would finance it and receive a share of the proceeds from the sale. The other solution would have been morally brighter but financially a loss.

Did I already say that working life is bestshould be considered a big (Monopoly) game? And there, too, there is a card "Go to prison".

And you cannot expect compliance with high moral standards from a system that is solely geared towards commercial goals.

2.3.5.14   employer holdsPromise of advancement not

Ask

I am a graduate engineer, late 40s, most recently AV Manager with the appropriate

scope. A few years ago, my employer at the time offered me a termination agreement because of economic problems. The managing director had already been fired, many top performers had left the company, I was also looking for a new job and had already made successful contacts.

I accepted the offered termination agreement and signed a new employment contract with my current employer (subsidiary). I managed to make the transition seamless.

The vacancy for my new position was for a managerial position. This was also clearly stated in the first draft of the employment contract, which was handed to me during the second interview.

In the third interview, I was then informed that the managerial function could only be assumed once the area manager had left. Then the current holder of "my" position would take over the management of the department and I would move up accordingly. One year was given as the time frame. In the new contract there was only a note that after one year there would be a "review" with regard to my function as manager.

Several years have now passed. The division head left more than two years after I joined. I worked very closely with him and my line manager. Both have assured me that they appreciate my performance and my commitment and would support my assumption of the management position.

Despite repeatedAt my superiors' efforts, nothing has happened so far. As a division head, my boss is also still the head of his "old" unit, which I was originally supposed to head. As part of this, he has now given me the technical responsibility for this group. The justification for my lack of disciplinary management responsibility is still pending. The division manager had indicated that the former managing director would have shied away from applying for a management position with the superior group unit and wanted to leave this to his successor. The new managing director has been with us for a few months now, and nothing has happened in my matter.

My options:

1. I remain. In principle, I feel very comfortable, the atmosphere is very good, everything is fine, I get on really well with my manager. In the meantime, I have taken on practically all of the technical tasks in the area originally intended for me.

   On the other hand, I have more than ten years of management experience. I often find it difficult to only be able to make suggestions and not have the power to make decisions. This makes me increasingly dissatisfied. The financial aspect also plays a role: in the interview, a significantly higher salary was promised for the management position originally planned. Subsequent applications are also difficult (break in the CV).

2. I'm changing employers. I currently have specific requests. I also see it as a risk that I was only employed by the last two employers for three to four years. Due to

my age, a wrong decision should hardly be correctable. How can I state my motives in applications without the applicant assuming that there is a lack of leadership potential?

I am very pleased about your risk assessment and recommendations for action.

___

Answer

With a person with my range of experience there is always the
drive that he hears "the fleas are coughing" - sometimes even when there are no little beasts of that kind. But here, in my opinion, they cough more than clearly. And so I believe that all the problems that come later go back to the initial situation described above, which sounds so "harmless". Which, of course, was never really harmless, but falls under the warning that has often been quoted here, which reads: "It is precisely the curse of evil deeds that, propagating, they must always give birth to evil" (Schiller, Wallenstein). It simply means: Nothing good can come from a wrong action.

What happened? The old employer had problems, had to cut costs and get rid of staff. He also offered you a contract that would annul your previous employment contract (we don't know whether that was a blanket offer that applied to everyone at the time or whether it was tailored specifically to you). In any case, the company would have been happy to get rid of you and urgently needed your signature on this termination offer. Nobody gives this signature voluntarily, so you have to entice them, "convince" them – whatever. The instrument for this is money, severance pay calls.

Hardly any other employee can get hold of such sums so quickly – and, as he thinks, so easily. Well, if a temptation didn't also seem appealing, it wouldn't be.

So the bait to get your signature was the severance package. And at the same time some pressure was exerted, the means of pressure is called time. Compensation offers are usually limited until ..... The threat is Sign by ..., otherwise we will have to give you notice".

To put it somewhat simply, the poor employee concerned is under pressure to find the "dream position of his life" externally within a short time on the labor market, for which such a change is really worthwhile. However, time pressure of any kind is "deadly" for this search, that is known.

And so you usually have your severance pay, but the thing with the dream position goes wrong.

It is strange that anyone who has no prospect of a subsequent position when they sign the termination agreement risks unemployment, but at least they know exactly what they are doing. However, anyone who has the prospect of a second or third-rate position looks at it through the rose-colored glasses of the severance payment, finds "the bride is more beautiful than feared" – and strikes. Then there he is. The third interview with your current employer was the time when you should have politely said goodbye to this company. But then there would probably have been difficulties with the severance payment that beckoned when the termination agreement was signed.

You were manager at the old employer, and had been at the previous one. Now the only option was a new position as manager. Even the possible "guarantee" that this would only happen after a year would have been unacceptable. The contract passage with the "review" (absolutely without guarantee) was a disaster. The combination of "We advertise a management position and state in the contract that it isn't one, but that we want to check after a year without obligation whether it might ever become one" is nothing but a request to"

withdraw the application - because who does that signing on the basis of your previous career disqualifies yourself.

I don't want to be misunderstood: I am far from criticizing you for your actions - what would I gain from it. In keeping with the aim of the series, I want to deter potential imitators.

Whatever "good" reasons you may have taken to accept this offer, which had deteriorated significantly in the course of the talks: there you were, the severance payment from your old employer in your pocket, but one delivered to the new company with a highly uncertain future (the contract was also limited!).

I must confront you with some serious circumstantial evidence (but not proof, as the term suggests):

a. Your two previous employers were solid medium-sized companies, your current company is a – albeit very small – subsidiary of a group. In principle, it is conceivable that you were qualified to be a manager by the standards of a medium-sized company, but not by those of the group. There is!

b. The company people noticed this during the application process, during which you were downgraded accordingly between the second and third interview. As a "dyed-in-the-wool" manager, you should never have accepted that, only incidentally – because you could clearly see how people assessed you in this regard.

c. Then they got to know you in the course of your work –

apart from the presentation of new "plum-soft" excuses, nothing happened. It all smells like heaven! The transfer of technical responsibility for

"Your" group, which the supervisor continues to lead disciplinaryly, underscores the assessment of you: technically competent + efficient, but probably too weak for disciplinary leadership. This group assessment sounds definitive and leaves little room for doubt.

d. As you approach an important age limit, I assume that if you stay, you stay what you are. As a consequence of your own mistakes. Because you don't go from a medium-sized company to a group at an advanced age - and then also overlook the "bang" warning signals in the contract negotiations.
With a little willingness to put a little personal effort into it, you might even be able to accept it all and become reasonably happy.

e. A change would only go back to the middle class. There you can then grumble vigorously about the "impossible group operation": First you were "lured" with an advert for a nice managerial position, then you were told that the actual task could only be taken on as part of a successor that was due in a year. Because of the "big name" of this company, you accepted the verbal promises. Then the succession was postponed for months, then for years. Again and again new promises, reassurances ("You are so great, you are our man"). Then you were admitted that the old manager didn't want to lose the savings effect that lay in your boss's dual function, so you were waiting for the new manager. He's here now, but he has to get used to it before he can do something so important

decided. That could take time. And now you have had enough! Although you would constantly receive recognition, praise and the like, you could also be responsible for everything professionally – but disciplinary changes in responsibility were only possible with the approval of the manager. And the - see above.

Credibility of such a story: around 50% (half somehow believe it). Corporations do this – but there are enough people who are too weak to lead. So partly, partly. Incidentally, you must not say anything about the deteriorated text of the contract after the second meeting, otherwise the person you are talking to will suddenly "everything is clear".

And then it is also important what your last two references look like. Hopefully they don't contain any hints of "insufficient assertiveness", "too weak as a manager" (in completely different words, of course).

I would have liked you to have made your request a year after you took up your duties. Then it would have been easier for me to decide. So I'm inclined to advise you to back off and stay - that is, to continue with the policy you have been practicing for several years. The alternative would require a fighter - are you one?

Since I also have my very own nastiness: According to your CV, you live in a city from which you can reach your present, previous and previous employers on a daily basis. That says to the expert: These were all changes of employer without moving. When you were young, you put six valuable years into a rather elite second degree, which is not absolutely necessary for your later career. Anyone who has said "A" so clearly should say "B" just as clearly later on, otherwise none of this is worthwhile.

2.3.5.15 Notes from practice

Answers that were important to me, even if there was no suitable question at the time

Thou shalt not fail

If they existed, the ten commandments of the market economy, then one thing would be: Thou shalt not fail.

Because? Because markets are a stage for winners, for winners. Followers without outstanding abnormalities are sometimes tolerated, sometimes even indispensable. Winners only stand out when they are next to non-winners. In this way, each group fulfills its individual purpose. We could only do without those of those who fail.

And its members certainly don't attach importance to being here.

Then why do they fail? Before that, a quick word about the terminology: When does someone, regardless of their level or activity, have to say or be told that they now belong? If - the market is a market, whether for products or work - buyers of a service stop buying out of dissatisfaction. In product markets they first stop purchasing and then stop making payments, in the labor market they simply terminate the existing contract and thus end the relationship for good. In the case of employees, "out of dissatisfaction" ultimately means "for personal reasons". The opposite – permitted within limits – would be operational causes, provided these are convincingly presented or, even better, proven. There's another little wickedness in failure: It's an active term.

Those affected are forced to formulate: "I'm failing." In

contrast, "I was fired" is so nicely passive. It happened, I was hit by it through no fault of my own, one might think—and somehow closer to a comfortable excuse. "I failed" makes that much more difficult.

So why do employees fail, from clerks to board members or managing directors?

1. Because they deny the principle. After all, while they can fail, they can't accept that notion. The problem with this: Of course, in the eyes of those around you, you still fail – but you don't learn anything from it because you refuse to accept defeat. An example:
"We, my boss and I, simply had different ideas about how to proceed in the future. I made no secret of my opinion, stood by my opinion and did not allow myself to be bent. I almost see that as a compliment for me – that's not why I failed. That would be me if I had made mistakes. But I showed backbone. Fine, I got laid off, but I can really explain that to everyone now." Well, at the top it says "market is market". Imagine the development and design manager justifying himself to his boss: "We, the customers and I, simply had different ideas about the product design. I made no secrets..., stood by my opinion,... didn't let myself be bent,... showed backbone. The company doesn't want a head of development with a stiff back, it wants sales. It doesn't come like this because there are no salable products. Conclusion: "Fine, I was fired." You would also call that a failure.

2. Because they deny not the principle, but the fact that it has already begun. Let's call it lack of sensitivity. One could also quote Ovid
ren: "Fend off the beginnings" - actually intended as a "cure against love",but equipped with multiple uses.

Nobody achieves - it is actually mostly an active process(!) - the displeasure of their bosses in the personal sphere in such a way that the characterization "suddenly" would be permissible. Apart from exceptional scenarios that are ready for a feature film, it is a process. It starts slowly, escalates, lasts, escalates further, reaches its peak and easily leads to termination by the employer. During this process, which often lasts several months, the employee is called upon to recognize signs – and to think intensively about reactions. Anyone who "suddenly" fails and "swears" that there were no warning signs beforehand for the reasons discussed here almost deserves his fate "because of a proven inability to recognize symptoms in good time."

Bosses give active signals before they get serious. They always do - anyone who hasn't seen them has been superficial or reckless.

Those who have mastered the discipline "I can feel what's going on" are in the right place. On the other hand, those who grope around "with the mind of a butcher's dog" live very dangerously.

These signs, which always(!) exist, are a problem. Because the superiors actually have the power to at least express themselves clearly - but they do not use it. Everyone would be helped if there were a clear announcement of this kind:

3. -"Mr. Müller, I can tell you quite frankly that, in my opinion, you simply work too slowly. The quality of your work is good, but I need more results per unit of time from you. You have to make progress here, otherwise I'll have to think about action. Just think

about how you can get this under control, your colleagues can do it too. I'm happy to help if you have any questions or if you need support. But it can't stay like this, I couldn't accept it."

This is a solid basis that Müller can do something with. In any case, he has been warned and, if he is already driving at his own maximum speed, can think about measures (go for another, possibly less well-paid area of responsibility, try to get an internal transfer to another area or write external applications. Or his working style adjust it to that of my colleagues, if that's still possible in any way). But then I wouldn't have to write this post. Unfortunately, bosses don't generally work that way. They formulate allusions, show tips of icebergs and do not talk about the overwhelmingly large potential threat that remains invisible under water. They do give signs, but only subtle ones. Something like this in the above case:

"Mr. Müller, I always wanted to tell you that the quality of your work is really good." Müller beams. He memorizes this sentence and quotes it him in the evening to his wife - that's almost all that sticks with him. Although the boss now goes on: "Of course I know that this quality doesn't just fall into your lap, it has to be worked for and can't be shaken out of the hat. And that it takes time to conscientiously complete everything. Well, I know that too, you are conscientious, I really have to say that." Müller beams even more intensely. Nothing of what is yet to come can shake him or get through to him. Although there is a bit more to come: "You know, maybe you could speed things up a bit in processing; You know the pressure we are all under. Give it a try - and come to me if you need help. But in quality you are really already there, where we have to go So, Müller, we understand each other."

They don't understand each other! Müller sees himself praised many times and he suppresses what came at the end of the boss's speech. And the boss? He is deeply convinced that he made it very clear to Müller that he would have to reckon with the consequences if he didn't finally "get up to speed".

And what happens afterwards? Nothing at first, because both parties sit back and are extremely satisfied. Until one day a disappointed boss decides to fire the unsuspecting Mr. Müller. Whereupon the one out of all the clouds...

4. Likeability and rejection are almost always mutual. In extreme: If you disrespect or despise your boss, you can't hope to be loved by him in return. Or as I once wrote: Your boss thinks of you as you think of him.

   It doesn't mean that you should force yourself to see him more positively at all costs - that is often extremely difficult. But if you can't relate positive feelings to him, be warned, you'll be walking on extremely thin ice in everything you do. Your rejection of him must be a warning to you of problems to come. And as a candidate with a choice, you shouldn't sign a contract if the prospective manager doesn't seem like the kind of person you'd like to place your destiny in their hands (positive feelings are useful indicators, but exclude e.g. the risk of a change of manager).

5. Even very good professional work does not reliably protect against the displeasure of the boss. "If I do my

work well and reliably, nothing will happen to me" is downright criminally careless. "Good work" is a self-evident prerequisite for "good money", nothing more. Even repeated praise for good work results does not automatically mean that the boss is completely satisfied "otherwise too".

Knowledge is power. I often ask in career counseling sessions, "If your boss was an old school friend of mine, I called him tonight and he asked about you, what would he say then?" And very often, after a moment's thought, comes the following: "I don't know, I really can't say that, I have no idea how he judges me."

That is unacceptable, on this basis one should not be surprised if at some point the great catastrophe is imminent. Just don't tell me that your boss in particular is so extremely reserved, because you don't recognize anything of the kind asked for. I don't believe that - and I can strongly support my doubts:

What would be a minimum requirement for you to have an answerto that existential question about your superior's assessment of your strengths and weaknesses(!)? That you are deeply interested in it. But what would the answer be from someone who is constantly and keenly interested (even if he hasn't found an answer)? He would say: "I ask myself that all the time, but I can't find a clear answer to it." But that's exactly what those who needed it didn't say. And they give themselves away: They were never interested in it.

6. By far the surest way to alienate your boss is to disregard them. An active variant is best, in which you act aggressively and then demonstrate it in front of an audience (his boss is a very good spectator, in front of

whom you demonstrate how little you think of your boss). What else falls into this category? Lack of respect, ridiculing him, showing your contempt. So if you want a mortal enemy, here's the recipe.

7.

8. So far so good. So failure is by no means completely inevitable. Just to be on the safe side: Did I say that you should constantly fawn over your boss, pay attention to his every emotional state, anticipate his every wish and become a helpless vicarious agent without any "backbone" of your own? Absolutely not, you won't read that from me either. In addition to all the other counterarguments: maybe the boss doesn't want it at all. Even the school principal in the "Feuerzangenbowle" smacks one of his teachers angrily across the mouth when he demonstrates obedience in anticipation of the principal's question about measures to be taken: "I agree with the principal's opinion." The boss angrily reprimands him rightly so: "I haven't expressed an opinion at all." And that somehow takes place in Kaiser's times.

9. No, for me it's enough that you know how and what your boss thinks about you. This alone will not prevent you from failing. But you can then develop an individual defense strategy based on this. Only The theory of the "failure that was completely through no fault of your own" cannot be based on a statement such as "I swear, I never noticed anything until the boss came with the termination agreement".

10. I cannot close this topic without stating one more uncomfortable truth. As a precaution, I approach the core cautiously:

Millions of people work together in our companies every day. Partly as bosses, to a much greater extent as employees under bosses. Both groups are "dynamic" in their composition, meaning they are constantly being mixed up. In some international corporations, bosses are routinely replaced every two to three years, while other companies generally have to cope with high fluctuation. New employees are constantly joining existing bosses, or existing groups are given new superiors. And all those involved "above" and "below" are individualists, proud to be an independent personality.

Can it work at all, if everyone shows themselves as they are in this whole interplay? Not really! Does it still work in practice? Actually yes!

The reason liesin a bit of tolerance, which bosses bring up and a lot of willingness to adapt, which employees invest in their employment that secures their livelihood. There is no other way. Therefore, those who fail in the sense of this article were very often not willing to make the degree of adjustment that would have been necessary. The employee is employed. Dependence requires a willingness to adapt. If it is missing, it crunches once.

recognize signals and interpret it correctly

When it comes to filling vacant (management) positions, a significant proportion of the hiring decisions made later turn out to be less fortunate than hoped. What is amazing is that if you analyze the whole process later, you will almost always find critical signs in the person, the documents or the behavior of the applicant. These signs – "signals" – were there from the start, were clearly visible, were also recognized, but did not lead to the candidate being excluded from the overall assessment.

One should learn from mistakes, so the decision-makers will at least know what they shouldn't tolerate when they are next recruited. Unfortunately it's not that easy. Of course, if you look afterwards, you will always find signals that had existed before. But there are at least as many examples of exactly these signals being seen in other cases – and meaning nothing at all.

The connections are probably much more complex than we currently know. So "too many employer changes in the last ten years" is less of a signal leading to exclusion, perhaps it will only be if the potential new boss has a factor of ⬚ 1.8 in terms of "irascible temper, unfair management behavior".

Why am I even telling you this? Certainly not to make you better HR consultants. But to remind you: Even if it is sometimes difficult to interpret signals correctly, they almost always existed before a later disaster in the personnel area. And you also have the "right to misinterpret" warning signals, but not one to ignore or overlook them.

As an example of the very different weighting of such

a signal by the giver and the recipient of the same: Your boss asks you, who is currently managing a project, whether you have any difficulties with the employees in the project team.

The signal is: He thinks you have these difficulties - otherwise he would not have "asked". He just didn't say what he thought out of excessive politeness, consideration or cowardice(!): "You're having trouble with the people on the project team, my dear."

And in response to the "question" you – of course – deny the problems, soothe here, reject there, make others responsible, spread optimism, assure something. This is the wrong way to deal with a "red signal": to pretend that it is not red at all or that you have to evaluate it completely differently.

And do you really think a boss who has an opinion ("this man has trouble with...") would let his subordinate talk him out of it? Bosses are reluctant to listen to employees when it comes to factual questions, and certainly not when they are accused. If he doesn't respond to your counter-arguments (anymore), it's only because he thinks it's pointless, because he doesn't believe you after all - or because, see above, he's polite, considerate or even cowardly. But what he still thinks must interest you, after all your existence depends on it.

And then that boss goes home and says to his wife: "Well, today I made it very clear to the miller ('Are you having troubles...?') that I know his weakness, will no longer tolerate it and that he expects huge consequences if he doesn't get the problems under control as quickly as possible." And he's proud of himself for his no-frills approach.

You now go home and report to your partner: "Today the boss, who must have heard some stupid rumours, asked if I had any problems with my project. I was able to prove to him crystal clear that all this is nonsense, that things are behaving very differently, that completely different people are responsible for it and that, on the contrary, I am the most responsible services in view of the previous successes. He was satisfied with that, said nothing more and left."

And you are – too – proud of yourself. A few months later, you're sitting in front of me with your severance agreement and time off, swearing you haven't the faintest idea why.
So much for signal processing.

Look, there isCEOs, they call an employee and say: "Oh Mr. Müller, if you have time, I would be grateful if you could come and see me." Which means: "To me, immediately." Every signal you receive means something. It is not always immediately clear what that is. But, that's for sure, you shouldn't ignore such signals. And what's most important to me: Being fired without knowing the reason is unacceptable for a professionally committed person. Then you would be extremely insensitive, which in itself would be a reason to make your survival at work questionable.

Help, I'm a generalist

Let's put it this way: Then you have a problem.

Imagine you have what it takes to be Federal Chancellor (BK). But you mustrecognise: You don't have what it takes to successfully follow the usual paths to get there. So district chairman of a party, member of state parliament, member of parliament, general secretary, specialist minister in the state or in the federal government – none of that suits you. But BK, you feel it, that would be in line with your talents.

What now? There should be a separate BK career: BK-Assi, deputy. Auxiliary BK candidate, auxiliary BK e.g. A. etc. up to the desired final stage. So that you, transferred to industrial conditions, can start your managerial career straight away without the tiresome specialization as development engineer, group manager design and technical manager etc. First as a general manager assistant, but then no longer back into the detailed environment of some department with the compulsion to first have to qualify as a pure specialist and later as a leading specialist in a narrow specialist area. Instead, you developed from an auxiliary GF through various intermediate stages of a generalist career up to the right sole GF (or chairman of a management board).

Well, you already know: there are no career paths like this, neither for the BK nor for the GF. Or to put it more generally: There is generally no generalist career path in industrial practice. So there is no chance of getting to the top somewhere without probation in a convincing specialist career (which is not officially called that) and the alleged generalist talent shortly after to achieve a breakthrough in your studies. There are always approaches in this direction, but there has not yet been an all-round groundbreaking solution.

So what are you left with? Just as the master always had to be an apprentice, the same applies to you: it doesn't help, you have to go through it. Without a successful(!) career in a specialist area, there is basically no rise to the general Olympus.

And that's a good thing (no, I'm not quoting, the simple sentence is common linguistic knowledge). Because one of our "golden rules" is: Whoever leads people should have previously held a function such as that of those being led. This cannot apply to all subordinates, but it can apply to some of them. And so the current MD, who is responsible for some areas, was usually the head of one beforehand. In order to become that, he was previously a department head in this area and long before that he was a clerk there.

So don't try to see yourself as a generalist when you're young and refuse to follow traditional career paths. It only brings you frustration. Fight for success in standard specialty careers until you are close to developing your "true" (generalist) talents. Our system has no room for failed department heads who would rather shine as a manager. Or do you think that there could actually be a convincing chancellor in many a rather pale and inconspicuous or even unhappily operating lower-level politician? What if you just let him?

Change Alert

Notice this: Changes of all kinds in the life around us are more likely to take a turn for the worse than the opposite. You don't have to be a pessimist to see that. Whether it's the climate, taxes, new speed limits on the autobahn or threats from your spouse, something is about to change here – it probably won't be as good afterwards, to put it mildly. That's the page. The other is that changes must be inevitable wherever there is life. I too bowed to this realization at some point, I had no choice.

And so there are constant changes in the professional environment; You can say "unfortunately" there, too, but just to be on the safe side, you should expect things to get worse or less good than before in key areas. In concrete terms: If something changes around you, you must not simply carry on as before. If you ignore this simple piece of advice, impairments that can even threaten your existence are possible.

To refine this recommendation somewhat: if something in your environment becomes "different", you must be willing to change your behavior. And that is one of the toughest demands you can make on a person; hardly anyone knows that better than me.

What was right, successful, and praised for ten or twenty years can suddenly be wrong, dangerously wrong. And while you usually tell a clerk what he has to do differently recently, a manager has to find that out on his own.

Such changes can lie in the economic environment - suddenly the company is fighting for its existence, while yesterday continuous growth was the order of the day.

Structural shifts must also be mentioned when listing the triggers, but at the top there are all kinds of personnel shifts. A new head at the helm of the company can downgrade any proven strategy to waste, a new direct boss can other" standards, you would not have thought that possible before. And even a new colleague is capable of forcing that oh-so-unloved change in behavior from you. Conclusion: If you don't change, your status will change, gradually or abruptly. With high probability
- so - for the worse.

Each key only fits into a specially designed lock (my standard example for applications and positions to be filled). If just one detail changes in this lock, yesterday's solid key is just a sample with no value. Or it has to be adjusted to the new conditions by filing. It doesn't matter whether he likes to endure it.

So alert attention, careful analysis of all new circumstances, thinking through all possible scenarios and the willingness to adapt flexibly to them – or alternatively to an unavoidable change of employer – are called for.

So be more than vigilant if you are an authorized signatory and the owner of the company suddenly brings her nephew into the business. After that, it will never be the same again, no matter how the nephew is "knitted". The boss solves one of her problems with this measure. And it can also be a change for the better for the nephew. But whether that also applies to you is an open question. A very open one. So be careful.

Career advice as a "total work of art"

Occasionally I meetto friendly people who don't just

claim to be dedicated readers of my career advice. No, they quote me so eloquently and thematically widely spread that I recognize in a slight pang of panic:You know more about my rules than I could so spontaneously gather from memory.

Actually, this corresponds to the ideal case I have in mind. And what more should an author expect than to be overwhelmed with quotations from his own works? But as is the case with formulations that begin with "actually": there is a catch! Even quite a large one: It is precisely these readers, who are so adept at quoting, that when they analyze their CVs, they usually quickly realize that theoretical knowledge and practical implementation are two different things: the immediately recognizable mistakes and rule violations silence all enthusiasm.

As restless as I can be, I was looking for a solution to this problem as well – and at least I found what I was looking for when analyzing the causes: These readers understand my rules and insights as a collection of diverse building blocks from which one selects those that suit your own taste. You shrug your shoulders and ignore others. In this way, although there is a central technical theme, one has changed employers far too often. Or you may have set a reasonable career goal, but started to implement the individual steps that are now required far too late.

No, dear reader, the rules and information presented here are not individual elements intended for random selection - they are rather links in a chain. Their number is predetermined, but you determine their strength. While you can disregard any link, design it very weak to begin with, or allow it to "rust" over the years, it is part of the whole and obeys the "eternal law of the chain": The chain is only as strong as its weakest link. If it tears, the catastrophe is there. And even if it doesn't break, the following still applies: The chain only carries the load that its weakest link can just about cope with.

Or to put it another way: the actual benefit is not gained from knowing as many rules and recommendations as possible, but from their comprehensive, consistent implementation.

It's like playing soccer, if you will. It is not enough to know how to avoid being placed in an offside position, for example, you must never put the ball into the opponent's goal with your hands. If the mistake has happened, it is of little use if you can confidently quote the rule you just disregarded.

Your career potential: Thetest

Where could your career path lead you, are your goals realistic, do you have what is needed "upstairs"?

Your professionally relevant past and present are the basis; Other essential building blocks asked about: your personal attitude (professional philosophy), your knowledge of important legalities ("rules of the game") and your willingness to pay the indispensable price for what you want. The test is divided into three segments that correspond to the three pillars on which a career is built.

restrictionsOf course, such a test can only provide indications for further professional development. Some of the statements are aimed at a future that encompasses 20 or even 40 years. We all know that changes of all kinds are possible in such periods, which make predictions about individual career developments extremely uncertain. After all, as always, luck and bad luck play a role. But there are basic patterns that impose themselves on the critical observer. We work with them.

An earlier version was published under the title "JOSH DOUGLAS's Career Test" for several yearswww.ingenieurkarriere.deoffered by the VDI news. This pattern has been extensively revised and supplemented.

Instructions on how to fill it out Nobody is watching you fill it out, you alone see your answers and the later evaluation. So be honest with yourself or you will falsify the results.

If you do not find yourself exactly in the answers to a question, choose the variant that comes closest to your circumstances.

We deliberately "shuffled" some of the answers, i.e. did not sort them in ascending or descending order.

THE END

9 798379 175764